SACRED GROUND

SACRED GROUND

Jamgon Kongtrul on
"Pilgrimage and
Sacred Geography"

by

Ngawang Zangpo

Snow Lion Publications
Ithaca, New York

Snow Lion Publications
PO Box 6483
Ithaca, NY 14851 USA
(607) 273-8519
www.snowlionpub.com

Printed in U.S.A. on acid-free recycled paper.

ISBN 1-55939-164-2

Cataloging-in-Publication Data is available from the Library of
Congress

Table of Contents

Dedicated to the memory of
Jamgon Kongtrul the Third,
Karma Lodrö Chökyi Sengé (1954-1992)

Preface

Jamgon Kongtrul's Pilgrimage Guide to Tsadra is a guide book for pilgrimage to a tiny area of sacred ground in Eastern Tibet. It was written in the mid-1800s for Tibet's Buddhists who could contemplate such a spiritual journey. It appears here in translation for a modern, non-Tibetan readership, to shed light on Himalayan Buddhists' concepts of sacred land, places of pilgrimage in tantric Buddhism, and how pilgrimage is undertaken. I have translated this book with the armchair or meditation-cushion traveler in mind. I do not intend to encourage readers to embark upon the difficult and dangerous journey to this remote place; I write wishing to enhance our appreciation of the world and its sacred aspect everywhere—first and foremost, wherever we sit now. I hope that this view of a remote land will enrich our daily life at home.

Sacred Ground presents the subject of pilgrimage places as understood by tantric Buddhists of the Himalayan region. In content and intent, this book follows *Jamgon Kongtrul's Retreat Manual* and *Enthronement*. Like these two books, *Sacred Ground* focuses on an important aspect of Tibetan spiritual life as explained by Jamgon Kongtrul, a major meditation master and writer of the nineteenth century. As in the preceding books, I have liberally supplemented the translation of one central text with excerpts or supporting documents culled from Kongtrul's extensive writings. My over-riding concern in each of these three works has been loyalty to the spirit in which they were written; thus my reliance on Kongtrul's work and inclusion of information specific to his life and times. Nineteenth-century Tibet is a context as far removed from our modern world as can be imagined, yet I feel that our study and practice of Buddhism can be improved by consideration of the ex-perience of that era's masters. At the very least, study of Kongtrul can help us understand modern Tibetans' spiritual life. At best, his work leads us to discover new aspects of our own experience and practice of Buddhism.

Sacred Ground includes a detailed description of a piece of land in eastern Tibet that is distant and inaccessible to most of us. Al-though Kongtrul wrote for an audience that could undertake the pilgrimage he describes, he also wrote the book to transmit a uni-versal message: that sacred ground is to be found everywhere. Buddhism has been called a "guest religion," a way of spirituality that adapts to its host culture. Shakyamuni Buddha tailored his teaching to the predominant spiritual and cultural reference points of his day, yet Buddhism was never constrained by the geography and mentality of India in 500 B.C. To find living Buddhism today, one must look not only to the land and people of its origins, but to such countries as Tibet, Thailand, Burma, or Korea. These coun-tries, which were once, in Buddhist terms, places of darkness, be-came imbued with enlightenment; they became sacred ground. This transformation continues nowadays: my teacher was fond of re-marking that "the sun of Buddhism is setting in the East and rising in the West."

If we are to fully experience our intrinsic enlightenment, our "buddha-nature," we must study, reflect upon, and put into prac-tice the path shown by those who have already uncovered their innate awakening. Our respect and appreciation for past buddhas and bodhisattvas should increase our respect and appreciation for our own and others' present inner wealth. Likewise, our faith and interest in the sacred ground far from home should enhance our sensitivity to the wonders of the world where we live. I believe this to be the spirit in which Kongtrul wrote this book and I have tried my best to honor it in this translation.

ON A PERSONAL NOTE

Many years ago, in 1976, I was among the first group of Westerners to enter a traditional Tibetan three-year, three-month meditation retreat. It was a courageous experiment for students and teachers alike. We braved the rigors of the traditional retreat: an intense
schedule of meditation, sleep in a seated position for the entire retreat, and all teaching, written or oral, in Tibetan, for our teachers
and their many meditation manuals came in only one flavor—Tibetan. The novelty of our situation prevented us from formulating
any genuinely informed preconceptions about the project we had
embarked upon, and our relative youth ensured that our concept
of Tibetan Buddhism, or any form of Buddhism for that matter,
was in the beginning relatively limited. But we were guided by
one of the greatest meditation masters of our time, Kalu Rinpoché,
and we were armed with high spirits, rambunctious enthusiasm,
and an awareness of our good fortune. On the negative side, well,
all that needs to be said is that we were fortunate to have teachers
endowed with the patience, sympathy and loving-kindness nor-
mally attributed to saints. I spent six and a half years at that first
retreat center; each year brought a deepening appreciation for Kalu
Rinpoché and for the retreat teacher he had designated as his teaching assistant and our on-site guide, Lama Tenpa Gyatso.

It was from Lama Tenpa that I first heard of the Himalayan tantric
concept of sacred ground. We had a million questions, from the
sublime to the ridiculous, and no sense of measure. No subject
seemed too minute, obscure, incongruous, inconsequent, or insig-
nificant. We had to ask.

The question that planted the seed for this book concerned
"Shangri-La," the land of *Lost Horizon*, James Hilton's thoroughly
delightful novel from the 1930s. Stripped of the devices necessary
for Western best-sellerdom—white faces in incongruous places—
the novel's central conceit was Shangri-La, an environment whose
inhabitants sought to preserve the world's cultural treasures and
to cultivate wisdom. This notion captured the imagination of a
world-weary post-World War One generation. It struck such a deep
chord of yearning that Shangri-La (translated from Tibetan, the
name means Shang Mountain Pass) became synonymous with a
spiritually charged refuge of tranquility where one could fully

appreciate the finest fruits of human endeavor and come to terms with life's deeper meaning. To Lama Tenpa we explained, as best we could, *Lost Horizon's* Shangri-La (leaving out such details as piano-playing Manchurian beauties and displaced Belgian priests) and asked whether such places existed in Tibet. To our surprise, his reply was unequivocal: "Many such places exist in Tibet!" This book attempts to put that statement into context by presenting a Tibetan view of areas of sacred ground, where prepared visitors can experience heightened awareness and take significant strides in their understanding of the world and their inner nature.

I might add that Lama Tenpa did not make claims that places exist where residents enjoy exceptional longevity, one of the main attributes of Shangri-La. Although Tibetans appreciate their lives as human beings as much, if not more, than most of us, and wish as we do to keep body and soul together, they often display a deep acceptance, however reluctant, of the fact of our mortality. While some lamas have lived exceptionally long lives, and many teach "longevity practices," their primary concern is with our happiness and well-being, not the survival of our physical organism. Doris Lessing reminds me of their attitude compared to our own in a passage from *The Sirian Experiments*, the third of her five-part series Canopus in Argos: Archives, my only foray into science fiction:

> How pettifogging and even pedantic the Canopean attitude to out-worn physical equipment makes ours look! We patch and replace, and transplant, and preserve—they throw an inefficient body aside and step into a new one without fuss, sentimentality, or regret.
>
> Klorathy had inhabited three different bodies since I had seen him last. And he told me that Nasar was at that time down in *our* Southern Continent I as a very small brown male, a hunter, bringing a species up to a new height of knowledge about its position in relation to "The Great Spirit." Which was the formulation suitable for that place. (p. 215)

From a Buddhist perspective, not only can we live in Shangri-La, we can take it with us when we die and be reborn there, regardless of the outer location of our birthplace. From that perspective, longevity in itself is not a treasured goal.

Shangri-La seems out of favor among scholar-journalists these days. Two recent books, *Prisoners of Shangri-La* (by Donald S. Lopez) and *Virtual Tibet* (by Orville Schell) make much of the perception-reality gap between Tibet and the West, and of some frightful reports from the front lines where the twain have occasionally met without the grace or humor that should accompany cross-cultural contacts. Yet the relevant question is not "How can we better understand Tibet?" but "How can we address the inner, long-gnawing desolation that makes us dream of a Shangri-La in a time zone other than our own?" To me, the answer seems to be this: to contribute in our own surroundings to the circumstances that make Shangri-La possible anywhere.

When I accompanied Kalu Rinpoché throughout the world as a translator, I never once heard him raise his voice for a free Tibet, and never once ask for money for materially poor Tibetan refugees in India, including those of his own monastery. His message was calm and clear: free yourselves and, if you have extra money, enhance your own communities. He encouraged people to make their Shangri-La at home, which is the only meaningful place to do so. When he sent his three-year retreat graduates into the world to teach, he told us: "Stay. Teach. And don't ask your students to send one cent back to this monastery (in India). If they have more money than they need, have them invest in Buddhism in their own country." It was a simple formula for success, worldwide, as long as people understand that Shangri-Las must be planned, built, and preserved through our collective endeavor. If Shangri-Las only exist in Tibet, it is not ordained so by geography but by the will and long-term dedication of the Tibetan people.

I hope this book will contribute to an accurate picture of how Buddhists throughout the Himalayas understand the concept of sacred ground and how they integrate this into their spiritual lives. The book's scope is limited, since Jamgon Kongtrul lived in the 1800s, wrote for a Tibetan readership, and never journeyed outside Tibet. Yet he tells us that the idea of sacred ground should be meaningful for us all. For him, every land has special places that provide clear windows onto the sacred nature of the world. He believed that, just as all sentient beings have "buddha-nature," all countries and lands have regions of sacred ground. James Hilton, a Westerner, imagined Shangri-La to be in Tibet; Jamgon Kongtrul, a Tibetan, agreed, but was convinced that actual and potential Shangri-Las fill the world.

Acknowledgments

I have dedicated this book to the memory of Jamgon Kongtrul the Third, the young reincarnate master whose life seemed, to those who knew him, to have ended far too soon. In 1991, the year before his death, he returned to Palpung Monastery and to Tsadra, the retreat center that is the subject of this book. By coincidence, my traveling companions and I met him on our pilgrimage and we followed him from Dergé to Palpung to Tsadra, our common destination. This gave us ample time to witness that the high esteem he commanded outside of Tibet was magnified in his own country. The people of Kham flocked to meet him as their own, and he responded in kind. He told me that he felt more at home in Tsadra than anywhere else in the world.

During that visit, the three-year retreat was not in session and by an incredibly kind gesture he invited us to live in the retreat center during his week-long residence there. If that was not enough, he watched over the health of my girlfriend, Késang Chödrön, who had come down with a severe case of septic pleurisy, brought on by the strain of the altitude and travel. He did nothing dramatic, but would gently and regularly mobilize the attention of the community toward her, as well as see her personally. She later credited him with saving her life. They had never met, but when Késang later talked with him, they discovered that their mothers had grown up in villages within sight of one another.

After we left Palpung, I never saw Rinpoché again. Although I returned to Tsadra in 1993, it is the memory of that initial visit to his true home and his overwhelming kindness in many ways that have become inseparably entwined with my impression of Tsadra.

If any readers wish to visit his virtual world, they may do so at www.jamgonkongtrul.org. If some of you have built your local Shangri-La and still have some resources which you wish to share with others, I would encourage you to consider contributing to Jamgon Kongtrul's work to preserve the Tsadra retreat center in Kham. Information on how to do so can be culled from the web site. Although I am far from being competent to judge anyone, I have the strong impression that Jamgon Kongtrul's impeccable integrity has rubbed off on every one of his lamas and attendants whom I have met. Specifically, I trust Tenzin Dorjé, his General Secretary, through whom any funds for Tsadra are passed, and the directors of the retreat in Kham.

CREDIT WHERE CREDIT IS DUE

Every translator needs expert guidance and generous sponsorship, and I have been very fortunate on both counts. First, Tsatsa Tulku of Dartsendo, Kham, and Tulku Thubten of Santa Cruz, California, were of invaluable assistance in understanding the Tibetan texts. Second, Tsadra Foundation sponsored my work on this book. Both the lamas and the sponsors have impressed me with their selfless wish to serve others through supporting translation. I appreciate the opportunity to try to keep their high ideals in mind in my work.

Lama Drubgyu Tenzin has in some ways been with me every step of the way in this work. He was another member of that first group of retreatants who heard of sacred ground from Lama Tenpa Gyatso. Lama Drubgyu and I made two journeys to Tsadra together and I would gladly do so again in his company. He read over this book and offered, as usual, many useful and important suggestions. I have found that two heads are better than one when it is his advice that is sought.

For their kind help along the way to this book's completion, I fondly recall Koji and Rutsuko Hirota, Faye Angevine and Howard Brewer, Kathleen Bryan and Richard Melton, Mei-Yen and Dwayne

Ladle (and their friends, Chi Shia, Celia Wang, Shan-shan Wang, Chou-Mou Huang, and Tsai-Farn Jan), Lama Denys Tendrup, Ge Wan-chang, Hogan Yie, Daniel Reid, and one of my sisters, Carolyn Littlejohns. Prior to the final editing of this book, I asked Sangyé Khandro and Chökyi Nyima, two translators whose work I hold in high esteem, to look over my work. I truly appreciate the encouragement they both gave me. Further, many persons in China, both Tibetan and Chinese, extended valuable aid. If I do not name them, it is due to their affiliation with the Party, not to forgetfulness or lack of gratitude.

Finally, I am forever impressed by Snow Lion Publications, both in their continued contribution to our culture and in my personal dealings with them. They set the bar very high in their professional bodhisattva lives and it is inspiring to associate with them. Grateful thanks to Sidney Piburn, Jeffrey Cox, and Susan Kyser, and to the editor who has carefully nursed the book to completion, Steven Rhodes.

INTRODUCTION

Sacred Ground describes two journeys: a journey outward, to a specific pilgrimage place on the globe; and a journey inward, to the sacred world of tantra, accessible through contemplation and meditation. Both journeys can be fascinating and inspiring, but neither destination can be reached without a guide to introduce some signposts a pilgrim might meet on the way. This introduction is intended as a short, general guide to both journeys, a paltry substitute for what both Buddhism and common sense would suggest as the indispensable guide in both cases — a human spiritual guide and companion.

Within the introduction, "The Inner Journey" presents pilgrimage as it is understood in tantric Buddhism. Kongtrul begins his main text with much the same information, albeit in a very concise form. For those unfamiliar with the concepts or the technical terms Kongtrul employs, this section presents some details of tantra pertinent to pilgrimage. "The Outer Journey" describes one route to the specific pilgrimage site Kongtrul wrote about, Tsadra, his home and retreat center in Kham (the Tibetan name for eastern Tibet). This includes information concerning the present and recent past history of his district in Kham and the influences that shaped his contemporaries' consciousness of their land as sacred. Lastly, "Life on Sacred Ground" relates Jamgon Kongtrul's personal experience of his sacred journey and his care for the sacred land.

Throughout this introduction, I have not spared the reader from the details of the Tibetans' experience of pilgrimage and sacred ground. Although we travel (and read!) to deepen our appreciation of the world and to add new dimensions to our lives, the fresh discoveries we seek cannot always be found in familiar settings, nor among persons with familiar, easily remembered names. This book will test the casual reader's ability to discern the path of meaning in a thick forest of challenging Tibetan names of places and persons. For those who read this book seated on a meditation cushion, I hope this journey proves a welcome opportunity to visit the home of Jamgon Kongtrul, one of the most loved, trusted, and respected spiritual companions of his time and ours.

The Inner Journey

Sacred Ground is a book that invites the reader into the world of tantra. For those who practice tantra, pilgrimage is ideally more than spiritual tourism: it is a one-way ticket toward the heart of one's spiritual life. While the pilgrimage journey necessarily implies outer movement from a known, lesser environment to one that is considered spiritually charged, the most significant landscape traversed on the journey lies within the world of tantra. The notion of the sacred, implied in the lower levels of Buddhist theory and practice, finds its full, explicit flowering in the tantras. The following pages present some aspects of tantra relevant to the appreciation of the sacred in our world and in ourselves.

This section has four parts: First, "Uncommon Travel to Inaccessible Places" explains why, apart from four traditional destinations related to the Buddha's life, Buddhist pilgrimage is the unique domain of tantric practice. Second, "The Ground of the Sacred" introduces the fundamental views of tantra that permit such a seemingly un-Buddhist concept as the sacred. Third, "First Steps on the Sacred Path" reviews the basic forms of tantric meditation, familiar to many readers from such works as Sarah Harding's translation of Jamgon Kongtrul's text on the subject, *Creation and Completion*. Finally, "Sacred Regions for Tantric Conduct" presents the full context and meaning of pilgrimage's inner journey.

Many fine books and articles on Buddhism, original or in translation, have introduced and explained the material contained under these four headings more clearly and thoroughly than what I
am able to present to you here. Further, many of us have had the
incredible good fortune to hear with our own ears the blessed words
of realized masters on these subjects. Most words on paper, my
own included, are as if drawn on the surface of a lake, whereas a
few simple words from a spiritual master can have the impact of
words carved on stone: they can open new horizons and change
unalterably the course of our life. Nevertheless, I have included
the pages below as an introduction for those who may not be familiar with tantra. For those who are, I hope they serve as a review
of tantric reference points in the context of pilgrimage, as expressed
in words often drawn from the works of Jamgon Kongtrul.

UNCOMMON TRAVEL TO INACCESSIBLE PLACES

Pilgrimage within common Buddhism is based on a single reference within its source texts, that of a few lines spoken by the Buddha close to the end of his life, here translated by Maurice Walshe
from *The Buddha's Last Days* (*Mahaparinibbana Sutta*):

> Ananda, there are four places the sight of which should arouse
> emotion in the faithful. What are they? "Here the Tathagata was
> born" is the first. "Here the Tathagata attained supreme enlighten-
> ment" is the second. "Here the Tathagata set in motion the Wheel
> of Dhamma" is the third. "Here the Tathagata attained the Nibanna-
> element without remainder" is the fourth. And, Ananda, the faith-
> ful monks and nuns, male and female lay-followers will visit those
> places. And any who die while making the pilgrimage to these
> shrines with a devout heart will, at the breaking-up of the body
> after death, be reborn in a heavenly world. (*The Long Discourses of
> the Buddha*, pp. 263-264)

These four sites are Lumbini, in Nepal; Bodhgaya; Deer Park, near
Varanasi; and Kushinagar, these last three in north-central India.
They are sufficiently close to one another that a harried modern
pilgrim could spend some "quality time" at all four places in the
space of two busy days.

It is noteworthy that the Buddha made no special promises for
those who survived the journey. He states only that faithful followers will visit them and that visits to those places should arouse

emotion. He does not command his disciples to turn toward these sites, does not obligate them to visit them during their lifetimes, and does not even claim these places as sacred. His encourage-ment of pilgrimage, when compared to his other teachings, seems fleeting and tepid, at best. Small wonder that even Bodhgaya, the Buddha's adamantine seat of awakening, center of the Buddhist world, fell into neglect and ruin for centuries before its rediscovery and renovation by, of all people, the English.

I have spent many happy months in Bodhgaya, in the company of pilgrims from around the world, and I have lived for five years in India, called the "land of the exalted" in Tibetan texts. Yet as inspiring and uplifting as I find that land, its history, culture, and people, I cannot casually recommend a pilgrimage there. For ex-ample, Bodhgaya, the crown-jewel of Buddhist pilgrimage places, is, on an outer level, a grubby Indian village lost in the center of the most unpromising state of India, Bihar. Pilgrims unfamiliar with how the majority of the world lives do not run any risk of meeting either outwardly pure elements or stress-free environments. Nor, from the viewpoint of Lesser Way (*hinayana*) or Great Way (*mahayana*) Buddhist texts, did the Buddha ever claim that such journeys are of vital importance.

It is only within tantric practice that pilgrimage assumes a cru-cial role in Buddhist practice. This idea, that pilgrimage does not form part of the Great Way but that it is central to tantra, is pro-claimed in the following long quote from a great Tibetan master, Sakya Pandita (1182-1251). One of the founding fathers of the Sakya lineage, Sakya Pandita is very highly revered within his own lin-eage, but enjoys a less enviable regard elsewhere in the Tibetan world, the difference between renown as an omniscient master and a reputation as a know-it-all. Since his time, few have dared argue with this author, yet many have tried to explain him away. For example, the book from which the following quote is drawn con-tains a typical gem that has caused headaches for centuries of Oral Instruction Lineage (Kagyu) masters and scholars:

> Concerning the blessings of Vajra Varahi,
> Marpa from Lhotrak doesn't have any!

The subject is Marpa, the first Tibetan of the Oral Instruction Lineage, and Vajra Sow, one of the main meditation deities offered by that school. This sort of broadside flowed from Sakya Pandita's pen and many of them have enlivened Himalayan debates ever since. Little wonder that when one Tibetan lama I know found this book in my collection, he asked to borrow it, explaining that for him it held the same irresistible fascination as American movies he had seen that contain scenes of exquisitely choreographed violence.

The quote below is pertinent in that it introduces the context of pilgrimage within tantric meditation practice, the theme of "The Inner Journey" and of the main translated text. When I first discovered and translated it for this book, I was unaware that it too had provoked centuries of controversy. (This came to my attention thanks to Professor Toni Huber, who sent me a copy of his fascinating article that describes the debate.[1]) The passage states unequivocally that pilgrimage belongs to the tantric path, a fact that Kongtrul accepted, although he always encouraged all persons to engage in pilgrimage and to bring to the practice whatever faith, devotion, and mindfulness they could.

This debate could be compared to one we can imagine in the present day: Some well-meaning persons might warn that a Kalachakra empowerment given by His Holiness the Dalai Lama should be restricted to advanced practitioners, and could prove dangerous for unsophisticated participants. Yet another equally well-meaning person might reply that, while it is true that such high tantric empowerments were never intended to be open, public events, if a participant who is unable to understand the words or the meanings of the ritual at least brings deep faith to the empowerment, pays sincere respect and makes an offering to the Dalai Lama, and later maintains pure views toward the Three Jewels, the lama, the deity, and the other participants in the empowerment, it would probably do more good to allow the person to attend. I think both opinions are reasonable: great minds never think alike. I believe the former to be like Sakya Pandita's view in relation to pilgrimage sites; the latter, like Kongtrul's.

Sakya Pandita also writes of pilgrimage in the regions of India and Tibet, how it was, even in his day, that Mount Kailash and Lake Manasarovar were confounded for what are described in Buddhist source texts as Snowy Mountain (Himavat), fabled mountain of the Indian sub-continent, and Heatless Lake (Anavatapta), legendary source of Asia's main rivers. He further explains the gap between the lyrical descriptions of holy places found throughout Buddhist texts and the often dreary reality of Buddhist sites as poetic license. He ends this subject by citing Charitra and Dévikotri, sacred places in India, which some Tibetan masters claimed to have located in central Tibet. This has a special resonance for this text, as the place for which Kongtrul writes his pilgrimage guide is related, according to Kongtrul and his sources, to both Charitra and Dévikotri.[2] Although Sakya Pandita appears to disagree with what he perceives as a dubious practice of locating "franchises" of Indian sacred sites in Tibetan territory, he uses the occasion to reiterate his first point, that only qualified tantric practitioners should frequent pilgrimage places, regardless of location. Sakya Pandita writes:

> After you receive the four empowerments in their entirety,
> Meditate in your own home.
> After you achieve stability, meditate in cemeteries and other
>   places.
> After you achieve a high degree of stability,
> Train in the physical
> And verbal signs,[3] and realize the nature of reality.
> To traverse the stages of awakening
> And to bring the sacred regions under your control,
> Travel to the thirty-seven major sacred regions,
> Such as the sacred places and higher sacred places,
> To practice the conduct of tantric discipline.
> This style of practice has been taught in the texts
> And commentaries of the highest yoga tantras.
> Those who know this kind of activity
> Can attain full enlightenment during this lifetime.
>
> These days, I have seen some who don't understand Secret
>   Mantra
> Concoct tantric traditions.
> The Buddha never said to go
> To the thirty-seven major sacred regions
> Without having first meditated on the two phases [of tantric
>   meditation, creation and completion].
> A great meditator who has not meditated
> On these two phases might be excellent,

But he/she is nothing more than a great meditator of the
    transcendent perfections [i.e., the Great Way and not of
    tantra].

The discourses [*sutras*] don't relate a ritual
For travel to such major sacred regions.
Further, if one hasn't meditated on Secret Mantra
But is conceitedly convinced that one has such understanding
And goes to those regions, obstacles will ensue.
A great meditator who [remains fixed within the absorption
    called] Nothing Whatsoever
Can visit them, but neither harm nor benefit will accrue.
Such sacred sites as Oddiyana, Jalandhara,
And the Himalayan Dévikotra
Might be populated with savages, fools,
Non-Buddhists, or nomads,
But do such as they achieve accomplishment [by contact with
    these places]?

An individual who has realization in Secret Mantra meditation
And who has the good fortune to encounter the signs and their
    meaning
Will be blessed
By the *dakinis* who reside in those regions.
For the meaning of this,
Refer to the highest yoga tantras.
Therefore, travel to the great sacred regions
Without having meditated on Secret Mantra is meaningless.

The texts of Glorious Kalachakra [Wheel of Time]
And *The Treasury of Knowledge* [*Skt: Abhidharma*]
Describe Snowy Mountain endowed with such features as
    golden sheltering cliffs,
Rose-apple [*jambu*] trees, and Raivata [Indra's elephant],
Surrounded by five hundred elephants;
And as being the residence of five hundred arhants.
The mountain [mentioned in these texts] is not Mount Kailash.
Heatless Lake is not Lake Manasarovar.
Elephants cannot be found there;
Similarly, where are the rose-apple trees?
And the cliffs of gold?

The proof of this is as follows:

[The tantras] of the Glorious Kalachakra,
State that Snowy Mountain
Is located to the north of the Sita River.
Beside the mountain are situated the 960,000,000 cities
Of [the kingdom of] Shambhala.
Within its ruler's supreme palace,
Known as Kalapa,
[Shambhala's] kings, manifestations of enlightenment,
Teach spiritual instructions for eight hundred years [each].
Various kinds of forests
And many varieties of orchards of fruit trees grow [in the
    kingdom].
During the degenerate time, the land of the exalted [India]
Will fill with uncivilized religions.
Barbarians there will use magical powers
To lead an army to Shambhala.
At that time, an emanation of Vajra-in-Hand [Bodhisattva
    Vajrapani],
A king known as Wrathful One,
Will defeat the barbarians
And spread the doctrine of the Buddha
To the exalted land.
Therefore, travel to Snowy Mountain
Without miraculous power is impossible.

The Treasury of Knowledge states,
"To the North from here, past nine ranges
Of black mountains, stands Snowy Mountain.
Between it and the Intoxicating with Fragrance Mountain
Lies a lake of fifty leagues in depth."[4]
This text describes these and other features in detail
And explains that it is not possible to travel there
Without miraculous power.
The present-day Mount Kailash
Has none of the features [described above].

Non-Buddhist religious texts state
That the Snowy Mountain range spans the region
From the East to the West, until the oceans.
According to Valmiki, [the Hindu god] Hanuman
Threw one piece of Snowy Mountain
Which became Kailash [where it landed].

Therefore, the place sacred to Maheshvara,
The ground where Raivata [the elephant] manifests,
And the region of the five hundred arhants
Is not this present-day Kailash.

Moreover, *The Discourse of the Great Peacock* states
That Snowy Mountain and Kailash are two distinct mountains.

Furthermore, *The Flower Ornament Discourse* states[5]
That Heatless Lake has a length and breadth
Of fifty by fifty leagues [*yojana*].
Its floor is covered with jeweled sands,
Its banks are fashioned from jeweled tiles.
Four rivers flow from the lake, as follows:
The Ganges River flows from an elephant's mouth,
Carrying silver sand in its current;
The Sita River flows from a lion's mouth,
Carrying diamond sand in its current;
The Sindhu River flows from an ox's mouth,
Carrying gold sand in its current;
The Vakshu River flows from a horse's mouth,
Carrying blue beryl sand in its current.
Each river
Measures one league in breadth.
The four rivers circle Heatless Lake
Seven times in a clockwise direction
Before flowing to the four cardinal directions.
Between the streams
Grow an assortment of flowers,
Such as blue, [red and white] lotuses,
And the area is completely filled
With various jeweled trees.
These and other features can be found, described in detail,
In *The Flower Ornament Discourse*.
The present-day Lake Manasarovar
Has none of these features [described here].

Further, some persons say
That Vulture Peak [site of the Buddha's teaching on transcendent
    knowledge] as well
No longer resembles the description found in *The Pinnacle of
    Jewels Discourse*.

Further, they say that all regions seem to be changing
Due to the force of these [degenerate] times.
I will explain this, listen:

Descriptions of the actual state of a thing
And proclamations of its faults or qualities are two different
    exercises.
If one makes known the faults or qualities of a thing
And follows the customs of poets,
One can state that Vulture Peak
Is round and high, etc.,
A major mountain in the exalted land [of India],
Like those [that rise from] the great plains of Tibet.

No one regards as faulty
Such descriptions on the part of poets.
Nevertheless, wise persons consider
Any additions, deletions, or errors
In descriptions of the actual state of a thing to be faults.

For example, in praising an ox,
One could say that it is a mass of snow mountains that knows
    how to move,
Or a fragment broken from a cloud.
Its horns' tips are like vajras;
Its hooves resemble sapphire;
Its tail, a wish-fulfilling tree, etc.
Or, if one praises a man,
One could say that his face is the sun or moon;
His teeth, a string of snow mountains, etc.
In general, large size can be compared to space;
Smallness, likened to atoms;
Coarseness, to Supreme Mountain;
A mouse, to an elephant;
The rich, to [the wealth god] Son of Renown [*Vaishravana*];
A minor ruler, to [the god] Indra;
An ordinary spiritual guide,
To the Buddha:
Such praises are not forbidden to poets.
But when [one purports] to report the actual state of something
Or to confirm its characteristics
And does not describe it as it actually is,

How could this please the wise?

Therefore, [the above-mentioned] praises of Vulture Peak, etc.,
Are related according to poetic custom.
[But a writer who intends] to describe Snowy Mountain,
    Heatless Lake, etc.,
As they are in reality
Yet strays [into poetry] is not omniscient.

The increasing influence of this time of degeneration
Can cause some deterioration [of these places]
But how can it be possible for everything [in a description] to be
    wrong?
[For example,] a sacred region called Charitra
Is located in the South [of India], by the sea.
This is not the [Tibetan place called] Superior Herb Tsari.[6]
Some say that Tsari
Is another location of Dévikotra.
The *Vajra Yogini Tantra* states:
"In Dévikotra, there stands a *bhatra* [tree]."
Further, the same text states:
"The co-emergent woman in the region of Tibet
Resides in a cave in the rock.
The goddess who stays in that region
Resides by the *bhatra* tree."
If a *bhatra* tree grows in that area [Tsari],
It cannot be denied that it is [Dévikotra].

However, even if Kailash, Tsari, and other places
Are major areas of sacred ground,
It is said [in the tantras] that persons who go there
Must have received tantric empowerment, maintain the
    commitments,
Know the signs and the replies,
Have stable realization in the two phases [of tantric meditation],
And travel there to engage in tantric conduct.
The tantras prohibit persons who do not have those
    qualifications
From visiting such places. (*A Thorough Delineation of the Three Vows*,
    pp. 62-67)

Persons familiar with the subjects of Buddhist geography and
pilgrimage will find this quote of rich significance, yet those accus-
tomed to Kongtrul's views will anticipate correctly that he is not

entirely in agreement with Sakya Pandita. As we will see throughout Kongtrul's writing on sacred places and pilgrimage, he felt all
tantric practitioners, if not all Buddhists, could benefit from pilgrimage. He takes this perspective to a point that would probably
have Sakya Pandita rolling his venerable eyes. Kongtrul writes the
following lines in a praise of Tsari in central Tibet (translated in
full later in this text):

> Even if you don't meditate or practice here as you should,
> [Pilgrimage here will cause you] to be reborn in the celestial
>   realms after leaving your body:
> That even animals who have died here leave relics is a sign of
>   this!
>
> If, with faith, you take seven steps in the direction of this place,
> The door to the miserable existences will be blocked to you at
>   death.

A reader of these two masters would guess that Sakya Pandita
would not have approved of Kongtrul's attitude, although to whom
would he have complained? In the Tibetan world of supra-tempo-
ral identities, Kongtrul was said to have been the reincarnation of
the very same Sakya hierarch.

A minor point that Sakya Pandita mentions is the necessary presence in Dévikotra of a species of tree called *bhatra*. *The Sanskrit and
Tibetan Bilingual Dictionary*, p. 664, offers us *bhatra-shva* as *thang shing*
in Tibetan. A Tibetan synonym for this in *The Great Tibetan-Chinese
Dictionary* is *ljon shing ser po*, which leads us to Sarat Chandra Das,
where that tree and *thang shing* are identified as the *deodara* tree (p.
471). *Webster's New World Dictionary* informs us that the English
name *deodar* comes from Sanskrit *devadaru*, lit., tree of the gods,
and defines it as "a tall Himalayan cedar (*Cedrus deodara*) with
drooping branches and fragrant, durable, light-red wood." While
this conclusion sounds plausible, I hope that others will pursue
this investigation beyond my superficial level.

What is important for us to retain from this passage by Sakya
Pandita is his refutation of pilgrimage as a practice outside the context of tantra and his affirmation of the vital importance of the practice for tantric adepts. He situates the place of pilgrimage at an
intermediate or advanced level, what we will see below (under the
heading "Sacred Regions for Tantric Conduct") as the second of

the five paths of Buddhism, the path of application. Before we embark on that path, however, we should review our reference points at the initial stages of tantric practice.

THE GROUND OF THE SACRED

From the last section, it is clear that, of the many vehicles we can employ to take the spiritual journey within Buddhism, it is that of tantra we must take to appreciate the context of *Kongtrul's Pilgrimage Guide to Tsadra* (hereafter referred to as the *Pilgrimage Guide*). To answer how a piece of land can be sacred, we must first identify the ground of the sacred within ourselves. This is the domain that tantra identifies and explores. This section presents two vast subjects in abridged form: our sacred nature and three approaches to it in Buddhism.

Buddhism begins with an idea that demands serious reflection: all beings, all of us equally, have buddha-nature, intrinsic enlightenment. The difference between ourselves and the men and women we call enlightened (buddhas), lies in the degree of our self-understanding. They know their nature entirely; we are often strangers to our better selves. The Buddha did not teach us how to create buddha-nature, but how to create the conditions for its discovery. That enlightenment is our true nature and that it can be realized by following a specific path stands as the central pillar of the Buddhist faith. Although the instructions of spiritual masters and companions act as vital catalysts to our self-understanding, the Buddhist path is grounded in the assumption, what should be called faith, that the journey and the destination are related to our inherently existent true nature. The sacred in Buddhism has not been granted by God or gods; it has not fallen from the sky; it is not the product of mysterious alchemy; nor has it been passed down to us as an ancient heirloom from time immemorial. The sacred is rooted in the primordial ground of our being.

I do not know how the word "Buddhism" became introduced into Western languages. It certainly does not reflect a translation from Tibetan, where the most common term to designate what we call a Buddhist is *nang-pa*, which literally means "an inner person" and implies inner spiritual cultivation. Most other religions are designated *chi-pa*, "outer," as their spirituality focuses mainly on the relationship between a human being (or a community of the chosen) and his or her god(s). To Buddhists, theistic religions do not value the ultimate nature of ordinary life: their initial message is one of the fundamental poverty of the human soul (not to mention that of animals!). A theist's concept of "original sin" is light-years from a Buddhist's "primordial purity." The sacred for theists must necessarily be "other" and experienced as a glimpse of a realm beyond the range of the viewer, who is reminded by the sacred of his innate insignificance. For a Buddhist, the sacred is seen as a manifestation of the enlightenment native to all sentient beings and as an invitation to communion with it through the cultivation of merit and of non-dual, timeless awareness.

The appearance of the sacred is like the sight of the sun through a break in thick clouds that covered it. The sun is always present but not always visible. The sacred is not the mundane, nor is it the extraordinary: it is reality, the truth, the nature of the animate and inanimate universe. It is natural, effortless, and spontaneously present. No god or buddha fashioned it: the changeless, enlightened essence of life is primordial liberation. A practitioner does not have to "attain" enlightenment or to "gain" liberation (although our human languages, Tibetan included, constrain us to talk in that manner), since that would amount to re-attainment and re-gaining that which in essence is already free and enlightened, our fundamental nature. Kongtrul here contrasts the fundamental changeless nature with the superficial, transitory changes that occur between who we are now and enlightenment. He here calls that enlightened nature "the continuity of the cause," a technical term in tantra we will return to below:

> As earlier stages of the path lead to later ones, the essence [of the ground of being] does not change. The continuity of the cause is neither destroyed nor changed by birth, old age, sickness, death, any form of sentient life [a person may take], links of causation, families of enlightenment, truths, the entering [of meditative states] without discursive thought, and, at the fruition, vajra-like meditative absorption. (*Encyclopedia of Buddhism*, vol. 2, pp. 619-620)

Despite this changeless nature, we experience ourselves differently, depending on the degree of our self-understanding. What

Buddhism teaches as our true nature is enlightenment; all else amounts to distortion due to what are referred to as "incidental" impurities. The term *incidental* implies that what we experience as the real, solid, frustrating limitations in our lives, such as karma, negative emotions, and ignorance, are in fact transitory and ephemeral, like so many clouds that appeared from and will dissolve back into the changeless, unmoving sky. According to Kongtrul, such distinctions as "ordinary being" or "bodhisattva" or "Buddha" exist in the mind of the beholder; from the perspective of ultimate truth, only enlightenment exists:

> When buddha-nature is made continually impure due to incidental stains, an individual is called a sentient being. When both purity and impurity are present, the individual is called a person on the path of bodhisattvas. At the time of extreme purity, the individual is called a transcendent one [i.e., a buddha].
>
> The circumstance of existence within the wheel of life created by karma and negative emotions is that of an impure [sentient being]. The circumstance of freedom from karma and negative emotions, but lack of freedom from the habitual tendency of ignorance, is that of a bodhisattva. Freedom from that ignorance is the circumstance of a transcendent one.
>
> These three have been presented here from the point of view of the distortions of relative reality; in the essence of the ultimate sphere, [their nature] is changeless. (*Ibid.*, p. 624)

Before turning to the specific subject of tantra, it might be useful to show that what we identify as sacred buddha-nature, and the view that it is innate, primordial, and permanent, do not represent a weird, marginal tantric perspective. *The Flower Ornament Scripture*, one of the monumental source texts of the Great Way, so marvelously translated by Thomas Cleary, is replete with such references to our buddha-nature. For example,

> There is nowhere the knowledge of the Buddha does not reach. Why? There is not a single sentient being who is not fully endowed with the knowledge of Buddha; it is just that because of deluded notions, erroneous thinking, and attachments, they are unable to realize it. If they would get rid of deluded notions, then universal knowledge, spontaneous knowledge and unobstructed knowledge would become manifest. (p. 1002)

This passage continues with a metaphor: suppose all the information concerning the billion-world universe were contained in every single atom (inscribed on an immense "scripture" in the Chinese version or, in the Tibetan version, on "a bolt of silk" as large and as wide as the universe), yet was of no use to sentient beings, since they could not see that fact nor access the knowledge.

> Then suppose someone with clear and comprehensive knowledge, who has fully developed the celestial eye, sees these scriptures inside atoms, not benefiting sentient beings in the least, and with this thought—"I should, by energetic power, break open those atoms and release those scriptures so that they can benefit all sentient beings"—then employs appropriate means to break open the atoms and release the great scriptures, to enable all sentient beings to benefit greatly.
>
> Similarly, the knowledge of Buddha, infinite and unobstructed, universally able to benefit all, is fully inherent in the bodies of sentient beings; but the ignorant, because of clinging to deluded notions, do not know of it, are not aware of it, and so do not benefit from it. Then the Buddha, with the unimpeded, pure, clear eye of knowledge, observes all sentient beings in the cosmos and says, "How strange—how is it that these sentient beings have the knowledge of Buddha but in their folly and confusion do not know it or perceive it? I should teach them the way of sages and cause them forever to shed deluded notions and attachments, so they can see in their own bodies the vast knowledge of buddhas, no different from the buddhas." Then Buddha teaches them to practice the way of sages, so they get rid of deluded notions, after which they realize the infinite knowledge of Buddha and aid and comfort all living beings. (p. 1003)

Although this passage mentions splitting atoms to reveal the secrets of the universe, this text originated in India and was translated into Chinese in the second century and into Tibetan in the eighth century. Modern or outdated idioms aside, the text repeats throughout its pages the same point: the true nature of sentient life is enlightenment.

Another metaphor for the relation between sentient beings and their buddha-nature can be found in Tibetan texts in this "life-is-but-a-dream" story, undoubtedly from Indian sources:

In a supreme mansion of jewels, ornamented with infinite wealth, two brothers slept. The elder brother, who had gone to sleep first, awoke with the power of clairvoyance to know his brother's mind. He saw that his younger brother had fallen asleep and dreamed of various states of happiness and suffering, related to the confused appearances in each of the six realms of existence. At that moment, he found it impossible to wake his brother, yet to allow him to remain sleeping was of no help. Therefore, when the younger brother [dreamed of] having taken birth as a god, etc., and experienced happiness or suffering, the older brother would approach him [in his dream], in whatever manifestation was appropriate— as a virtuous practitioner or as a brahmin, as a man or as a woman, as a buddha, a listener, a solitary sage, a bodhisattva, or an ordinary individual, etc. He would teach him spiritual instructions, such as, "Alas! All composite phenomena are impermanent! They have no essence! They are not true existence! These appearances of confusion are false: do not be attached to their reality! Practice the spiritual teachings!"

Due to [these interventions, the younger brother] rejected negative acts and practiced virtue. Thus, during repeated lifetimes, in his seemingly real [dream] experience, he enjoyed the happiness of the higher realms and was born as a person who practiced spiritual teachings. Thus his immediate circumstances were happy. As his sleep thereby became lighter, he understood the wheel of life to be false and with this [realization], he awoke. He saw that he had not moved from his bed, [that what he had experienced] had been dreams, and that his older brother had guided him through having manifested in his dreams. Although there was no difference between the two brothers, for the period [that one slept and the other was awake], there seemed to be a qualitative difference.

To use the moral of this fable of the two brothers as an example, buddhas and sentient beings are equal masters in the palace of essential wisdom. However, their momentary difference can be compared to whether or not they have woken from the transitory obscuration of sleep. (Longchenpa, *The Precious Treasury of Philosophies*, pp. 125a-b)

Although these two passages are from pre-tantric Buddhism, they elucidate the relationship between sentient beings and enlightenment, the mundane and the sacred, which continues in the tantras.

Many elements of the view, path, and conduct distinguish tantra from the spiritual paths that precede it, but there is much territory that is contiguous among the three ways of spiritual development in Buddhism. Before we enter tantra by itself, let us see the common ground of the three paths—the Lesser Way, the Great Way, and tantra, also called Secret Mantra or the Vajra Way.

The key point in the Lesser Way is renunciation. In *Words of My Perfect Teacher*, we find the story of Buddha's cousin, Nanda, who was ostracized from the monastic community until he changed his motivation. Neither his conduct nor his meditation were called into question—outwardly, he seemed a perfect monk. Yet the Buddha told the other monks to have nothing to do with Nanda until his wish for a better rebirth gave way to determination to find freedom from the entire wheel of life. (pp. 95-96)

The heart of the Great Way is compassion. In the same text, we read of Geshé Tönpa, who comments favorably on hearing of three students who devoted themselves, respectively, to teaching; to fashioning representations of the Buddha's body, speech, and mind; and to meditation. When the same messenger tells the master of another disciple who stayed apart from others and wept constantly with his face hidden, Geshé Tönpa removed his hat (a gesture of respect), joined his hands in prayer, and burst into tears, exclaiming it was that student who truly practiced Buddhism. The student he praised had been crying when considering others' sufferings. (p. 210)

Renunciation is indispensable to the Lesser Way; compassion, to the Great Way. Similarly, like it or not, devotion anchors the practice of tantra. In the same text, this point is made in many passages, such as:

Geshé Kharak Gomchung says:

You may know the whole Tripitaka [the three collections of the Buddha's teaching], but without devotion to your teacher that will be of no use to you.

Particularly in all the paths of the Secret Mantra Vajrayana, the teacher has a unique and paramount importance. For this reason, all the tantras teach the practice of Guru Yoga, and say that it is superior to all the practices of the generation and perfection phases. In one tantra it says:

Better than meditating on a hundred thousand deities
For ten million kalpas [eons]
Is to think of one's teacher for a single moment. (p. 310)

Tantra is not a dead language, such as Latin or Sanskrit; it is not an arcane subject of study, the province of eccentric professors in dusty libraries; and it is not an opera of the soul that elite connoisseurs patronize for their own and others' refined edification. Like the other forms of Buddhism, tantra is a contact spirituality (as in contact sport). The contact begins with the spiritual master and it is characterized on our part by devotion, a state as difficult to define but as unmistakable as love. Respect, love, appreciation, generosity, attentiveness, patience, gentleness, etc., are welcome elements in a relationship with a spiritual master, but without the torrid core of devotion, it might be authentic Buddhism, but it isn't tantra.

> Better than meditating on a hundred thousand deities
> For ten million kalpas [eons]
> Is to think of one's teacher for a single moment.

This is not a testimony to the superpowers of the teacher but to the power of a relationship grounded in devotion. In fact, in tantra, devotion is not the beginning of something else, be it a friendship, a collaboration, or any externalized, materialized relation. Devotion is the point. Many great teachers, of yore or of today, had little or no outer relationship with their spiritual masters, apart from receiving empowerments and instruction. Otherwise, they were abandoned and ignored at best, or forcefully expelled from the master's circle at worst. In any case, they left their teacher with what was most precious intact: the devotion that would power their practice until enlightenment.

Buddhism in practice is up close and personal. In the Lesser Way, we examine ourselves, body and mind, piece by piece, to discover that what we thought was a whole, a self, was nothing but a collection of pieces, glued together by a potent mixture of positive or negative karmic appearances, emotional states, habitual patterns, and lack of self-examination. For those who innocently come to Buddhism for just a little psychic home improvement, the Buddha first offers the wrecking ball of selflessness.

In the Great Way, we examine our connection to others, beginning with the consideration that all sentient beings have been our mother at one time or another during our series of lifetimes since time immemorial. We deliberately develop compassion for others, starting with our common first other, our mother in this life. She was the human being in whose body we gestated. Hers was the first heart we heard, the first physical heat we felt. After our birth, unless she died putting us into the world, she was the person we most often saw, heard, tasted, touched, and smelled. Later, it was most often she who fed, cleaned, clothed, and cared for us. We recall, or imagine what we have forgotten, with new or renewed gratitude and make that the basis for the development of compassion (regardless of how we remember our conscious childhood or adolescent memories of our relationship with our mothers).

Once we feel intense compassion for our mother, we turn our attention to other beings, with the aim to feel the same gratitude and compassion for each and every one as we do for our mother. Compassion begins at home, the unavoidable up-close-and-personal aspect of the Great Way.

This compassion is based on the Lesser Way's glimpse of our lack of an intrinsic self. Therefore, the Great Way's vaunted training in love and compassion does not amount to well-meaning but heavy-handed brainwashing. For instance, it is not a coercive replacement of an existent, devalued negative emotion, such as hatred, with an existent, treasured positive emotion, such as love, which a separate, existent "I" feels for a separate, existent other. Without the Lesser Way's renunciation and selflessness, the Great Way risks becoming a cosmic materialistic humanism or sentient being-ism that produces social workers dedicated to provide warm and fuzzy security blankets for all beings until the end of time. Rather, Buddhism at this stage idealizes the inseparable union of compassion and emptiness, epitomized by dreamlike bodhisattvas who make dreamlike vows to work for all dreamlike sentient beings' dreamlike liberation from the dreamlike wheel of life.

In tantra, we begin with a solid foundation in the Lesser Way's renunciation, and the Great Way's union of emptiness and compassion. Each of these is as indispensable to incorporate in the practice of tantra as the Lesser Way's renunciation was at the outset of the bodhisattva path. Then we examine the nature of being, enlightenment. It is not as if this hasn't been the concern of earlier forms of Buddhism, but the subject is brought into perfect focus in the person of the spiritual master. As mentioned above, enlightenment is our eternal, changeless nature, but this nature goes unrecognized or remains diffused, like the sun's rays. The spiritual master is like a human magnifying glass who gathers and focuses our enlightened nature's energy into one point, creating a fire of wisdom that consumes our dualistic experience. This will seem like empty, meaningless words until we have met a qualified spiritual master to whom we feel unadulterated and uncontrived devotion. Tantra works as long as our devotion lasts; the minute it stops, tantra becomes very intricate mind or energy "work," perhaps useful to make money, gather crowds of seekers, or gain credentials in this new-age world, but without devotion it amounts to a travesty of the Buddha's path to enlightenment.

The tantric master must be "qualified," a Buddhist code word to indicate that the man or woman who inspires our deep devotion should be capable of leading us on the path of tantra from wherever we are to full and complete enlightenment. Their capability is rooted in their personal realization and, necessarily, in their preservation of a pure, unbroken lineage that they received in exactly the same way in which they transmit it to us. Primordial enlightenment is like a power plant; the line of masters from the original buddha to the present day is like an electrical cord. It must be perfectly intact, unbroken, if we are to benefit from it. What we receive should be no different from what was ever transmitted or received at any point. If the lineage is unbroken and the master is qualified, there is no difference between him or her and the original buddha. This is the premise and the promise of tantra.

Do such persons even live on this planet? Yes, I certainly believe so. I cannot judge anyone's realization, but in my blind confusion, I think I have met many such masters and I continue to follow them as best I can. Over the years, many of my teachers have exchanged their worn-out bodies for new ones, while some continue to inhabit the bodies I first met. If a reader wanted some names of qualified tantric masters still living whom I could personally recommend, I would vouch for any of the following: Sakya Trizin, Chojé Trizin Rinpoché, and Dzongsar Kyentsé Rinpoché of the Sakya tradition; Tai Situpa, Gyaltsab Rinpoché, and Bokar Tulku Rinpoché of the Kagyus; and Chatral Rinpoché, Trinley Norbu Rinpoché, Do-drup-chen Rinpoché, Namka Drimé Rinpoché, and

Lama Tharchin Rinpoché of the Nyingma tradition. My only criterion for including these names on the list is my own experience: these are the living masters from whom I have sought and received tantric empowerments.

There are many, many others whom I believe to be equally qualified, but I have not had the good fortune to meet them or, if I have, to receive empowerment from them. For women who feel uncomfortable with enlightenment in a male form, I highly recommend Khandro Tsering Chödron of Gangtok, Sikkim; Jétsun Ku-chok-la of Vancouver, Canada; and Khandro Rinpoché of Clement Town, India.

This is nothing but one person's list, but that is the nature of the up-close-and-personal aspect of tantra: it comes down to you and a qualified master that you have deliberately sought out and chosen. Tantra does not exist outside that context. Once your devotion is awakened, you can set foot on the path of tantra, seeing each and every technique of tantra as nothing but aspects of the master's enlightenment. If you take empowerment and continue to practice with that attitude, like a plunge off Lovers' Leap, you are sure, sooner or later, to hit the ground. In this case, it will be the sacred ground of enlightenment.

I have dwelt here on the subject of devotion as the fuel of tantra because it is never again mentioned in this book. Kongtrul writes at an advanced level of tantric practice and does not cover such essential preliminary reference points. No doubt he thought his readership did not need such reminders. Our advertisements for cars never mention that we must also buy gasoline; we sell lightbulbs assuming that the buyer's home is equipped with electricity. Kongtrul wrote of tantra secure that we would know that it runs only on high-octane, direct-current devotion, the purer and the stronger the better.

A General Map of Tantra

This section provides an indication of the initial entry to tantra and Jamgon Kongtrul's overview of the field of tantra, a general map on which he situated any aspect of tantra, from beginning to end.

Tantra promises to lead to enlightenment within what is, in Buddhist terms, a very short time: in this very lifetime or in a matter of lives. Tantra also compares itself favorably to other Buddhist paths and remarks how adaptable it is to practitioners' circumstances and how it is relatively easy.

These claims, of tantra's efficiency, adaptability, and ease, presuppose that practitioners would have what only the richest and poorest among us have these days: time. It is no accident that the first prerequisite for Buddhist practice, what is called the "precious human birth," is defined first and foremost by the simple presence of leisure time. If spiritual paths were reflected within the realm of food, tantra would be the most elaborate, extravagant banquet imaginable, a grand occasion in which every participant—the chef and staff, servers, musicians, the host and hostess, and guests— bring the best in themselves to the event. Tantra is designed for those with enough leisure to regularly summon and refine their most acute sense of themselves, others, and the world. It may be that tantra is better suited to more relaxed and reflective times than our own, as its gentle ease in relation to time is obviously out of place in a culture geared to a diet of time-micro-managed spiritual fast food. I do not at all mean to imply that tantra is impossible these days, quite the contrary, but I do feel that few of our own grandparents, let alone the Tibetans of another era, could have imagined to what an amazing extent we have mastered space and yet have lost control of time. For many modern persons setting out on the tantric path, the first challenge seems to be to learn to truly take time.

Apart from such culture-specific considerations, how does anyone enter the path of tantra and what is needed? Kongtrul first gives the standard reply that we can enter tantra after having trained our mind in more elementary forms of Buddhism, specifically that of the Great Way, but he adds that it is also possible and appropriate to embark on the tantric path directly as a beginner. What any individual must come equipped with is faith, energetic application, and transcendent knowledge. The first step on the path is that of the development of confidence—confidence in tantra; confidence in one's inspiration and guide, the spiritual master; and confidence in oneself. Kongtrul writes:

> Ordinary individuals enter this path after having trained the mind
> in the general path of the Great Way. Special individuals can enter

this path at the beginning of their practice. Either approach is appropriate. Individuals who enter this path must be endowed with three special qualities. The first is inviolable faith in the methods of the cause, path, and result of the Vajra Way [*vajrayana*]. The second is unrelenting, intense diligence in the subjects of study, reflection, and meditation, with the wish to reach enlightenment during this lifetime or in the intermediate state after death, etc., for the benefit of all sentient beings. The third is the supreme good fortune of innate and acquired transcendent knowledge and other qualities that develop when the special power of the Great Way's inherent buddha-nature awakens.

As an indispensable preparatory stage, persons entering tantra must develop two forms of confidence. The first is confidence in the profound tantras of Secret Mantra, what one intends to enter. The second is confidence in the illustrious spiritual masters, through whom one enters tantra. Beyond these two, those who meditate on this path need a third form of confidence, self-confidence. On this subject, the illustrious master Drimé Özer [Longchenpa] states:

> In the Mantra Way, the Honored Buddha taught three forms of confidence. At the outset, for a while, one develops confidence in the tantras; then one develops confidence in the spiritual master, then self-confidence. With these three confidences, the path to authentic, complete enlightenment will be perfectly pure.
>
> Otherwise, without these three confidences, any path the master teaches the student will not lead to the result of authentic, complete enlightenment. Because the student has a fool's faith, the path's relative truth will lead to a worldly result.
>
> Moreover, confidence in the tantras is the conviction that the tantras, having been spoken by the perfect Buddha, are reliable and authoritative. Confidence in the spiritual master is the conviction that the succession of the lineage, from the Buddha Vajra Bearer until one's spiritual master, is unbroken and that no broken tantric commitments have contaminated it. Self-confidence is the conviction that by putting the meaning of what one hears from the master into practice, appropriate experiences will arise. (*Encyclopedia of Buddhism*, vol. 2, pp. 655-656)

The individual who has developed these forms of confidence engages in the tantric path like those who practice other ways of spiritual development within Buddhism—by listening to the master's teaching, reflecting upon it, and meditating. Exceptionally, tantric meditation consists of two phases, creation and completion, and is preceded by empowerment and the acceptance of the commitments that define the parameters of the tantric path. What is noteworthy in the following passage is that the entire path of tantra (referred to as "mantra," one distinctive element of tantric meditation) is simplified into two stages, that of empowerment, the catalyst for spiritual maturation; and meditation, the path of liberation. These subjects will be returned to later in this introduction. Kongtrul continues:

> An individual who has the two confidences must first understand the meaning of the tantras. After having listened to the tantras and their commentaries and gained a good understanding, one begins meditation on the meaning of the tantras, the two phases [creation and completion]. As a preliminary to those meditations, an individual must receive an authentic empowerment in the proper manner and maintain well the tantric commitments.
>
> In brief, all stages of tantric paths can be summarized as the initial reception of empowerment that brings spiritual maturity and acceptance of tantric commitments; and, as the main practice, the path that brings liberation—the two phases of meditation. *The True Measure of the Doctrine* states:

> > The path is taught to entail both maturation and liberation.
> > The path taught by the spiritual master
> > Brings the disciple to full maturity.
> > The instructions taught by the Buddha Vajra Bearer
> > Are based entirely upon two phases [of meditation] —
> > The phase of creation
> > And the phase of completion.
> > Having balanced these two phases,
> > He who holds the vajra taught the spiritual instructions.
> > (*Ibid.*, p. 656)

We now come to a general map of tantra, which at first view can seem intimidatingly packed with uncommon words and concepts. The challenge of navigation within a new technical language does not always tempt us; it gives us pause. Perhaps we can imagine ourselves as a driving instructor to a FOB Tibetan (fresh-off-the-boat). Our friend wants to learn to drive, having seen its benefits (the first confidence), sees us as the instructor of an unbroken lineage, materialized in our driver's license (the second confidence), and, although the prospect of putting our Tibetan friend behind the wheel is at the least worrying, he or she bubbles over with enough exuberant self-confidence for both of us (the third confidence). So far, so good. Now comes the question of language. We have managed to find a translation of the fundamentals of navigation—speed limit, right of way, one way street, etc.—and the basic parts of the car—key, ignition, gas pedal, brake, etc.—in Tibetan, but our friend stubbornly resists learning the words. "I just want to learn how to drive!" we hear. Of course. And of course it is possible to learn to drive without having learned the most basic language of the road. But in all good conscience, can we allow our friend, for his/her sake and for others', to drive without it?

To be able to articulate to ourselves and to others what we are doing on the path of tantra, there are some basic reference points we need to know. We don't need to become the equivalent of automotive engineers or car mechanics—how many of us can explain in detail how our car really works? Or could identify problems and fix our machines? We don't have to become lamas or scholars. We do need to give ourselves the opportunity to become alert, informed practitioners, a learning process that implies learning a new set of words and meanings beyond the names of lamas, deities, practices, and mantras.

A vital point to be noted at the outset of any description of the tantric view is that tantra purports to describe the mind and life the way they are. While some may construe tantra as spiritual steroids for psychic bodybuilding, this is not how tantra views itself. The word *tantra* denotes continuity, specifically in three aspects: the continuity of our fundamental enlightened nature; the continuity within the path of techniques, such as meditation, for us to realize that basic nature; and the continuity of the result—stable, perfect enlightenment. Kongtrul asserted that to comprehend the highest level of tantra, we must understand the subject of the three continuities. As if to underline that, he explains them in the following passage twice, first as a definition of terms, then as a synopsis.

Kongtrul mentions that every level of Buddhist practice has different names for the changeless, enlightened nature of our being and he uses one such name from the highest yoga tantra to elucidate enlightenment's qualities—the Sanskrit syllables *é* and *vam*.

As foreign as these syllables are to most readers, they can be considered a form of tantric shorthand, akin to the Taoist *yin* and *yang*; the *é* represents emptiness, transcendent knowledge, the feminine; *vam*, appearance, skillful means, and the masculine; their union, the ultimate.

Kongtrul wrote the pages below to introduce tantra in his *Encyclopedia of Buddhism*. He used this outline of the three continuities to provide a format for details of every aspect of tantra, over a hundred pages' worth. This framework does not make for easy reading, but seems essential for us to study and learn if we are to understand tantra or, at the very least, to follow Kongtrul's lead on that path. Kongtrul writes:

> Different styles of encapsulating the meaning of the highest yoga tantra's content have appeared, based on the enlightened intention of [specific] tantras or masters. The principal one is presented in *The Latter Tantra of Quintessential Secret* (*Guhyasamaja*):
>
> > Tantra is expressed as continuity.
> >
> > Moreover, this continuity can be classified into three aspects:
> > The basis, its intrinsic nature, and
> > Immutability.
> > Its intrinsic nature is [the continuity of] the cause.
> > The basis is known as [the continuity of] technique.
> > Similarly, immutability refers to the result.
> > The meaning of tantra can be condensed in these three.
>
> Since this abridgement [of the meaning of tantra] into three continuities is universally recognized, I will explain it here:
>
> Tantra itself is the ever-excellent mind of enlightenment, with no beginning nor end, intrinsic luminosity. As this is uninterrupted from time immemorial until [the attainment of] enlightenment, it is continuously present. Tantra's three aspects are as follows:
>
> 1. from the perspective of the fundamental cause, the intrinsic nature or *continuity of the cause*
> 2. from the perspective of co-emergent conditions, the basis or *continuity of the technique*
> 3. from the perspective of awakening, which includes magnificent benefit for oneself and others, immutability or *continuity of the result*.

As this constitutes the single vital key to understanding [the highest yoga] tantra, I will explain this encapsulation in brief here.

[Continuity of the Cause]

This is the mind's intrinsic nature, which abides like space, in an unchanging manner, from [the time of one's experience as] an ordinary sentient being until enlightenment. Any number of names are given to it: In the discourses, it is given such names as the inherent constituent, or buddha-nature, or the naturally present potential for enlightenment; and in the lower tantras, it can be called the ultimate self or the mind of awakening or the ever-excellent mind, etc. However, in the upper tantras, those of highest yoga tantra, it is joined to the meaning of the union of *é -vam.*

To explain this, the meaning of the syllable *vam* has three features: mind's intrinsic nature that remains unchanged from [the time of experience as] an ordinary sentient being until enlightenment; inner awareness that has the characteristic of individual self-awareness; and supreme, unchanging great bliss. It is expressed with such names as the ultimate nature, vajra holder of the cause, and original buddha.

Further, the meaning of the syllable *é* is as follows: Due to the vital point that this ultimate nature is the mind of the nature of reality, it can have form or an appearance. In an impure state, [this ultimate nature] appears as the psycho-physical aggregates, etc. of an ordinary being in the wheel of life. In the [relatively] pure impure state, it arises as the infinite visions that appear within a practitioner's meditation. In the extremely pure state, it arises as the appearances of the inexhaustible circle of ornaments of the body, voice, and mind of enlightenment. This ultimate nature that naturally has various forms is given names such as emptiness endowed with sublime aspects, the all-appearing, and the all-powerful.

This union of *é -vam* is referred to as *cause* since it is the underlying basis of awakening. *The Unsurpassable Continuity* states:

Unconnected to sentient beings' obscuring emotions that
    cover it,
The nature of mind
Is from time immemorial without stain.
It is said to be beginningless.

It is referred to as *continuity* since it dwells in the nature of mind from time immemorial and is continuously present from the time of one's experience as an ordinary being until enlightenment.

Intrinsic nature is defined in *The Root of Transcendent Knowledge*:

Intrinsic nature is that which is uncontrived
And does not depend upon other [influences].

The fundamental state of the essence of mind not newly contrived or embellished by conditions is its intrinsic nature.

[Continuity of the Technique]

A broad definition of the basis or continuity of the technique includes all possible forms of the spiritual path to be traveled from the point one's enlightened potential is kindled until awakening is attained. A narrow definition of the basis is the empowerments that foster spiritual maturation and the path, with all its aspects, that brings liberation. [It is called *basis*] because these paths act as a support for the accomplishment of, and rest within, the result of awakening, just as earth provides the basis for the growth of plants. [In this context,] *continuity* refers to the uninterrupted connection between the two achievements, temporary and ultimate, and the [tantric] path's two phases. These two phases of meditation are themselves connected to the support, tantric commitments; and the commitments are in turn connected to the entrance gate to tantra, empowerment.

It is called *technique* because the path itself constitutes the co-emergent conditions that create the actualization of the result, awakening. There are both remote and proximate techniques. Remote techniques include all paths from any of the three ways of the transcendent perfections up to, and including, yoga tantra. Proximate techniques are the path of the highest yoga tantra's two phases and their branch practices, preceded by empowerment.

[Continuity of the Result]

When the fundamental cause is freed from all incidental impurities, it changes into the body of enlightenment of the two purities, manifest perfect awakening, the support for others' benefit. What is referred to as *immutability* is to enter this state in permanent stability, without regression due to occasional obscuring obstacles or without entering a state of inferior transcendence. This latter state is characterized by the interruption of awareness, which causes damage to or loss of the life that works for others' benefit.

As long as space exists, the number of sentient beings will be endless. As long as sentient beings exist, awakening likewise will not be interrupted. Because it has this enduring quality, it is called *continuity*.

What is referred to as *result* is the principal, ultimate goal, desired intently by all bodhisattvas who practice after they enter the door of tantra. These points have been presented here as clearly taught in *The Harvest of Profound Instructions*.

[A Synopsis]

These topics can be explained in very easily understood terms as follows:

The unimaginable force of karma of each of those commonly known as sentient beings, grouped into five classes, produces the entire range of their experiences, a total immersion in place, body, possessions, moment of time, perception, mind, and discursive thought. Like optical illusions that appear to those with impaired vision, all this experience of sentient beings is only the distorted appearance of what is undivided appearing as duality through the force of beginningless habitual ignorance. Even while such appearances arise, the basis of their experience, naturally luminous mind, abides free from the impurity of habitual, distorted appearances. This is what is called *continuity of the cause*.

The profound instructions of the holy spiritual master teach neither to remove nor to accept whatever appears, but to familiarize oneself with the very essence of luminosity. Or, those unable to undertake such practice immediately can enjoy these appearances as the forms of male and female deities in the transcendent ones' celestial palace, which has limitless adornments. This technique of unceasing enjoyment of objective experience is employed as a preliminary, then joined to the wisdom of luminosity. Stable application to familiarization with this wisdom, like the stream of a river, is what is called *continuity of the path*.

What is the effect of such continual familiarization? The entire array of the mind's knowledge appears unobstructedly. However, since stains from distortions of reality are completely extinguished, no dualistic appearances arise. [The array of knowledge] becomes the integral essence of the great wisdom of intrinsic awareness, free from all obscurations. At the same time that this state has not the slightest stain of concept, discursive thought, and dualistic appearances, sentient beings (whose numbers fill the limits of space) are viewed impartially and, according to the precise interests, dispositions, and capabilities of each, the entire benefit they desire is unceasingly, completely achieved in spontaneous enlightened activity. This is what is known as *continuity of the result.* (*Ibid.*, pp. 612-616)

FIRST STEPS ON THE SACRED PATH

Journeys to sacred places do not only entail travel plans, reservations, luggage and checklists. Nor is tantric pilgrimage different from tourism only in the outer activity done once the destination is reached, e.g., sitting on a meditation cushion as opposed to lying on a beach. As Sakya Pandita so emphatically stated, we prepare for pilgrimage by gaining stability in tantric meditation practice in a controlled environment, one's own home, for example, and in uncontrollable, challenging environments, such as charnel grounds (as they existed in ancient India or Tibet) or, for example, in a big city hospital (our modern equivalent). Then we can set out to encounter and to benefit from the charged environments that regions of sacred ground have to offer.

The previous section presented the sacred foundation of our faith and practice, buddha-nature, and a general map for navigation in the realm of tantra. "First Steps on the Sacred Path" focuses on what was mentioned above by Kongtrul as the continuity of the path (or technique) and, within that subject, the two phases of tantric meditation, creation and completion.

Here Kongtrul supplies a textbook definition of these terms, by translating their Sanskrit names:

> The literal meaning of the phase of *creation* [can be understood by providing a definition based on its Sanskrit name] *utpanti,* which means "contrived," referring to the fact that it is created by thoughts or contrived by thoughts. It has also been called "the phase of conceptualization" and "contrived practice."
>
> The term [in Sanskrit for] *completion, nihapanna,* means truly existent or natural, referring to the fact of it being truly existent in reality, natural or present in the nature of things. Therefore, this term denotes meditation not on something newly created, but on what is fully existent from before.
>
> *Phase* refers to a stage of the path. (*Encyclopedia of Buddhism*, vol. 3, p. 160)

Tibetans called the first phase that of creation (or development), since this practice involves the creation of a parallel sense of oneself and the world, that of "meditation deities," pure forms of nonmaterial enlightenment. There does not seem to be any limit to the number or variety of such tantric deities, but the point of any of their practices remains the same, to overcome our habitual tendency to make something out of nothing and to believe in its solidity. Although this diagnosis of our basic sickness does not change from one level of Buddhism to another, the prescription of tantric practice is very different from the cures offered in pre-tantric Buddhist ways of spiritual development. Instead of renunciation, or mind-training in antidotes, or a dose of straight emptiness, the deities of the phase of creation provide a stepping-stone away from conventional experience and toward sight of reality by using the energy of the disease itself. Fire is fought with fire. Kongtrul writes:

The Hévajra Tantra states:

> Discursive thoughts can be purified by discursive thoughts,
> Existence by existence,
> Just as water that blocks the ear
> Can be drawn out by more water.
> Discursive thoughts of reality
> Can be definitely purified in the same manner.

Further,

> The unbearable karma of an individual,
> By which he/she is constrained, whatever it is,
> Can, through skillful means,
> Cause liberation from the constraints of existence.[7]

Conventional discursive thoughts can very effectively be blocked by discursive thoughts of the deity. This process can be compared to the immediate blocking of the thought that a certain person is one's enemy by developing the thought of him/her as one's friend, a change difficult to effect through other means, such as meditation on emptiness. Similarly, conventional desire can quickly be reversed by meditation on bliss and emptiness, whereas exclusive meditation on emptiness or other means will not produce the same result. When an individual purifies desire that he/she has deliberately engendered into emptiness, without attachment, this process

has the side effect of purifying into a state without attachment the
desire that arises from within. (*Ibid.*, pp. 164-165)

It does not take much imagination to recognize that tantra's approach is different and replete with opportunities for misunder-
standing. Kongtrul does not dwell on the obvious possibility for
us to mislead ourselves on this path and I think all that needs to be
said is, once again, that regular requests for guidance from a qualified spiritual master seem an indispensable element of any successful journey on the path of tantra.

Kongtrul continues with a more explicit explanation of what is
wrong with our usual mode of experience and how the phase of
creation can set us on the path to recovery:

At the outset of the practice of the phase of creation's wisdom, we
must recognize what must be renounced. *The Vajra Tent* states:

Correct meditation is proclaimed
As that which overcomes conventional discursive thought.

["Conventional discursive thought"] refers to both conventional
appearances and attachment to those appearances. Meditation practice on the appearance of the deity and attachment to the deity
immediately blocks manifest attachment to [ordinary] appearances.
Knowledge that the deity's appearance has no intrinsic nature
blocks attachment to the reality of both conventional appearances
and those of the deity. [Phase of creation meditation has these ef-
fects] because it vigorously confronts with specific antidotes three
[aspects of conventional experience]: appearance, attachment, and
belief in the reality of appearances.

To compare this style of meditation to the way of the transcendent perfections [i.e., the Great Way], the latter overcomes the cause
of suffering, negative emotions, and thus impedes the result, future suffering. On the other hand, the phase of creation begins with
the transformation of one's present impure appearances, the truth
of suffering, into the sacred configuration of the deity. This immediately impedes the appearance of suffering.

Therefore, in the phase of creation, one meditates on the vivid
appearance of the deity, which thwarts conventional appearances;
on pride in oneself as the deity (such as [a wrathful deity, called] a
héruka), which thwarts one's self-image as an ordinary human being; and on conviction in the illusion-like nature of these appearances, which thwarts clinging to them as real. Once vivid appearances arise in the [practice of the phase of creation, these three aspects

of conventional experience] are immediately blocked. Moreover, such clear appearances can easily arise, like the vivid appearance of a woman seen in the mind of her ardent lover. (*Ibid.*, p. 166)

Kongtrul here compares Great Way practice to that of tantra: the former is preventive medicine, in that it attacks the cause of future suffering—negative, obscuring emotions. The phase of creation applies itself to suffering already present, the appearances of life itself, and overcomes it with potent antidotes to appearances, attachment to them, and the belief in their reality.

His final point, that the appearances of the deities can easily arise, is an important one. In the phase of creation, we are confronted with what might seem to be a daunting demand, that we visualize an elaborate set of forms, objects, and colors. Kongtrul assures us that this is an easy exercise by relating it to another form of visualization with which most of us are familiar, that of a loved one. A lover is captivated, enthralled, possessed by the image of the other. The world seems to naturally slip away, to fade into insignificance against one's better judgment and in spite of one's best intentions, replaced by the image of one's loved one. He reasons that, since human beings are capable of such intense visualization practice without ever having been taught it, surely the phase of creation should not pose insurmountable problems.

We often hear complaints that the phase of creation must be easier for Tibetans than for Westerners, yet logically it should be the opposite. Outside of temple settings, Tibetans had fewer opportunities to visualize than we do. Orienting ourselves in the modern world requires visualizations of a complexity undreamed of by most rural Tibetans. Each of us can visualize clearly the *mandala* of our local supermarket, from the fruit and vegetable department to the ice cream freezer. We can give directions, as we visualize them, to friends on the phone who will visit our home for the first time. A few bars of an old song can unlock intense memories of times long gone. We can review in our mind's eye any number of scenes from films or TV shows we once saw. The list is endless. Yes, we are unfamiliar with the deities and many seem to feel that it is a nuisance to have to familiarize ourselves with them, in the same way that some of us stubbornly resist learning to drive or to use a computer. But it is a fact that our culture has given us more than ample training in the basic exercise of visualization. What we need is to be convinced that it is worth our while to include tantric deities in our cornucopia of daily visualization practice.

Kongtrul mentions here a few suggestions concerning phase of creation meditation, how to approach it at first and what to expect in terms of duration. He suggests visualization at night for beginners and reassures us that stability in the practice takes a year for most persons. He assumes, I believe, that we will make a major time commitment to our chosen deity during that year.

> For beginners in Mantra, meditation mainly at night facilitates accomplishment of vivid appearances in deity practice. Once stability is reached, meditation can be done continually, regardless of the time of day.
>
> On the subject of duration, if one wishes to practice in a specific manner—to make the phase of creation one's principal practice, or with the wish for common accomplishments, or even with the intention to accomplish the lesser forms of enlightened activity— one should meditate until one has attained stability in the vivid appearance of the deity. In general, it is said that this takes one year. (*Ibid.*, pp. 185-186)

Most meditators first stabilize the phase of creation before they embark on the phase of completion. The deity meditations on the phase of creation, although vital, represent only a step on the path and not its destination. Kongtrul here mentions the limitations of this first phase, yet insists that it is indispensable on the tantric path to enlightenment:

> Ordinary persons who live within the bounds of discursive thoughts are unable to train from the outset in the phase of completion without discursive thoughts. Therefore, like planting coarse seeds to prepare a field for more delicate crops, the initial complex practice of the phase of creation purifies conventional thinking. Once the nature of discursive thoughts is known, simple, non-discursive meditation on the phase of completion can be undertaken. This has been stated in *The Commentary to The Vajra Essence*.
>
> Until stable, specific realization arises within the natural, uncontrived phase of completion, one must rely upon the contrivance of the conceptual phase of creation. Once such realization arises, one no longer needs to pursue meditation on contrived practices, such as the simple, conceptual phase of creation, just as the

boat one needed to cross a river is not needed after arrival at the far shore.

Nevertheless, neither the phase of creation separate from the phase of completion nor the phase of completion apart from the phase of creation can by themselves lead to supreme attainment. To reach the state of integration of Buddha Vajra Bearer at the time of the result, one must have practiced during the path an integration of the phases of creation and completion, without lacking balance between appearance and emptiness. The phase of creation constitutes the skillful means aspect of the practice of integration; the phase of completion is its transcendent knowledge aspect. An integration of the two is essential in meditation. *The Lamp of the Path* states:

> Skillful means without transcendent knowledge;
> And transcendent knowledge without skillful means
> Are in any circumstance called restrictive.
> Therefore, do not renounce either of them.

Does this contradict the statement [made above] that once specific realization within the phase of completion has arisen, the conceptual phase of creation is unnecessary? No, since although at that point, meditation on the phase of creation based only on conceptual thought is unnecessary, it is definitely essential for the appearances of the illusory circle of the phase of creation's deities to arise. (*Ibid.*, pp. 163-164)

This quote makes the point that tantra aims to find a balance in the phases of creation and completion. That said, the order in which each practitioner approaches the two phases is left to the discretion of his or her teacher and, in this, the teacher is given the considerable leeway that typifies tantra. Kongtrul writes:

> Due to the different capacities of individuals, there is no definite order for meditation on the two phases. In general, however, average persons who begin practice on the path of liberation at the highest level of tantra begin with the phase of creation, followed by the phase of completion. *The Five Phases* states:
>
> > Those who rest stably on the phase of creation,
> > Who wish for the phase of completion,
> > Were taught these techniques by the perfect Buddha,
> > Like steps up a ladder.

Many masters, such as Nagarjuna and his spiritual successors, taught that one meditates on the phase of completion after first gaining stability in the phase of creation. Their point is the consideration that for untrained, unsophisticated meditators, each stage of practice must be stabilized before the next is begun, like climbing a staircase.

The accomplished masters Saroruha-vajra, Durjaya-chandra, and others taught that the first part of a meditation session should be devoted to the phase of creation; the latter part, to the phase of completion. Their point is the consideration that, for those somewhat familiar with meditation or of middling capacity, training in the two phases should be alternated, like walking.

Some Tibetan masters have taught that from the outset the two phases can be meditated upon together. Their point is the consideration that, for those of acute capacities who are very familiar with meditation, it is appropriate to meditate on an integration of the two phases, like a bird which spreads both wings when taking flight.

However, all agree that training in the path of liberation for individuals who develop gradually should begin with the phase of creation, followed by the phase of completion. (*Ibid.*, pp. 162-163)

As pilgrimage is situated in tantric practice at the level of the phase of completion, the information in the next section will relate almost exclusively to that phase. Here, two points can help us distinguish it from earlier forms of Buddhist practice.

First, when we shift from the phase of creation to the phase of completion, we leave behind an overriding concern with intricate and elaborate visualizations of deities. We no longer "keep up appearances." In the phase of completion, the key words are co-emergent, non-discursive, and all-inclusive. Each of these signals a significant shift from previous forms of meditation, as Kongtrul explains:

The phase of completion must be presented as well in terms of basis, path, and result. Moreover, each of these has [three characteristics], as Drimé Özer [Longchenpa] states:

The stage of completion is co-emergent, non-conceptual, and all-inclusive. That is to say, it has no concept of [a deity's] face, hands, color, and shape.

This means that the stage of completion has three characteristics: co-emergence, non-conceptuality, and all-inclusiveness. The effect of the first facet, co-emergence, cuts through meditative states, such as those of cessation or those that resemble unconsciousness, the extreme diminishment of appearance and awareness. The second, non-conceptuality, cuts through meditations that involve discursive thought, such as the phase of creation. The third, all-inclusiveness, cuts through meditative states focused on awareness alone, states that do not include the symbolic appearance of wisdom. (*Ibid.*, p. 210)

Second, some crucial reference points from pre-tantric Buddhism are reincarnated in tantra in slightly different forms. We saw this above, where the buddha-nature of the Great Way appears in tantra in verbal guises (such as *é-vam*) that require a reintroduction. The same can be said for the union of compassion and emptiness, familiar to us as the core of the Great Way. Kongtrul says that this is shared by tantra, but then informs us that, while the meaning is the same, the language and context of practice undergo a radical change. Specifically, the word "compassion" in the Great Way becomes "desire" in the phase of completion. Kongtrul explains:

In the general context of the Great Way, it is well known that the root of the path is the mind of awakening, the essence of emptiness and compassion. Moreover, within the specific highest path of spiritual maturation and liberation in the Vajra Way, and within the phase of completion, the mind of awakening of inseparable exceptional emptiness and great compassion must be considered the ultimate subject of study, meditation, and result. (*Ibid.*, p. 211)

This subject [of inseparable emptiness and compassion] represents the essence of the entire doctrine of the discourses and tantras, and specifically, the essence of the highest Secret Mantra's phase of completion. Therefore, the highest tantras, such as Kalachakra, present it as the ultimate purpose [of their teaching], the meaning of *é-vam*, and the source of the 84,000 collections of teachings. Moreover, what is called Vajrasattva Kalachakra [literally, the adamantine being of the wheel of time] has the characteristics of the union of emptiness and compassion. Thus, the precious tantras clearly present it to be the heart of their doctrine.

On the subject of how it forms the root of the spiritual path, the general custom of the Great Way teaches that [emptiness and compassion] effect renunciation of the extremes of existence [*samsara*] and perfect peace [*nirvana*]. Moreover, any overview of the phase of completion necessarily presents extraordinary emptiness and compassion as effecting renunciation of the two extremes, existence and perfect peace. How they cause the cessation of the two extremes is as follows: emptiness ends the formulations that result from grasping to the characteristics [of phenomena as real] and compassion prevents the abandonment of sentient beings' benefit. Within the specific context of the phase of completion, compassion is called "desire": the extraordinary great bliss of desire must be accepted as the skillful means of great compassion. This effects the renunciation of the extreme of perfect peace. Since desire takes the form of attachment toward sentient beings, it must be understood as the skillful means of great compassion. This is a special feature [of the phase of completion].

Therefore, inseparable emptiness and compassion is called the vajra practice that integrates skillful means and transcendent knowledge. [This integration] exists during the basis, path, and result. On the path, during the purification of the obscuring emotions, such as attachment, the wisdom of great bliss is said to have inconceivably greater power than that of ultimate truth [i.e., emptiness]. In the beginning, [realization of] emptiness purifies, then great bliss arises from emptiness. Such bliss can purify every habitual pattern. Of bliss and emptiness, emptiness is the initial purifier and great bliss, the principal factor [in the process of purification]. (*Ibid.*, pp. 212-213)

As we will see in the next section, concepts and terminology from earlier Buddhist paths are borrowed by the phase of completion, sometimes with different values and sometimes they are totally unrecognizable. In fact, each stage of Buddhism, from the Lesser Way to the Great Way, and through various levels of tantra, is accompanied by a radical departure from the reference points of the previous level. Such courage on the Buddha's part to enter previously uncharted territory was not always greeted warmly by his audience. Chögyam Trungpa Rinpoché would fondly recount the reception given to Buddha's first elucidation of emptiness by some followers, proficient at one level, who could not cope with the challenge of taking their spiritual path to another level: "Heart attack, dead on spot." (That "Form is emptiness and emptiness is form" and so on of *The Heart Sutra* no longer causes cardiac arrests is a tribute, I hope, to our sophistication and not to a symptom of attention deficit disorder!) This would not be the last time the Buddha's word proved earth-shattering. When the Buddha assumed the form of Joyous Vajra (*Hévajra*) and taught tantra to a circle of *dakinis*, they reacted to the teaching this way:

> Then all the goddesses...and the other yoginis, numerous as the atomic particles in Mount Meru, were all overcome with great astonishment. Hearing such words, terrified, they fell senseless to the ground. (*Concealed Essence*, p. 227)

History records that they recovered and the teaching continued.

Our first act in relation to the Buddha, his Teaching, and Community is to take refuge. We may construe that with a need for security within the wheel of life, but the Buddha seems to have been more concerned with teaching the truth. His truth was pure, simple, and virtuous in the beginning and remains, in fact, pure, simple, and virtuous throughout. Yet the scope of the truth becomes increasingly powerful and pervasive. To the fire which the Buddha started with small kindling, he adds larger and larger fuel until it consumes anything and everything, yet it remains all the while the same fire.

It is easy to speculate that the repeated transformation of the linguistic and conceptual decor along the Buddha's path to enlightenment is meant to prevent complacency, a false sense of security, or attachment to the path. Easterners or Westerners, we sometimes seem to content ourselves with attaining the state of Buddhist-hood rather than buddha-hood. One antidote to that is to make Buddhism less familiar, to rewrite the signposts in a new language, and to bring new, unexpected dimensions to the spiritual path, related to the cutting edge of our growing spiritual maturity. If this in fact was the point of the radical shifts along our path, the Buddha succeeded splendidly once again when he taught the phase of completion.

SACRED REGIONS FOR TANTRIC CONDUCT

The phase of completion's view of the body and the world is radically different from what is proposed in the lower paths of Buddhism. For tantric practitioners at this level, enlightenment dwells within this very body and in this vivid world, regardless of who we are and where we live. In particular, those who follow the mother tantras (of the highest level of the four classes of new tantras, or *Anuyoga* in the old tantras) are invited to discover enlightenment rooted within our present embodiment and enworldment. In the following quote, Kongtrul describes our human birth and body as ideal for tantric practice. Our body corresponds to the "vajra" body, a pure form inherent in our nature. The tantra he quotes here, *The Joyous Vajra (Hévajra) Tantra*, is a mother tantra:

> [The life that provides] the supreme support for a qualified recipient of the Secret Mantra Vajra Way is the impure body of manifest enlightenment, complete in every respect—[that of human beings] born in the eastern, southern, or western continents of this world-system and, particularly, those born here in this [southern] continent, the land of karmic activity, called Land of Jambu. Since this body is endowed with the six elements, it has all aspects of the vajra body, the basis of purification [to be effected through tantric practice].
>
>   The body's psycho-physical aggregates, constituents and sources of consciousness are produced from its inner channels, energy, and vital essence. These, in turn, arise from the nature of mind, with impurities, buddha-nature. For this reason, it has been affirmed that [human] birth within existence itself constitutes the impure supreme manifest body of enlightenment. *The Joyous Vajra Tantra* states:

>> The walls of the womb are themselves the Buddhist robes.
>> Similarly, the mother is the preceptor.
>> The [gestating] child joins his/her palms at the head in
>>   homage to her.
>> [The child] is engaged in the discipline of worldly activity.
>> The mantras recited are *ah* and *hom*.
>> The circle of the womb is *ah*;
>> The appearance of great bliss is *hom*.
>> Naked, hair and beard shaved,
>> The child is a fully ordained person of the ultimate Mantra
>>   Way.
>> Due to these conditions, all beings
>> Are the Buddha, beyond any doubt.
>> The ten months [of gestation] constitute the [ten] stages of
>>   awakening:

Human beings are born lord [bodhisattvas] of the tenth stage.[8]

(*Encyclopedia of Buddhism*, vol. 2, p. 632)

As mentioned here, our body's channels, energy, and vital essences form the bridge between our aggregates, constituents, and sources of consciousness and our buddha-nature. This is a critical domain of practice within the phase of completion, one that eventually leads to travel to external sacred ground. In brief, the body is made of innumerable channels, or meridians, through which different energies circulate, carrying with them the "the seed or vital essence of great bliss" (some texts call this "mind of awakening," thus borrowing and relocating a key term, *bodhichitta* (Sanskrit) or *jang-sem* (Tibetan), from the Great Way vocabulary; it is referred to below as vital essence).

In recent years, the concept of circulating physical energy—*chi* in Chinese, as in *Tai-chi*—has been introduced throughout the West, and those who have witnessed or experienced acupuncture treatments have had direct experience of the meridians through which energy travels. These invisible channels permit a doctor to plant fine needles in one part of the body that have dramatic, curative effects elsewhere. Chinese and Tibetan medicine describe this network as it actually is in order to target health and well-being; tantra postulates an idealized configuration, to target enlightenment. The tantric system of channels, energy, and vital essence is not meant to be scientific, any more than depictions of human-like deities with sixteen arms and four faces represent material, sentient beings. Although the West has discovered Tibetan/Chinese medicine and tantric theory at roughly the same time, we should clearly discern that the former strives to describe the human body as it is, whereas the latter is only concerned with the anatomy of deities, sacred anatomy, if you will. However, the basic terms and concepts used at the point of departure, channels and energies, are the same.

What tantra calls vital essence remains an unfamiliar concept in the West, except in the domain of sexuality. In tantra, two basic kinds of vital essence are identified: the first is white, centered at the upper extremity of the central channel—the crown of the head—and called "spring" (Tibetan, *dpyid*), since it forms like frost melting and brings joy to beings' hearts. The second is red, centered at the junction of the three main channels below the navel, and called "circle" (Tibetan, *thig le*), since it supports the experience of pleasure or bliss. According to the tantras, these vital essences are intimately related to consciousness, bliss or pleasure, and enlightenment. Kongtrul states:

> Fundamental consciousness, along with the great life-force energy, rests between these white and red [vital essences]. Thus, if they are symbolized by an outer location, they are the essence of Vajra Seat, Heart of Awakening [Bodhgaya, north-central India, site of Buddha's enlightenment]. In brief, because the white component stimulates bliss, [it is called] "spring"; and because the red component stabilizes bliss, it is called "circle." Since they are the place where enlightenment is actualized, they are known as the Vajra Seat. (*Ibid.*, p. 642)

Tantra's techniques that employ the channels, energies, and vital essences in meditation are collectively called the phase of completion, as Kongtrul states:

> The essence of the phase of completion is the cause and effect of the extraordinary wisdom produced when the body's energies and the mind are made to enter, remain within, and dissolve into the central channel. (*Ibid.*, vol. 3, p. 160)

Meditation on the phase of completion is both at-home work and, once one reaches a level of stability, necessitates travel to sacred places, since it is taught that the channels, energy, and vital essences of the body correspond to outer environments. Where can such sacred places be found? In the mysterious East? Surely, but they are also present in every corner of the globe and in every sentient being's body.

According to the mother (also called "*dakini*" or "transcendent knowledge") tantras of the highest yoga tantras, pilgrimage becomes part of spiritual life once a practitioner has traversed the first of the five paths within Buddhism, the path of cultivation. Here is a textbook definition of some familiar features of that initial path:

> The example [of the path of cultivation] is any act motivated by the wish for complete awakening performed after one's initial entry into the Great Way until the arising of the path of application. Such acts can be summarized by the following: ethical conduct; control of the senses; conscientious consumption of food in proper

measure; diligence in meditation practice during the first and last parts of the day, instead of sleeping; joyful, mindful living within the bounds of correct conduct; to not regret virtuous acts; interest, faith, devotion and other virtues that cause freedom; and transcendent knowledge gained from study, reflection, and meditation. [These and other virtuous acts] cause the path of application to arise. (Longchenpa, *The Precious Treasury of Philosophies*, pp. 102a-b)

Once a tantric practitioner enters the path of application, mastery of the body's energies through tantric practice offers a swift path to awakening. At that point, travel to outer regions and communion with their enlightened aspects can provide a potent catalyst for inner evolution. Each region is related to a point in the body's channels; each region's native enlightened beings, to the body's vital essence. In the following quotes, Kongtrul calls these beings "female messengers," although in later passages he also mentions their male counterparts:

The regions to which one travels for tantric conduct are mainly the well-known thirty-two major regions of the Land of Jambu and regions concordant with them in Tibet and in every country. These great regions are considered to be complete in each country and even complete within a single city. "Complete" can be understood in this case to indicate that the female messengers of the major and minor ten stages of awakening all reside in these places and will assist the practitioner in the realization of those stages. Therefore, the major regions of sacred ground are located in different principal lands.

No travel to sacred fields exists within the conduct of the father tantra's path, since those tantras do not teach the mantras of the yoginis as critical. Supreme Bliss [*Chakrasamvara*] and other tantras state that in the context of special conduct, gatherings with female messengers achieve various special results. This is the reason why travel to the sacred fields is essential. Because they include this method, the tantras of transcendent knowledge (i.e., mother or *dakini* tantras) are outstanding and constitute a swift path. (*Encyclopedia of Buddhism*, vol. 2, p. 544)

We have reached the point where Sakya Pandita's words at the beginning of this section draw their meaning. And we have obviously entered territory radically different from that of other Buddhist paths. Even major, familiar signposts change. In the following passage, Kongtrul leads the reader through the ten stages of awakening (Sanskrit: *bhumi*) as seen by the mother tantras, where the Great Way names for these stages (such as Completely Joyful, etc.) are replaced by the following: sacred place, higher sacred place, field, higher field, *chandho*, higher *chandho*, gathering place, higher gathering place, cemetery and higher cemetery. An eleventh and a twelfth stage are called drink-severer and higher drink-severer. Although this passage describes stages on the paths of seeing and meditation, we will see later that the same place-names can be applied to stages on the path of application.

> The non-Buddhist language of *yoginis* is used to affix unusual names to the common [stages of awakening]. Thereby, the first stage of awakening, Completely Joyful, is called by the name "sacred place." A place indicates a support. The ultimate, never before glimpsed throughout the course of one's lifetimes in the beginningless wheel of life, is directly seen, therefore this stage is mainly completely joyful. Because this first stage of awakening serves as a *support* for excellent qualities for one's own benefit—including meditative states and clairvoyance—and, based on the perfection of generosity, serves as a *support* for excellent qualities for others' benefit—satisfying the minds of infinite numbers of sentient beings—it is called "place."
>
> The second stage of awakening is called "higher place". . . since this stage serves as the support for the pure ten virtues based on the perfection of ethical conduct and for control of meditative states and clairvoyance.
>
> The third stage of awakening is called "field" since, like an abundant harvest that grows in a field, the perfect culmination of the perfection of patience produces uncontaminated meditative absorption, the basis for the growth of the great illumination of spiritual instruction.
>
> The fourth stage of awakening is called "higher field" since the perfection of diligence causes the growth of even more good qualities than before.
>
> The fifth stage of awakening is called *"chandho-ha."* *Chandho* means aspiration or wish, referring to the aspirations for one's own and others' benefit; *u-ha* means "I will follow my aspirations with deeds," i.e., the donning of the armor [of determination]. [At this stage,] based on the perfection of mental stability, beings are brought

to spiritual maturity and the instruction of the buddhas sought has been found and perfected.

The sixth stage of awakening is called "higher *chandho-ha*." Based on the actualization of the perfection of transcendent knowledge, the qualities referred to before are integrated to a high degree.

The seventh stage of awakening is called "gathering place." Because this means to bring together, it is called gathering, but it also means "to attain." Based on the perfection of skillful means, non-material qualities, such as meditation and spiritual freedom, are gathered by effort, thus "gathering place."

The eighth stage of awakening is called "higher gathering place": based on the perfection of aspirations, the complete purification of realms of worlds and beings is achieved effortlessly and spontaneously.

The ninth stage of awakening is called "cemetery," because *cemetery* has the significance of selflessness. Based on the perfection of force, one realizes the selfless nature of all phenomena and reveals this to others, completing one's goals for oneself and others. Thus this stage is called "cemetery."

The tenth stage of awakening is called "higher cemetery." Based on the perfection of wisdom, one's goals for oneself and others are brought to successful completion and one achieves the ultimate powers, thus "higher cemetery". . . .

The eleventh stage of awakening is called "drink-severer." Drink refers to negative emotions; sever, to virtuous conduct. Alternatively, this could indicate that [this stage] cuts through the cluster of negative emotions. Or again, that based on the special path of the tenth stage of awakening, rebirth in miserable states, has been severed, thus "drink-severer". . . .

The twelfth stage of awakening is called "higher drink-severer." At that stage every [negative influence], including habitual tendencies, has been abandoned and, thereby, exceedingly great wisdom has arisen; it is called [the level] of great wisdom.

Why isn't the thirteenth stage of awakening mentioned here? Because the stages listed before all pertain to the bodhisattva stages, whereas the thirteenth stage is that of [the Buddha] Vajra Bearer. (*Ibid.*, pp. 527-529)

Once again, this list of the stages of awakening designates stages on the paths of seeing and meditation. Nevertheless, the same progression (sacred place, higher sacred place, etc.) is employed in the following passage, where Kongtrul provides the correspondence between the ten stages on the path of application, general names of areas of sacred ground (such as place, higher place, field, higher field, etc.), specific names of twenty-four locations in India (such as Jalandhara, Oddiyana, Dévikotri, etc.), and points of the body where the channels, circulatory energies, and vital essence are made to enter the central channel.

The reader will note that the first paragraph of this passage provides the key to understanding tantric pilgrimage. It mentions the level of practice needed before setting out on tantric pilgrimage, that of initial stability within the practice of the phases of creation and completion, and to the purpose of travel to specific places once such stability is reached. To render the information here more accessible to the eye, I have placed it in a chart, although this was not the case in the original.

> Once the body of enlightenment formed entirely of mind and inner energy has been accomplished [through tantric meditation], one enters the outer environment of the twenty-four great regions and obtains a special gathering with the vajra female messengers of these places. On an inner level, this impels the body's elements and energies to be constrained within the central channel, which causes the gradual traversal of the ten stages that belong to the path of application.
>
> For example, when the subtle potency of the channels, energies, and vital essences of four sacred places dissolves into the central channel and is constrained there, the realization of the first stage of the path of application arises.

STAGE OF AWAKENING	SACRED GROUND	INDIAN PLACE NAME	PLACE IN BODY
First	Sacred Place	Pulliramalaya	Head
		Jalandhara	Crown of head
		Oddiyana	Right ear
		Arbuta	Neck
Second	Higher Sacred Place	Godavari	Left ear
		Rameshvara	Eyebrows
		Dévikotri	Eyes
		Malava	Shoulders
Third	Field	Kamarupa	Armpits
		Odra	Breasts

STAGE OF AWAKENING	SACRED GROUND	INDIAN PLACE NAME	PLACE IN BODY
Fourth	Higher Field	Trishanku	Navel
		Koshala	Nose
Fifth	*Chandho*	Kalinga	Mouth
		Lampaka	Middle of throat
Sixth	Higher *Chandho*	Kanchika	Heart
		Himalaya	Secret Channel
Seventh	Gathering Place	Pretapuri	Genitals
		Grihadéva	Anus
Eighth	Higher Gathering Place	Soraktra	Thighs
		Suvarnadvipa	Calves
Ninth	Cemetery	Nagara	Fingers
		Sindhu	Heels
Tenth	Higher Cemetery	Maru	Big Toes
		Kulata	Knees

As was just explained above, when the channels, energies, and vital essences are purified in the central channel at the two places in the body to which each pair [of geographical locations] is related, the realization of the corresponding stage arises. Thus the ten stages are gradually traversed. Following them, on the path of seeing, the body of non-dual wisdom is attained in drink-severer and higher drink-severer. (*Ibid.*, pp. 514-515)

The twenty-four areas for tantric conduct are listed here with Indian place names affixed. Some of these places have disappeared from modern maps, others thrive; yet in either case, travel to those specific locations in India is not what the tantras intend. A note to Matthieu Ricard's translation of *The Life of Shabkar* states:

It must be remembered that sacred geography does not follow the same criteria as ordinary geography. Kyabje Dilgo Khyentse Rinpoche (1910-91), for instance, said that within any single valley one can identify the entire set of the twenty-four sacred places. Kyabje Dudjom Rinpoche (1903-87) also said that sacred places, such as Uddiyana, can shrink and even disappear when conditions are no longer conducive to spiritual practice. The twenty-four sacred places are also present in the innate vajra body of each being. (p. 442, n. 1)

Why twenty-four places? On an outer level, this number finds its origin in *The Tantra of Supreme Bliss*, a mother tantra, from which the following passage retells the first part of the legend of its origin. I have added English equivalents to some Sanskrit words in square brackets:

> The world was once ruled by Bhairava [Terrifier], the wrathful form of Mahadeva, who made the land of Magadha [north-central India] the seat of his power. It is said also that four devas [gods] and four gandharvas [celestial musicians, literally "smell-eaters"] descended from the sky and established their dominion in eight places known as the eight Celestial Abodes. Likewise, four yakshas [harm-bringers] and four rakshasas [cannibal demons], already on the earth, made their way to Jambudvipa [the Land of Jambu, the southern continent], where they established themselves in eight Earthly Abodes, while four nagas and four asuras [demi-gods] came to Jambudvipa from beneath the earth, to settle themselves in eight Underground Abodes. (*Ibid.*, p. 343, n. 10)

According to the legend, these beings and their abodes came under the influence of the wrathful god Terrifier. When Buddha Vajra Bearer assumed the form of Supreme Bliss to subdue the god, the abodes of the gods and demons were transformed, as Kongtrul relates (in the *Pilgrimage Guide* below):

> All the places, regions, and charnel grounds above, on, and below the ground that the arrogant spirits had controlled were consecrated as the manifestations of the three circles of deities surrounding Supreme Bliss. They thus became an inconceivable number of major and minor natural sacred places, the domains of spiritual warriors and *yoginis*.

Although the twenty-four sacred places listed above are definitely located on the earth, they are nonetheless divided into three categories that correspond to the three abodes—celestial, on the ground, and underground. The first eight, from Pulliramalaya until Malava are the celestial abodes; the second set, from Kamarupa until Himalaya, are the earthly abodes; the last set, the underground abodes.

The tantras relate these three sets of eight to the mind, speech, and body of enlightenment and to the twenty-four major channels. They claim that a correspondence exists between the body's energy and the outer environment. For example, when internally the white component of vital essence descends within those channels in the body, externally male and female manifestations of enlightenment, called spiritual warriors and *dakinis*, gather at the locations. As in the case of the locations that were listed above, each of the body's twenty-four major channels has a name, as do the male and female enlightened beings. For example, the outer location of Dévikotri corresponds to the inner channel called Meditator, a male spiritual warrior called Vajra Light and a female spiritual warrior called Powerful Woman of Lanka. Kongtrul states:

> The eight locations of enlightened body, the Underground Abodes; the eight locations of enlightened speech, Earthly Abodes; and the eight locations of enlightened mind, Celestial Abodes, are specifically related to the twenty-four principal channels.
>
> According to such considerations as whether the vital essences [within the body] and *dakinis* [in the environment] are always present or occasionally present, locations are designated as inner or outer, sacred places or higher sacred places. The sacred places and higher places have four outer locations each [as listed on the chart above], the eight regions of the circle of enlightened mind.
>
> The field and the higher fields, the *chandho* and the higher *chandho*, each have two locations, the eight regions of the circle of enlightened speech. The gathering places and the higher gathering places, the cemeteries and the higher cemeteries each have two locations, the eight regions of the circle of enlightened body.
>
> In each case, internally, the white component descends [to the location in the body]; externally *dakinis* gather [in the corresponding region of sacred ground]. (*Encyclopedia of Buddhism*, vol. 2, p. 643)

To continue with a presentation of the main concepts of the phase of completion, tantra explains that three main channels (or meridians) run parallel, straight from the crown of the head to above the genital area. Of the three, the middle one is called central channel and is by far the most important focus of meditation; many phase of completion meditations aim to have the two other major channels enter it.

The channel that runs parallel to the right of the central channel is called *roma* in Tibetan, indicating residue or degeneration. "Sun" energy and red vital essence circulate mainly in the twenty-four thousand *roma* channels, the network of channels that branch off from this major meridian. The channel that runs parallel to the left

of the central channel is called *kyangma* in Tibetan, indicating un-
polluted or unadulterated. "Moon" energy and white vital essence
circulate mainly in the twenty-four thousand *kyangma* channels,
the network of channels that branch off from this major meridian.
"Rahu" (a celestial body) energy circulates mainly in yet another
set of twenty-four thousand channels, the network of channels that
branch off from the central channel.

The chart above listed twenty-four vital points of the body: these
constitute the major gathering points of the body's channels. At
each point, the three main channels—central, *roma*, and *kyangma*—
diffuse into a network of increasingly fine channels, much as we
can imagine the network of our veins, arteries, or nerves. (Kongtrul
states that in fact, when we count further subsidiary channels, three
and a half million channels exist throughout the body.)

Energy and vital essence circulate within these channels. Tantra
calculates twenty-four "constituents" of vital essence, each of which
separate into three, called dissolution, enjoyment, and authority.
These relate respectively to past, present, and future, and to the
circulation of energy, white vital essence, or red vital essence. Just
as the twenty-four vital points of the body's channels divide to
become seventy-two thousand (or more) tributaries, spread
throughout the body, the twenty-four constituents of the vital essence can be subdivided to include seventy-two thousand varia-
tions of constituent and action. Kongtrul gives an overview:

> Each of the twenty-four elements [i.e., vital essences] that descend
> through the twenty-four major channels is divided into three—
> dissolution, enjoyment, and authority—[a total of] seventy-two.
> Dissolution, the residue that results from completed action, is the
> component of the past. Enjoyment, the elements' essence in on-
> going action, is principally the white component, the present. The
> creative authority is the source of both essence and residue. Since
> it is the cause, the mixture of energy and blood, it is the component
> of the future.
>
> The twenty-four elements as a unit are further multiplied by
> three times one thousand, seventy-two thousand in all: twenty-
> four thousand elements of dissolution, consisting mainly of en-
> ergy; twenty-four thousand of enjoyment, mainly the white com-
> ponent; and twenty-four thousand of authority, mainly the red
> component. These constitute the three elements of the moon, sun,

and Rahu. They descend, penetrating the entire network of channels, to the extremities of the body's pores. (*Ibid.*, pp. 643-644)

In other texts, such as *The Profound Inner Meaning*, a lengthy commentary to a text by the Third Karmapa, Rangjung Dorjé, Kongtrul wrote far more on the subjects of channels, energies, and vital essences, and their practical application in phase of completion meditations, such as inner heat, illusory body, dream, and clear light. My criterion for including the passages above is to help readers unfamiliar with these concepts understand the keys to tantric pilgrimage as Kongtrul presents them. Specifically, in a passage in the *Pilgrimage Guide* below, he explains the correspondence between outer and inner sacred places. It is Kongtrul at his best—succinct, precise, and complete. In fact his explanation is quite simple and straightforward. I imagine that he trusted that his reader would either understand right away or not have any trouble finding someone who did. Faced with the same questions—Can a reasonably intelligent reader understand this or not? Are there resources readily available to help him or her do so?—I was less confident than Kongtrul and hope that the material above helps render the following passage more accessible.

A final note: the framework he uses here—outer, inner, and "other" levels—is the technical language from one specific tantra, Kalachakra (Wheel of Time), in which outer indicates the environment; inner, the body; and other, the pure bodies and environments of meditation deities.

> Why are sacred places categorized into principal and subsidiary places? The locations of the deities within the "other" supreme, ultimate, essential configuration (the result of purification) correspond to the elements of the true nature of reality (the basis of purification). The impure channels, circulatory energy, and vital essences of the inner vajra body (that which is purified), arranged in a pattern of structure and contents, appear in the outside world in the form of sacred places, sacred regions and *dakinis*.
>
> To illustrate this, the moon, sun, and Rahu circulatory energies descend through the major channels that have the nature of enlightened body, speech, and mind. These are twenty-four channels (in three groups of eight) that branch off from the main right, left, and central channels. The twenty-four major channels (including one called Undivided at the forehead, for example) appear in the

outer world as the twenty-four great sacred places (including Jalendhara). The spring and the circle vital essences, etc., based in these channels at the forehead, appear outwardly within the sacred grounds as the twenty-four male spiritual warriors (such as the one named Piece of Skull) and female spiritual warriors (such as the one named Very Fierce). Each of the twenty-four channels is further subdivided by dissolution, enjoyment, and authority, to produce seventy-two subsidiary channels. In the outer world these appear as the three sets of each of twenty-four places—actual, subsidiary, and hidden—bearing similar names. Further, [when outer sacred places that correspond to] the supports for the five subsidiary circulatory energies and the three main channels are added [to the twenty-four sites], thirty-two great sacred regions appear externally. Such subdivisions are limitless.

In conclusion, on the "other," pure, level, in the pure lands abide twenty-four male and female spiritual warriors, each surrounded by seventy-two thousand spiritual warriors and *dakinis*. On an inner level, in the vajra body, there are twenty-four main channels, surrounded by seventy-two thousand subsidiary channels. In the outer world there are twenty-four main sacred places, each having seventy-two thousand subsidiary places. On the ultimate level, all of these are bound together within the single equanimity of inseparable bliss and emptiness, the natural, innate essence of the masculine and feminine principle in union. Therefore all the sacred areas exist as symbols of the union of skillful means and transcendent knowledge.

This, then, is the context of the path and destination of the inner journey that is taken parallel to an outer pilgrimage journey. It is this inner journey that Sakya Pandita refers to when he insists that pilgrims be prepared spiritually as well as materially for their pilgrimage. It is this understanding that allows us to find sacred ground not only on the other side of the globe in strange and exotic lands but close to home, in lands and cities we sometimes disdain as hopelessly mundane. Like charity, pure vision can begin at home.

Sakya Pandita's dire warnings aside, it is not my intention nor, I believe, that of Kongtrul, to discourage pilgrimage to any site in Buddhist Asia. The cultivation of merit and wisdom can accompany our travel anywhere and many of us find that virtuous activity seems easier in faraway places where no familiar forms of entertainment or distraction exist. Wherever pilgrimage of the kind described above, related to the phase of completion, takes place, it should not be construed as different in feeling-tone from one's spiritual path in general. The key concept of the phase of creation is the union of appearance and emptiness; and of the phase of completion, the union of bliss and emptiness. The male or female messengers that one meets at sacred sites are manifestations of enlightenment, not gods, ghosts or ghouls.

And, as one would expect from Buddhism, by the time one has become familiar with this landscape on the path, one realizes that new horizons await. Once mastered, this essential passage of the inner journey will be put aside, as have so many others before, and the lessons learned on sacred ground will be applied to the next part of the path.

This section has provided some background information to help the reader situate sacred environments within tantric theory and practice. For many, this territory, the basis of the phase of completion, may be new and its seeming complexity may not be inviting. Yet it is no more complex or challenging than any other path within Buddhism and it is no less suffused with the wisdom of enlightenment.

NOTES

[1] "Where Exactly Are Caritra, Devikota, and Himavat? A Sacred Geography Controversy and the Development of Tantric Buddhist Pilgrimage Sites in Tibet," *Kailash, A Journal of Himalayan Studies*, vol. 16, nos. 3-4 (1990), pp. 121-165. A warning: Prof. Huber regrets that the article as published has many errors because he was not given proofs to check before publication.

[2] In writing the Sanskrit names of sites, such as Dévikotri and Charitra, I have endeavored to use a single spelling, whereas Tibetan texts often offer two or more spellings for the same location.

[3] The signs referred to here and once below in this passage refer to coded greetings by which tantric adepts identify themselves to the yoginis at sacred sites and gain acceptance into their circle. For a stylized example of this code, see pp. 71-75 in *The Concealed Essence of the Hevajra Tantra*.

[4] See *Abhidharmakoshabhasyam* by Vasubandhu, translated into French by Louis de la Vallée Poussin and from French into English by Leo M. Pruden, vol. 2, p. 456 and n. 394. Readers should be alert to the fact that this multilayered translation (Sanskrit to Chinese to French to English) relies mainly on a Sanskrit to Chinese version that differs from the reading of the translators from Sanskrit to Tibetan.

[5] See Thomas Cleary, *The Flower Ornament Scripture*, p. 841.

[6] See Toni Huber, *The Cult of Pure Crystal Mountain*, pp. 82-83, point 3, for the meaning of this name for Tsari.

[7] These two passages can be found in *The Concealed Essence of the Hevajra Tantra*, pp. 172-173.

[8] It was at this point in the teaching of the tantra that the circle of goddesses and yoginis fainted with astonishment, as mentioned in the immediately preceding quotation.

The Outer Journey

This section has four parts. The first, "To the Heart of Kham," will lead you on what is now in fact a short journey. From your home, wherever you are in the world, you can probably reach Hong Kong, Singapore, or Bangkok in less than twenty-four hours. From there, Chengdu is but a few hours away on a direct flight. And from Chengdu, an all-terrain vehicle can get you to our destination in three days of overland driving, with stops along the way. After all, it's just one thousand kilometers of highway from Chengdu to Tsadra, roughly the distance from one end of California to the other, or round-trip from New York City to Niagara Falls. This section provides some background information for what you would see en route: the journey itself is the goal.

The second part, "Tsadra and the Twenty-Five Areas of Sacred Ground," introduces our destination as an area of sacred ground, one of many inaugurated in eastern Tibet during the mid-nineteenth century. This section will explain how that time and these places signaled a major change in Tibetans' consciousness of their land's sacred geography.

The third part, "Tsari, Mother of Tsadra," shows how the eastward shift of sacred ground was in this case explicitly modeled on a well-known pilgrimage site in central Tibet.

Lastly, "An Invitation and a Supplication" presents a translation of Jamgon Kongtrul's encouragement to pilgrims to visit the sacred ground at Tsadra and his prayer to evoke the blessing of that site, once they had arrived.

Before I begin this section, praise for another book: Any attempt at understanding Tibetan geography was once a fool's errand for a non-Tibetan, as no reliable books existed in English. This is no longer the case, thanks to the incredible work of a Westerner named Gyurmé Dorjé and his *Tibet Handbook*. No superlative seems excessive in praise of this book: anyone wanting to situate a Tibetan place-name in space and time must consult it first before searching out further details in a more specialized study, should one exist. And of course, no one should venture into Tibetan territory without it (he even includes the Kathmandu valley and Bhutan in his *Tibet Handbook*).

I have never met Gyurmé Dorjé, but I have had an experience probably shared by many pilgrims throughout Tibet. I arrived unannounced at a stranger's home in eastern Tibet, close to the end of a long day's hike and horse-ride, and seemingly not far from the end of the earth. Imagine my surprise when, with the usual fare of tea, roasted barley flour, and dried yak-meat, my host showed me the calling card of one Gyurmé Dorjé who had passed there some years before.

TO THE HEART OF KHAM

The *Pilgrimage Guide* describes a pilgrimage place called Tsadra in southeastern Tibet, close to the heart of what is known as Kham. This section will provide a general account of one modern route to this place, with special attention given to the influences from the past that have shaped the local people's experience of their land.

My two journeys into this part of Kham were pilgrimages to my spiritual homeland: the majority of the masters I had met, the literature I had read, and the meditations I had practiced originated in Kham. Specifically, the life and work of Jamgon Kongtrul occupied a central place in my spiritual life, undoubtedly due in large part to the fact that my personal spiritual guide, Kalu Rinpoché, was his reincarnation. I was a visitor in Kham, but not a tourist.

The route I took into the region was the only one open to foreigners at the time. It began in Chengdu, the city that serves as the administrative capital of Sichuan, China's largest and most populous province. Readers familiar with the writing of a trio of modern Chinese women—Han Suyin (*The Crippled Tree* and many others), Jung Chang (*Wild Swans*), and Anchee Min (*Red Azalea*)—have glimpsed life in this country-within-a-country. Everyone knows the name of Sichuan's most famous modern native son, Deng Xiaoping.

For those interested in Kham, Sichuan is critical, since most of Kham falls within its borders, rather than those of the "Autonomous Region of Tibet." That Kham is administered from Chengdu, rather than Lhasa (or Beijing), has practical effects: the colonial presence of soldiers and administrators, so stifling in Lhasa, was nowhere to be seen in areas I visited in Kham. Pictures of the Dalai Lama and other great masters who fled in 1959 to India and Nepal are sold openly in shops. Monasteries and retreat centers thrive. Kham in Sichuan is not an independent paradise, but much of what revolts Tibetans and foreigners alike in central Tibet reflects policies that do not apply in Kham.

Why is Lhasa, a showcase of Chinese colonialism at its worst, open to foreigners, while Kham was closed to outsiders until recently? Some might imagine perfidious Chinese plots at work, but I do not think that the Chinese authorities have coordinated their policies toward Sichuan and Tibet. In Tibet, some infrastructure for food and lodging exists in the large cities, whereas such facilities in Kham were/are rudimentary and served only the local population. An influx of foreign tourists would put impossible strains on a well-run but local system. Once one leaves Chengdu, many familiar reference points are left behind—languages other than Chinese and Tibetan, telephones, hot water from taps, private bathrooms, flush toilets, menus in any language in restaurants, etc. And once off the main road in Kham, there are no paved roads, stores, hotels, restaurants, or electricity. At the risk of seeming to apologize for the Sichuan government, I can sympathize with their wish to spare themselves the nuisance of unaccompanied foreign tourists.

The first stop of interest between Chengdu and Kham, a small village named Luding in Chinese, Chak-zam-ka in Tibetan, has a unique attraction—a bridge which is a pilgrimage place for Chinese

Communists and Tibetan Buddhists alike. For those whose hearts soar remembering the Long March, the crossing of the Luding Bridge marked the final, decisive battle between the Marchers and the Kuomintang army. Anthony Grey, in his novel of the Long March, *Peking,* recounted the fight in all its heroic detail (pp. 278-297). The March could have ended in Luding but Mao and his followers crossed the bridge, where a shrine now stands to those whose sacrifice allowed the revolution to continue.

Tibetan Buddhists visit the bridge to honor the person they believe is its maker, the "Iron Bridge Man" (Chak-zam-pa in Tibetan), Tang-Tong Gyalpo (1385-1509). The bridge at Luding was one of many he constructed with his trademark—iron links. Statues or paintings of this Tibetan spiritual hero show him holding a chain of iron links in his right hand, in remembrance of his engineering work so beneficial to Tibetans (and their Chinese cousins) over the centuries.

Tang-Tong Gyalpo's influence can be found in a number of facets of Tibetan culture: he composed the much-performed Lhamo opera, for example; and as will be mentioned below, the city of Dergé, the heart of Kham, owes its inception to him. In the context of Tibet's pilgrimage places and areas of sacred ground, he is noteworthy because he furthered the work of the Chinese princess of the Tang Dynasty, Wen-cheng (seventh century).

Wen-cheng Gong-ju (*gong-ju* means princess) exercised an enormous influence on Tibetan history: she brought Tibet's most revered statue to Lhasa from China; she designed the capital's main temples, as well as a series of temples throughout the land. This was not just a self-flattering exercise in design and construction: she made Tibetans understand their land. Tang-Tong Gyalpo was a significant example of the few who followed her example and constructed temples and stupas on vital points throughout greater Tibet. These vital locations were geographical acupuncture points, which, if controlled by the needles of buildings and monuments, allowed the country's energy to circulate for the common good. Negative forces, both human and natural, such as earthquakes, could be neutralized by such construction. Wen-cheng's work is best described in brief by Gyurmé Dorjé (*Tibet Handbook,* pp. 672-673) or in detail by the late Michael Aris in *Bhutan,* pp. 3-33.

The thread that connects the lives and work of Wen-cheng Gong-ju (seventh century), Tang-Tong Gyalpo (fourteenth-fifteenth centuries), and Chok-gyur Déchen Lingpa (Jamgon Kongtrul's inspiration and friend of the nineteenth century) is their work to improve the state of Tibet through construction on sacred sites. Like our bodies' changing state of health, the state of the land's energy needed regular checkups and occasional major tune-ups. Whether construction of temples and Buddhist monuments on strategic points can save a country from calamity is a matter of faith. At the very least, these three Buddhist masters' wide-ranging efforts made a major contribution to their country's self-consciousness. All lived at times of extreme political tension, are considered to have exercised a significantly beneficial influence on their period, and are still widely honored.[1]

On leaving the bridge at Luding, one rises to Kanding, the unofficial border between Kham and China. For the Chinese, Kanding is renowned as a source of love-songs; for the Khampas, who call it Dar-tsen-do, it is either the point of departure before a plunge into the swirling sea of China, or the first hint of the high and dry land on the way home. Like most border towns, it is rough, tough, and fascinating: here we find two Tibetan monasteries, a Chinese temple, and a Christian church. One Christian missionary who stayed in Kham until the Communists threw him out, probably in the 1950s, told me that he considered the Tibetans the vilest people on earth: no one has succeeded in converting any significant number of them and he seemed to genuinely feel he had wasted his young, enthusiastic years on souls far too wretched to save.

Perhaps Princess Wen-cheng first felt the same: her marriage to Tibet's king in the seventh century was a minor clause in a peace treaty between her country and the Tibetan then-non-Buddhist savages to the Northwest. She was bundled off to the Land of Snows, most likely against her very lively will, the Jo statue as part of her dowry. We follow her route after Kanding and find a major temple she built at Lha-gang (Ta-gong in Chinese), seventy-seven kilometers beyond the 4,300-meter pass above the border town. She had left China but had not ventured far into Tibet before she called a halt, designed and had a temple built, and placed a Jo-like statue in the main prayer hall. These, and an impressive number of stupas in the courtyard, still stand and attract many pilgrims.

Inside the temple, one finds a row of small stupas, each dedicated to a great master of the past. One bears the inscription that it is the reliquary for the remains of Wen-chung's son, for the oral history passed among Tibetans reports that she sojourned in Lhagang because pregnant. A book in the temple contradicts the common, thirteen-century-old gossip that the main Tibetan peace negotiator in China, government minister Gar, was the father. Not so, claims the record: it was a fellow wanderer, an Indian prince, who had the honor. Whatever the case, it could have become a diplomatic blunder of epic proportions, but peaceful Sino-Tibetan relations survived, probably because the unfortunate child did not. No text explains his demise, though perhaps the fact that his birth was politically inconvenient for everyone involved was deemed too obvious to be worth mentioning.

Further up the road, two towns carry further memories of the time of Princess Wen-cheng. The first, just sixteen kilometers away but over a 4,420-meter pass, is called Garthar, meaning "Gar's Release." When government minister Gar reached this village on his way back home, he felt he had traveled far enough from China to breathe easily. He had tarried in Chang-an (the modern Xian, then capital of China) at the insistent invitation of the emperor. He was shown the finest hospitality, but he felt as if he had been incarcerated in a five-star prison. He fled, with his overly eager hosts in pursuit. Be it ever so humble, the village of Gar's Release felt like home to him. How many Tibetans returning from China smile when they reach that place and remember their countryman, a true patriot, of so long ago?

Not far away, in a major town called Ganzé, Wen-cheng again built a small temple which still stands on a plain outside the town and houses another Jo statue look-alike. These are old stories, ancient even by European standards, but as distant as they might seem to us, the tales of Princess Wen-cheng, Minister Gar, and their king form part of the heart of Tibet's identity. They lived thirteen centuries ago, but it seems like yesterday.

The land here has little in common with central Tibet, except the altitude. Here, at a distance of a number of four thousand-meter passes from China, the monsoon rains still penetrate. The rivers are unimaginably strong; the ground appears to be very fertile; grass and flowers of every hue cover the landscape. Trucks and rivers carry huge logs downward; some wood stays to construct the attractive log homes so popular here, as they are in wooded mountainous regions throughout the world. Kham is impressively rich; the people are strong, willful, and often exuberant. This is not the arid desert of Tibet. This is Tibet's Wild East. Khampas, as they are known, ride on horseback into Ganzé, rifles slung over their back. They are both cowboys and Indians: red skins, with cowboy hats and boots. They play pool on tables placed on what might have been originally conceived as sidewalks. Life is earthy, real, and really boring. Small wonder that those young adults who survive what seems to be a hormone rush of Himalayan proportions eventually gravitate to the monasteries and meditation centers for some basic instruction in what has made their culture work for centuries. Khampas work hard, play hard, and when they dedicate themselves to meditation, do not know how to practice half-heartedly. In Kham, today's hopeless juvenile delinquent may very well be tomorrow's spiritual master, just like his or her parents.

Kham. The name evokes hot-blooded warriors and otherworldly lamas. The people of Kham gladly acknowledge that their region produces both the finest human beings on earth as well as the most bloodthirsty, the incarnations of universal compassion and the embodiments of brutish savagery. The Khampas take pride in both extremes and remark favorably on these qualities that distinguish them from their tamer and (according to them) less spiritual cousins in central Tibet.

Ganzé, a pleasant town on an open plain, was visited by a contingent of the Long March. A modern Tibetan artist has recreated the scene, depicting a warm welcome shown by the local monastic officials to the fleeing remnants of Mao's following. The reincarnate lama responsible for this reception was Géda Lama, or so he is named in Robert Ford's account of his years in Kham, *Wind Between the Worlds*. Ford recounts how Géda traveled as far as Chamdo during the Chinese-Tibetan conflict of 1950 and lost his life under highly suspicious circumstances while waiting for permission to travel to Lhasa to negotiate a settlement.

Thirty-six kilometers beyond Ganzé lies a series of villages collectively known as Rongpatsa, birthplace of the First Karmapa (1110-1193). A house stands at his birthplace; water considered holy flows inexplicably from the back wall in the stable where he is said to have been born. There is no special shrine at the site, nor is there any mark whatsoever to inform strangers that stupas containing possessions of this most famous resident of the village stand in another house on a hill a few kilometers away. Monasteries faithful to Karmapa can be found throughout Tibet, yet the stupas remain untended; only a few paintings that cover the walls—whitewashed during the Cultural Revolution—have been made visible.

This same curious disregard for history is evident in another part of the village. Across the river, another famous lama, Kalu Rinpoché (1905-1989), was born, descendent of the First Karmapa's family. High on a hill, a stupa rises out of forlorn ruins at the site of his birthplace. The stupa was built not by local residents but by Lama Lodrö, a Sikkimese disciple of Kalu Rinpoché, who lives and teaches in San Francisco. Along the same hills, a few miles away, stand the ruins of the monastery Kalu Rinpoché attended in his youth and the dilapidated house where he spent some years in retreat. In a garden of a nearby home, one can find a dozen of his carvings of various buddhas and bodhisattvas, on thick slabs of rock (perhaps slate) stacked up one against the other, slowly being etched by the wind, rain, and snow. In a land now free, why does no one seem to care for history, either long past or recent? I feel very close to the people of these hills; we talk of those we know in common and they often cry. In a country now relatively free, I cannot understand or accept their refusal to preserve the past, for it is their collective memory.

In this I feel closer to another native of this village, the person I feel is the most extraordinary woman I have ever met, Khandro Tsering Chödron. Many readers have been introduced to her by Sogyal Rinpoché, another Rongpatsa native son, in his *The Tibetan Book of Living and Dying*. Her unfathomable qualities radiate by themselves, but she is often cited as having been the wife of the most widely respected lama of this century, Dzongsar Kyentsé Rinpoché. Since his death in 1959, she has lived simply in a small shrine room dedicated to his memory in Gangtok, Sikkim. Her devotion and care for our heritage has not prevented her from pursuing her own spiritual life to quiet, resplendent success. Were there another like her in her homeland, Kalu Rinpoché's retreat cabin would not crouch feebly, abandoned and rotting, nor would his artwork have become the shelter of small animals and insects.

To this point, we have traveled from Luding, on the borderline between China and Kham, to the Ganzé region. This represents 436 kilometers over numerous passes and unpaved mountain roads. In a good four-wheel drive vehicle, this could be done in a day, but what a day! We have passed through regions with a number of languages and cultures, all Tibetan, but all mutually unintelligible and as distinctive as if we had driven through Germany, Denmark, Holland, and Belgium. I speak both Lhasa Tibetan and Mandarin Chinese fairly fluently, but I rarely met anyone in this area who spoke either with ease. Khampas would say flatly, "I'm not Tibetan; I don't speak Tibetan." This is not the equivalent of, "I'm not American; I'm Canadian", rather, "I'm not Canadian, I'm Quebeçois; I don't speak English." Kalu Rinpoché used to speak the central Tibetan language during his teaching of Buddhism, but as his translator, I sometimes had the unenviable role of "translating" his heavily accented speech for Tibetans who couldn't understand him: I had to repeat his words in Tibetan, with my Canadian Anglophone accent, for communication to be possible.

The next eighty kilometers of road westward winds slowly upward through sparsely populated hills and valleys. One eventually comes to a long wall of stones, which on closer inspection proves to be an impressive collection of rocks, each carved with the mantra *Om Mani Pémé Houng*, the Tibetan six-syllable national anthem. All human beings, Western or Oriental, Chinese or Tibetan, want to have a happy and comfortable life. Yet throughout this country, then and now, people have put such considerations as fame and fortune aside to carve mantras on millions of stones or to travel these long, dusty roads toward Lhasa three steps at a time, followed by a full-length prostration. In other countries, determination and concerted effort are applied to organizing sports events, building skyscrapers, improving technology, or sending men and women into space. Here, the energy of generations is focused on faith, pure and simple, humble and anonymous. Nevertheless, the man responsible for the etching of these mantras (Sonam Namgyal) is now renowned for his having attained what is called "rainbow body" at death. His body dissolved into light, leaving just hair and nails behind. Trungpa Rinpoché wrote the following account of this event in his autobiography, *Born in Tibet*:

On the third day we stopped at Manikengko as we had been told the story of a very saintly man who had died there the previous year. We went to the house where he had lived, and met his son and his wife who recounted the miracle that had occurred at the old man's death.

In his lifetime he had erected a group of '*Mani* stones' on which he had carved a great number of *mantras* and *sutras* and he had also set up a *chöten* (*stupa*) among them.

In his youth he had been a servant with a wealthy family, but in middle age he left his employment to receive meditational instruction in a monastery. Though he had to work for his living by day, he spent most of his nights in contemplation only allowing himself two to three hours' sleep. His compassion was so great that he always helped everyone in need, and opened his house at all times to pilgrims and the very poor. While carrying out his daily work he used to practice meditation in his own way, though his son who was a monk told him that he should carry out more formal spiritual exercises, but this he could not accept. Though he had hitherto always been in good health, three years before his death he fell ill and his family began to be very worried, yet he himself appeared to become increasingly happy. He composed and sang his own songs of praise instead of traditional Buddhist chants. As his illness became more and more serious, lamas and doctors were called in, with his son telling him that he must now remember all the teaching that he had received, at which he smiled, saying, 'I have forgotten it all, and anyway there is nothing to remember; everything is illusion, yet I am confident that all is well.' Just before his death the old man said 'When I die you must not move my body for a week; this is all that I desire.'

They wrapped his dead body in old clothes and called in lamas and monks to recite and chant. The body was carried into a small room, little bigger than a cupboard and it was noted that though the old man had been tall the body appeared to have become smaller; at the same time a rainbow was seen over the house. On the sixth day on looking into the room the family saw that it had grown still smaller. A funeral service was arranged for the morning of the eighth day and men came to take the body to the cemetery; when they undid the coverings there was nothing inside except nails and hair. (pp. 95-96)

Other modern Tibetan writers have also written of this event, which seems to have marked deeply the consciousness of the young Khampas of that generation, a saint hidden in their midst who showed the highest signs of accomplishment at death.

Close by the "mani wall," one arrives at a major fork in the road. One road leads northwest—to monasteries such as Dzok-chen, Séchen, and eventually Zurmang and Trangu, among many others. Perhaps Princess Wen-cheng took that route, since around the corner from Trangu Monastery she built a temple that contains towering statues of the eight bodhisattvas. She also had the last passage of *The Flower Ornament Discourse,* called *The Prayer of Excellent Conduct,* carved in the stone of the sheer cliff. As Gyurmé Dorjé notes (pp. 483-484), once again local legend has it that the princess was pregnant and miscarried at this now-desolate site, although I did not see there any official indication of that event, nor a text to name the father, as I did in Lhagang.

The road the princess did not take, the one that leads straight west, braves a 4,916 meter pass soon after the junction. Just before reaching the peaks, one can see one of the most beautiful settings in Kham—Yi-lhung Lha-tso, the divine lake of Yi-lhung. Its setting—a glacier-fed lake, framed by forested, eternally snow-topped mountains—is strikingly similar to that of Lake Louise in Canada. But the scale in Kham is grandiose: Yi-lhung Lake is larger and the highest mountain behind it reaches 6,168 meters. It was here that Kalu Rinpoché finally found a peaceful cave to meditate, above the snowline. He had wandered for many years between his homeland and this point, changing caves or sites for his tent whenever word that a lama was in retreat brought visitors (or his worrying, well-intentioned, but meddlesome mother) to his door. Yi-lhung is stunning, but it seems impossible for anyone to have tried to live there beyond the short summer and survived. This is yogi country; Milarepa would have felt right at home.

After a long descent from sharply jagged peaks through narrow canyons, we arrive in Dergé, capital of the kingdom of the same name, the heart of Kham. At first sight, Dergé's renown seems to dwarf the town itself, for the collection of buildings huddled in the limited confines of a tight valley pale beside the splendor of its renown. Despite the diminutive size and drab appearance of their town, the people of Dergé do not lack *chutzpah*, their writers in particular. One example is Tsultrim Rinchen (1697-1774), a lama who in 1743 wrote a lengthy catalogue to the Dergé edition of the collection of Indian Buddhist masters' treatises (the *Ten-gyur* in Tibetan). He covers close to twenty pages with his description of the glories of Dergé!

Jamgon Kongtrul gives a later example in his catalogue for a temple built in Dergé. To accurately locate Dergé's place on the Buddhist map, he begins with a short tour of the cosmos, before settling on Tibet, and Dergé in particular. While it might be presumed from this passage that Kongtrul felt Dergé was not only the heart of Kham but close to the center of the universe, we should recall that he wrote this for the royal patron of the temple, for whom Dergé might have been nothing less than God's (or Buddha's) Own Country. Kongtrul writes:

> The confluence of oceans of the victorious ones' compassion and sentient beings' actions has created this support, the environment of the expanse of worlds that spreads to the bounds of space. Among these worlds, the realm called Flower-Adorned Base and Heart is the domain of the body of enlightenment's perfect splendor, Illuminator of Form [*Vairochana*], Lake of the Himalayas. This victor's every pore holds oceans of realms equal to the number of atoms in all realms. On his palms, in an ocean of scented water, grow lotuses that support twenty-five world-systems, arranged in tiers. The thirteenth of these, our world-system Endurance, comprises a galaxy containing one billion four-continent worlds. Each four-continent world in turn contains eight lesser continents. Among these [major and minor continents], the place where supreme manifest forms of enlightenment attain buddhahood is ours, the southern continent, Land of Jambu, distinguished by the Seat made of Vajras [i.e., Bodhgaya, India] and *jambu-bricha* (rose-apple) trees. In the other continents, beings experience [the result of past actions]; this is the place for creative action. Buddhas do not appear elsewhere: this is the excellent place where buddhas appear.
>
> The central region of this Land of Jambu is Vajra Seat [Bodhgaya] in Magadha [a district in the modern state of Bihar, north-central

India]. It is surrounded in every direction and interstice by lands, such as Mahatsina [greater China] to the east, and the twenty-four major sites of sacred ground. Among these, the northern Himalayan province of Tibet was foretold:

In the region of Tibet, dwells the co-emergent,
Peaceful woman of distinct form.

Tibet is well known as the great province of medicinal *sal* trees and as the implement held in the hand of the exalted bodhisattva Lord of the World. The upper region of this Himalayan province contains the three circular ranges of Ngari; the middle region contains the four parts of Ü and Tsang; and the lower region contains the six ranges of Amdo and Kham.

Among these lower districts, known as Four Rivers-Six Ranges,[2] this region is known as Zalmo Range. The Yangtze River winds pleasantly in its descent through the region, circled by the enclosure of eternally snow-covered summits that pierce the blue sky. The great deity Dorjé Lodrö, nine other beneficial brother *genyen* gods, and many other powerful deities naturally reside here and guard the land. This region has the ten virtues of a region and is connected to various great indestructible sacred places blessed by the vast ocean of the victorious Three Sources [masters, deities, and *dakinis* and protectors]. All the many general and specific conducive features of land from the viewpoint of geomancy are here complete, so every written edict of the powerful, divine religious rulers has been respected by [literally: "placed on the crown of the head of"] all great leaders in the region. Many hundreds of erudite and accomplished persons have come from this area: it has served as the source of the lotuses [i.e., masters] that fill the Victorious Buddha's doctrine impartially. In particular, Tang-Tong Gyalpo, leader of an ocean of accomplished masters, here bound all malevolent spirits, including gods, cannibal demons, and *nagas* under oath and blessed animate and inanimate life in this region with his great, timeless wisdom. (*Dergé Temple Catalogue*, pp. 16a-17a)[3]

Of the two major Buddhist travelers and builders whose lives and work gave definition to the land we have traveled through—Princess Wen-cheng and Tang-Tong Gyalpo—it is the latter who is related to Dergé's history, as Kongtrul underlines in the same text when he discusses the lineage of Dergé kings:

His brother, Déchen Sonam Zangpo, on the prophetic advice of [the Seventh] Karmapa Chödrak Gyatso (1454-1506) and Ngu

Chökyi Dorjé, followed the Dri River upstream and arrived before the chief of Ling. He received the name of Dergé. Of his four sons, Bo-tar (also known as Tashi Sengé) invited Tang-Tong Gyalpo to the area. This marked the inauguration of the family's royal power and the founding of Lhundrup Teng Monastery. (*Ibid.*, p. 18a)

Lhundrup Teng Monastery, built in 1448, was razed during the Cultural Revolution and has since been rebuilt on the same site at the center of Dergé.[4] It and many of the surrounding buildings and homes bear the mark of fidelity to the Sakya monastic system: the walls are painted a deep gray and are circled with a horizontal multi-colored band. On the main throne in the temple sits a portrait of Jamyang Kyentsé Chökyi Lodrö, well known to readers of Sogyal Rinpoché's *The Tibetan Book of Living and Dying*. A small, old temple hidden in the neighborhood is said to have built by Tang-Tong Gyalpo and caves in the cliffs overlooking the town have been blessed by his meditation.

Dergé's kings are renowned in modern times for their sponsorship of the printing press. Founded in 1729 by the forty-second of the royal lineage, Tenpa Tsering (1678-1739), the printing press became a major center of religious and cultural life in Kham. The royal family sponsored the printing of the Buddhist Canon, for which the great Eighth Tai Situpa, Tenpa Nyin-jé (1700-1774), wrote the catalogue in 1733. This major work was followed ten years later by the printing of the collection of Indian masters' commentaries mentioned above. Since that time, thousands of texts have been carved in wood, preserved, and printed by hand on handmade paper, as they still are here today.

The printing press was saved from destruction through the courageous determination of a handful of individuals who stood firm against the destructive tide of the Cultural Revolution. Today, hundreds of books are printed there as of old, employing hundreds of people. The main building, which looks like an enormous temple, is filled with an extraordinary collection of hand-carved woodblocks and an equally extraordinary collection of workers very busily printing mountains of texts. The administration of the press is housed in an adjacent modern building: it is an impressive undertaking by any measure. The printing press attracts more pilgrims than the rebuilt monastery: people circle it continuously in prayer or even by prostrating on the ground as they walk. It has become a monument to the resilience of Kham's spiritual life.

What has made Dergé a center of History and Tradition, unlike many of its neighboring towns and districts? Perhaps the people of Kham needed a royal family to provide a focus for their collective memory. Perhaps the predominance of the Sakya tradition in the region taught the people a love of the written word, unlike the carefree and sometimes careless meditative traditions. It is perhaps both, in a typically Tibetan volatile mix of politics and religion, which made Dergé outshine any other dynasty in Kham. Kongtrul finishes his short history of the Dergé kings with these lines:

> In conclusion, each member of this line of sovereigns of enlightened activity and legacy has acted as patron to the entire doctrine of the Buddha through wide-ranging sponsorship of Buddhism and protection of the many persons in their domain according to royal laws in harmony with tradition. Among Dergé's rulers, those dating from the religious king Tenpa Tsering have been conferred sovereignty over the land by the god of heaven, the great emperor [of China]. The emperor further bestowed edicts granting them the rank "Tu-zhu Dergé Xuan-wei-shi," a title that has become manifestly renowned from the great ocean in the east [i.e., the Chinese Pacific Coast] to the fields where nutmeg grows in the west [i.e., India]. [5] (Ibid., pp. 19b-20a)

The kings had thus a dual contract—law in harmony with Buddhism and support of religious projects on the one hand, thus ensuring the blessing of the lamas; and acknowledgment of the Chinese throne, which evidently had sufficient political power to accord sovereignty. It is noteworthy that Kongtrul makes no mention of similar recognition and power flowing from Lhasa. At the time, Lhasa's recognition had little worth: five Dalai Lamas sat on the throne during Kongtrul's lifetime! He never lived to hear of one who survived beyond twenty-one years of age in the turbulence of nineteenth century Lhasa politics. Small wonder that the kings of Dergé looked east for support—after all, Chengdu was less than one thousand kilometers away.

Dergé natives are often seen in pictures taken in Lhasa: the tall, long-haired, dark-skinned men stand out from their milder Lhasa cousins; while the sight of traditional Dergé women inevitably sends tourists scurrying for cameras. The women weave turquoise into their hair and after marriage sport a large turquoise circled in gold above their foreheads. From Kanding to Dergé, some Khampa women wear traditional dress and hairstyles; others have relaxed into more practical, western styles. But almost none, except for nuns or dedicated meditators, will wear her hair cut short. I was told that the women of Kham were twice forced by government order to cut their hair and they will never willingly do so again. It has become their collective badge of defiance.

The destination of this journey—Palpung Monastery and Kongtrul's retreat center—is a long day's journey from Dergé. At a distance of about two hours from Dergé, heading west toward Lhasa, a small stupa marks a turn-off that leads to a series of farms and the end of a vehicular road. At that point, one must find a farmer willing to rent a horse and to part with a child or two to lead them. Palpung's setting, described in detail by Kongtrul in the *Pilgrimage Guide* below, lies on the far side of a number of high passes, the highest of which is said to turn the traveler's hair white. None seem as high as 5,000 meters, yet every pass is high enough to force one to dismount from the strong Khampa horses before reaching the summit.

The approximately eight-hour journey on horseback and on foot takes one within sight of Alo Paljor Monastery, home of the Eighth Tai Situpa, Chökyi Jungné (1700-1774), who founded Palpung Monastery in 1727. The locals joke that Alo Paljor was first the mother monastery of Palpung, whereas now Palpung, the child, has far outgrown her progenitor.

Most pilgrims' first sight of Palpung is almost an aerial view, as one approaches from the final high pass.[6] One can easily see how the idea of a major building on such a stunning site recurred to lamas over the centuries, as Kongtrul describes in the main text. Palpung means Mound of Glory: the monastery sits like a jewel on the crest of a round hill that stands above the junction of two rivers. So far, the land around Palpung has been spared from the loggers' axes. It is densely wooded and the air, far from roads or industries, maintains an alpine pristine quality. The main temple stands by itself, the lowest structure on the mounded hill. The small community's homes ring the temple from above, like amphitheater seats around a stage. The courtyard holds an active monastic college. Further up the hill, we find the printing press where so many of Jamgon Kongtrul's works were first published, written backward on wood blocks by scribes, carved, and printed by a team who must smear ink on the block, place the paper (often handmade) on the wet surface, press it down, in a movement like taking a credit-card imprint, and then hang the page on a clothesline to dry. After drying, the backside of the page is printed. It is labor-intensive work and requires large storage areas for the wood blocks.

Around the printing press building, forlorn ruins sag, slowly dissolving into the earth. They look as if they date from Druid times, but in fact, not so long ago, some of those walls held the residence of Beru (or "Palpung") Kyentsé Rinpoché. His home met the same fate as the main residence of the Tai Situpa, founder and leader of the monastery. His home sat perched above, beside one of the three-year retreat centers, as the uppermost structure on the hill overlooking the temple. The retreat center has been reconstructed and is in session at the same location; the remains of the lama's residence are practically invisible, but for a few stones lying on the ground.

A visitor to Palpung cannot see Kongtrul's retreat center at Tsadra Rinchen Drak from the main monastery. As is clear from Kongtrul's accounts, he lived in Palpung for some time without knowledge of the exact location of an abandoned retreat center at what would become known as Tsadra. He and some friends set out one day to find it, but lacking a guide, followed a vulture who had set down on the lower retreat center before winding up the hill and over the small pass. Kongtrul and his friends pursued it and spied the abandoned retreat. Most persons now follow the same route Kongtrul took that day, but have no trouble seeing the retreat once over the crest of the hill. The short stroll can be a humbling experience: the hill seems perpendicular at times and the altitude, over four thousand meters, is daunting. What is worse for the ego is to be passed by Khampa men and women who walk very quickly, as if the ground were level, singing *Vajra Guru* mantras at the top of their leather lungs as they speed along.

The history and the topography of the area around the retreat center are described in full in the *Pilgrimage Guide* below. Spiritual

considerations aside, it is a lovely spot, a slightly hidden face of
the mountain that seems to be protected and dominating at the
same time. Visitors cannot ignore history here: Guru Rinpoché,
Yeshé Tsogyal, and so many other masters of the distant past meditated here; Jamgon Kongtrul, Jamyang Kyentsé Wongpo, and Chok-
gyur Déchen Lingpa followed in the mid-1800s; and even now, on
a small grassy meadow above the retreat, two large trees grow, one
planted by the first reincarnation of Jamgon Kongtrul, named
Kyentsé Özer, son of the Fifteenth Karmapa, and the other by another of Kongtrul's reincarnations, Kalu Rinpoché, at the place
where they would sit and meditate together. Left to itself, Tsadra is
a meditation-friendly environment.

Like the Dergé and Palpung printing presses, the main temple
of Palpung was spared destruction during the Cultural Revolution. The local people "occupied" it, "expelled" the monks, put up
sheets over the frescoed walls, and claimed it as a "people's medical clinic." Once the nightmare frenzy had passed, the people left,
the sheets were removed, and the lamas invited to return. It was a
small but significant victory in a war that was long and cruel. The
two retreat centers were demolished, countless treasures wasted,
and the mummified remains of the Tai Situpas and of Jamgon
Kongtrul desecrated. A woman who was forced to participate in the
destruction of Kongtrul's retreat center spirited Kongtrul's heart away
and was able years later to present it to Jamgon Kongtrul the Third.
Statues described in Kongtrul's works as being dear to him were
hidden by one of Kalu Rinpoché's nephews, the only surviving ritual
master of Palpung (there were seven at the beginning of the Cultural Revolution). He was publicly tortured during that time of mad-
ness but lived to return the treasures to the rebuilt retreat center. He
also put back in circulation the sole copy of many priceless texts
once owned by Kongtrul that Kalu Rinpoché had left in his care.

I first met that ritual master, named Omdzé Zopa, in France in
1982, and had no idea of his then-recent past (the Cultural Revolution ended in 1977). Kalu Rinpoché sent him into our three-year
retreat to teach rituals and yoga exercises. Later I accompanied him
on pilgrimage in India in 1983, after which he returned to Palpung.
I had no clue then of the enormity of his decision to return. He had
circled the globe with Kalu Rinpoché and could have chosen to

live anywhere in the world, whether as a teacher or as a man enjoying a well-deserved retirement in a western Shangri-La. Instead, he chose to leave a relative paradise, to return to Palpung, scene of so much horror in his life, to lead the community there and to teach a new generation of ritual masters from all over Kham. I stayed at his home during both of my visits to Palpung and remain in awe of his monumental courage. It is conceivable to me that he could have survived the dark and desperate years. But he has done far more than simply survive: imprisonment, public humiliation and torture have not blunted his enormous energy for preserving and continuing the transmission of the spiritual life and values he holds dear. In France, in India, and at home in Kham, I have watched his enthusiasm light those around him, high and low, and I have marveled at his memory during his teaching; his mind is as fresh and as clear as if he had just finished his training.

He is not alone or unique in his context, yet he is unusual, even an exotic character when compared to Western persons. I dwell on him because he represents the kind of person Palpung Monastery and the surrounding retreat centers were meant to produce. He is a ritual master who knows by heart countless Buddhist liturgies, as well as the texts of commentary describing the accompanying visualized meditations and their meaning. He is also an accomplished yogi: after his three-year retreat (the first that Kalu Rinpoché taught at Palpung), he decided to join the once-a-year walk that retreat graduates could choose to participate in. At the coldest point in winter, at dawn after a sleepless night spent singing the songs of realized masters of the past, a group walked slowly, single-file, singing, from the retreat center to Palpung Monastery, a stroll of a few hours. They wore only a short cotton yoga-exercise skirt and perhaps a cotton shawl. The ceremony was to prove in public their mastery of inner heat yoga—*tummo*. Omdzé Zopa said he started self-confidently on his first outing but soon became convinced that he was going to die of cold before the morning was through! During the following year, he practiced inner heat meditation during his spare time and claimed to have had no discomfort when he participated the following years, even though as a ritual master, he was obliged to play the cymbals while walking, although these would freeze instantly were it not for his inner-heated hands.

What is truly remarkable in this man, and in many women and men of Tibet, Kham, and Amdo, is an enduring communion with life that defies the gravity of their experiences. They have every reason to have become professional victims, pools of cynicism, bitterness and self-pity—no one would deny them that right. While they remain perfectly lucid and reflective concerning the pain they have borne and what their culture has lost, they are inhabited by an infectious lightness. They live and breathe deep well-being, peace, and energy. They do not allow themselves to be diminished by the horrors they have witnessed or experienced—those evil acts and the sordid attitudes that spawned them are totally "other" to most Tibetans and will always remain so. Their attitude seems to be that there are simply more interesting things to study, reflect, or meditate upon in life than their own individual sufferings or others' political struggles.[7]

Palpung Monastery is located deep indeed in the Himalayas— electricity is new, extremely limited, and very faint. There are light bulbs, but no outlets. No stores existed when I was there: nothing could be bought, except from neighbors, and I imagine that any exchange is made through barter rather than money. Homes are made from wood; windows are covered with paper; no glass is used. The homes, buildings, temples, food, clothes, and people all reek of butter in varying degrees of rancidity. People are poor, dirt poor. But here, on the edge of sacred ground, money can buy next to nothing. At first glimpse, the life of the community here seems not too different from James Hilton's version of Shangri-La in *Lost Horizon*. Here are three short passages from that delightful book:

> Shangri-La was always tranquil, yet always a hive of unpursuing occupations; the lamas lived as if indeed they had time on their hands, but time that was scarcely a featherweight.

> "What do the lamas do?" she continued.
> "They devote themselves, madam, to contemplation and to the pursuit of wisdom."
> "But that isn't *doing* anything."
> "Then, madam, they do nothing."
> "I thought as much."

> "... [in Shangri-La] you will achieve calmness and profundity, ripeness and wisdom, and the clear enhancement of memory. And, most

precious of all, you will have Time—that rare and lovely gift that
your Western countries have lost the more they have pursued it."

"To the Heart of Kham" has taken us back through centuries of
history, over land once trod by a Chinese princess, Wen-cheng; an
Indian master, Guru Rinpoché; and countless Tibetan lamas and
yogis, kings and queens. Palpung Monastery marks the final stop
before arriving at the area of sacred ground where Kongtrul lived,
wrote, taught, meditated, and founded a retreat center. I am in love
with this land and with its history, but most of all, I love the people
I have met here. They incarnate life lived on a human scale and
they preserve human and spiritual values with their simple, deep
lives—they are the salt of sacred ground.

TSADRA AND THE TWENTY-FIVE AREAS OF SACRED GROUND

Dergé remains a fascinating center of Khampa self-consciousness.
It is surrounded by major monasteries of the Sakya, Nyingma, and
Kagyu traditions and prides itself on the number of reincarnate
masters who are its native sons and daughters. Kongtrul claimed
that by his time in the mid-1800s, this Khampa Buddhist pride was
more than hollow patriotism. At the end of his biographies of the
many treasure revealers who appeared after Guru Rinpoché, he
advances the view that Kham had become the center of Tibet's
spiritual life:

> Each of these treasure revealers guided beings through a variety of
> means for enlightened activity, principally those of spiritual instruc-
> tions and consecrated substances. Directly or through [subsequent]
> lineages, they relieved temporal disharmony and increased posi-
> tive conducive influences in the lives of an infinite number of be-
> ings, high and low, even in those of animals. Ultimately, they pro-
> vided beings with refuge from rebirth within the lower realms and
> the wheel of life, and placed them within the complete freedom of
> spiritual liberation. When conditions of their historical period war-
> ranted it, some saved Tibet from the danger of invasion. In these
> and others ways, their kindness has been outstanding; each and
> every one of them has been the embodiment of prodigious enlight-
> ened activity. However, each has appeared only as the display of
> the compassion of the Tibetan land's sole refuge, the precious mas-
> ter from Oddiyana, Guru Rinpoché. [A treasure text] states:

I, Lotus-Born Master, have filled the whole world with
   treasures—
Inexhaustible gifts of spiritual instructions for beings of the
   future.
Those who retrieve them are my manifestations.
Their dress and behavior are uncertain and can take any form
   whatsoever.
Within the experience of faithful persons, sometimes faith will
   be lost.
It will be difficult for everyone to accept many of them as
   authentic.

As stated here, these treasure revealers surely appear from the
inconceivable kindness of Guru Rinpoché and his consort [Yeshé
Tsogyal]. It is wise to keep their kindness sincerely in mind and to
satisfy their enlightened minds by such acts as giving them the
offering-clouds of one's life, body, possessions, and virtuous acts,
and energetically praying to them whole-heartedly.

These genuine treasure revealers, holy individuals, first began
to appear mainly in upper [western Tibet], the Ngari area; then in
central [Tibet]—Ü, Tsang, Lho, and Mön; and finally in the upper,
middle, and lower parts of Amdo and Kham. (*Lives of the Treasure
Revealers*, pp. 230b-231a)

The sun of Guru Rinpoché's treasures rose in western Tibet,
moved eastward, and reached its zenith over Kham during
Kongtrul's lifetime. With the birth and activity of treasure revealers
in the neighborhood came knowledge of Kham and Amdo's relationship with Guru Rinpoché, thanks to histories recounted in new
treasure texts. Traditional histories had told of Guru Rinpoché's
activity in central Tibet, but no mention had ever been made of the
Indian master's specific travels to, and meditation at sites in, eastern
Tibet. Yet Kongtrul was able to affirm this:

[Guru Rinpoché] also traveled throughout Ü [central Tibet], Tsang
[western Tibet], and Kham [eastern Tibet] through the uninhibited
play of his miraculous powers. There is no area of Tibetan soil larger
than a horse's hoof that was not touched by his feet. He consecrated all isolated mountainous regions as places of meditation
practice. (*Encyclopedia of Buddhism*, vol. 1, p. 510)

This statement looks tame to us, but it proposed validation of
eastern Tibet as ground sacred to Guru Rinpoché's followers at the

same level as central Tibet. For some, it might have seemed as out-
rageous as a fraudulent claim that Buddha Shakyamuni had once
visited Lhasa. While less explicit words alluding to Guru Rinpoché's
presence in Kham and Amdo might have been written by masters
before him, it was only during Kongtrul's lifetime that this became
a real fact of spiritual life for Khampas. For example, if we look at
The Life of Shabkar (the great master, a native of far eastern Tibet,
Amdo, who lived from 1781-1851), we see that his numerous pilgrimages did not include sites in Kham and that he made no mention of the twenty-five areas of sacred ground in eastern Tibet that
Kongtrul repeatedly proclaims. This can be easily explained: the
existence of the twenty-five areas of sacred ground was revealed
only in 1857, after Chok-gyur Déchen Lingpa unearthed *The Location List of the Twenty-Five Major Sacred Sites of Amdo and Kham*[8]
from Powerful Hero Cliff (Pawo Wongchen Drak, also known as
Horse-Neck Hero Cliff). Kongtrul includes the last lines of this text
written by Guru Rinpoché in his *Pilgrimage Guide*:

> [To express the benefits of sacred ground,]
> Prostrations and circumambulations done in these places shut
>   the door to rebirth in the miserable existences.
> Service rendered here leads to rebirth in the higher realms.
> The offering of one vajra feast completes a great cultivation of
>   merit.
> A second vajra feast offering purifies all the ripened effects of
>   past acts.
> A third vajra feast offering ensures that you will meet me, Lotus-
>   Born Master from Oddiyana,
> In a symbolic form either in real life, in meditation, or in the
>   course of a dream.
> One hundred vajra feast offerings lead to rebirth in the pure
>   celestial realms.
> If you wish to attain supreme accomplishment, practice single-
>   mindedly: you will attain it!
> How marvelous are these sublime sacred places that help others
>   through any connection to them! (pp. 19a-b)

This must have proved a wonderful revelation to the people of
Kham: in the treasure text which Chokling revealed, Guru Rinpoché
indicates five central and twenty-five major sites, representing the
body, speech, mind, qualities, and activity of enlightenment; plus

four special places and eight locations of manifest activity to tame beings, all blessed by his presence and all in their immediate vicinity. Khampas no longer needed to travel to Tsari (the major central Tibetan pilgrimage site, explained in the next section); Tsari would come to them, as Kongtrul promises in his *First Notice of Gathering at the Sacred Place* (translated in full in the Appendix):

> Now especially, from the first day of the sixth month of the Iron Sheep Year until the new moon, the palace and deities of the circle of wisdom from the supreme sacred place of Charitra will actually come here. During this period, the effect of one circumambulation around the outer extremity of this area will definitely equal that of seven hundred million recitations of the six-syllable mantra or the *Vajra Guru* mantra; similarly, three such circumambulations equal that of a circumambulation of the whole area of Tsari [Tib.: Tsari Rongkor].

Thus, Tsari Rongkor, one of the most arduous and dangerous pilgrimage routes that took between ten and fifteen days to complete, could be equaled by three circlings of Tsadra, which could be done in as many days. If nothing else, this was definitely a bargain, available every Sheep Year, as this marked the anniversary of Tsadra's inauguration. (The critical year for pilgrimage gatherings at Tsari is the Monkey Year, commemorating its inauguration by Tsangpa Gyaré. Mount Kailash, the most famous of western Tibetan pilgrimage places, is at spiritual high tide during Horse Years.)

To return to the shift of sacred sites to Kham, Chokling's treasure text's unveiling of over thirty locations consecrated by Guru Rinpoché marked a new dawn for Buddhism in eastern Tibet. If their spiritual compasses still pointed West toward Lhasa, it was with less urgency—Kham had become authenticated as sacred ground.

I mentioned above that Chok-gyur Déchen Lingpa revealed the first list of Amdo and Kham's sacred sites in 1857. The last words of Guru Rinpoché in that text and the colophon Kongtrul added to it recount the circumstances of the text's concealment and rediscovery:

> To foster joy throughout the entire Tibetan land,
> I, the Lotus-Born Master from Oddiyana,
> Have composed this list and have concealed it,

Sealed at Powerful Hero Cliff.

[The protectress] Ékajati guards the scroll of teachings:

If there is need, give it to someone who has a karmic connection

And at that time make it resound with the seal of skillful means
   and transcendent knowledge.

Samaya Gya Gya Kha-tham Gu-hyé

[This treasure was revealed] in response to a request I had made due to a positive connection with Terchen Chokgyur Déchen Lingpa, reincarnation of [King Trisong Dé-tsen's son] Prince Murub Tsépo. On the first Joy [i.e., the first day] of the waxing moon of the miracle [i.e., first] month of the Fire Snake Year [1857], at Horse-Neck Hero Cliff (itself located in front of Trori Dorjé Ziltrom, to the east of the palace of the great spiritual king of Dergé), he removed nine seals from the front side of the white rock, where there is a distinct self-arisen [form of a deity]. Then, before twenty fortunate persons, he removed a triangular leather box, shaped like a large [?].[9]

[Later, Chokling] re-illuminated the sacred ground of Dévikotri and authenticated the treasure in the isolated hermitage of Kunzang Déchen Ösel Ling, situated to the left of the meditation cave of Guru Rinpoché. This cave is located at the center of the upper reaches of the third Dévikotri, Tsadra Rinchen Drak, which has the self-arisen form of the eight deities gathered around Great Glorious *Héruka*.

On that occasion, before the lion throne in Yiga Chödzin, the private residence of the omniscient Lord Maitreya Tai Situpa, at the main monastic seat of the Palpung temple, we opened the treasure. It contained yellow parchment that measured a hand-span long, and four finger-width's wide. This text comes from the interpretation of the symbolic letter *Ha* written by Guru Rinpoché in the sixth line.

The one called Péma Garwong, Lodrö Tayé, or Yonten Gyatso [three of Kongtrul's names] wrote this down in his own hand. May the illumination of virtuous portents, encompassing Buddhism and beings, pervade all time, space, and circumstances! *Sarva-tha Mangalam* (pp. 19b-20b)

This colophon finds Kongtrul and Chokling in the Tai Situpa's quarters, opening and deciphering a treasure that was to have a huge impact in their lives. Even more importantly, it was to change the spiritual geography of Tibet: Kham became newly empowered or enthroned from that moment on.[10]

This was not a political event. For Khampas, Chokling's discoveries redefined their history and introduced them to many close-by centers of Guru Rinpoché's living presence. As is mentioned below in the section "The Best of Times and the Worst of Times," the mid-1800s were a time of extreme turmoil in Lhasa, Beijing, and in Kham, which weathered a popular, bloody revolt that engulfed the whole region for almost twenty years before the Lhasa authorities sent in troops to quell it. In reflecting on this period, if we are to understand these three wise men (Kyentsé, Chokling, and Kongtrul) who reoriented the spiritual consciousness of Tibetans during the 1800s, we must consider more than the brutal facts of that day's politics. Although these three sometimes interceded in the current events around them, it seems likely that all they wanted from those who wielded power was peace and quiet. They were authentic spiritual masters, conscious of the extraordinary chance their association gave them. Impartial judges would place Kyentsé and Chokling among the most prolific treasure revealers and visionaries that ever lived; Kyentsé and Kongtrul, among the greatest Tibetan minds and encyclopedists. Their lives and work, through which the rivers of Tibetan Buddhism's practice traditions flowed, were centered in Kham. There was no better time for Kham's hidden sacred ground to be revealed. If one believes in Guru Rinpoché's treasures, their timeliness at this juncture was not political in nature, but an expression of timeless wisdom.

The following passage from Kongtrul's *Autobiography* deals with these critical weeks of his life, including the events he mentioned in the colophon above. Kongtrul begins by recounting that Öntrul Rinpoché, chief administrator of Palpung Monastery after the death of the Ninth Tai Situpa, informed him that he must make a long journey to central Tibet to accompany the young reincarnation back home. This led to the ceremony of installation (Kongtrul's inaugural address preceding it is translated in *Enthronement*[11]).

> [In 1856, I was informed by] Öntrul Rinpoché that it was imperative that I go to Tibet next year to invite the supreme manifestation of enlightenment [the infant Tenth Tai Situpa] to return to his monastic seat. To prevent obstacles for this journey, I attended the daily

rituals in each of the protector temples and then returned to the retreat center, where I performed the intensive practice of the *Gathering of the Enlightened Families of the Immortal Three Bodies of Enlightenment.*

On the third day of the twelfth [lunar] month, Chokgyur Lingpa drew the treasure texts of the *Three Classes of Great Completion* from the Lotus Crystal Cave at Dzam-nang. I received news of this from both Terton and Tulku Rinpochés [Chokling and Kyentsé], who sent me immediate word of the event. Right away, I used the necessary articles I had on hand for feast, *torma*, and other offerings, to mark the occasion with meditation practice and offerings. For a few days around this time, an unbearably strong wind arose, the miraculous display of local deities, as clearly related in the master's [presumably Chokling's] biography. I performed the traditional year-ending Vajra Dagger rituals.

Then on the twenty-third day of the month, the treasure revealer [Chokling] arrived. We welcomed him with hoisted banners, sounds of conches, fragrant bonfires, etc. Snow mixed with flowers fell; "An auspicious event!" he declared. I worked as scribe for the transcription from the yellow parchment [of treasure texts] related to the empowerment ritual and other texts for the practice of White Buddha of Longevity. The auspicious signs of virtue during this work were also positive. I dreamed that I was close to eighty years old and that I acquired many special texts related to Slayer of the Lord of Death [*Yamantaka*]. Chokling gave me the empowerment, reading transmission, and instructions for his treasure Lotus Pure Crown Protuberance; the practice of [the deity called] Emptying the Depths of Cyclic Existence from the cycle of *Seven Profound Treasures* that he had revealed from [the place called] Karma the previous year; and the part of the treasure with which I had a connection, Chief of Longevity, Slayer of the Lord of Death.

Although it would not have been useful in the past, the time had now come: I asked Chokling to compose a guide to the sacred features in the area of my home. He replied that it was one of the twenty-five sacred areas of the Amdo and Kham region: it was therefore unnecessary to write such a guide, as it would have already been concealed as a treasure [by Guru Rinpoché long ago].

Chokling gave me a treasure he had retrieved from Yelpuk Cave that was related to me, a statue called Blazing Fire.[12] It is of [Six-Armed] Protector, carved by the exalted master Nagarjuna from a black stone from [the Indian charnel ground] Cool Grove. "I need a meditation support, any at all, to replace it," Chokling said. I gave him a special, old statue of Guru Rinpoché that I had.

Since I was actively collecting the most important treasure teachings [for what would become *The Treasury of Rediscovered Teachings*], I asked Chokling to perform divinations for precise indications concerning such questions as whether certain texts were reliable or not. To this he replied that, before long, he would reveal some concealed declarations and treasures. Around that time, he would meet Guru Rinpoché in person and have the opportunity to ask questions. He told me he wouldn't forget my requests. After leaving, on his way to Jadra, he made feast fulfillment offerings at Powerful Hero Cliff; at Lion Cliff he retrieved [from the treasure location] *The Additional Declaration*.

On New Year's Day of the Fire Snake Year [1857], *The Location List of the Twenty-Five Major Sacred Sites of Amdo and Kham* came into Chokling's hands. He returned here and we performed the authentication of the treasure. Concerning the subjects of my request for divination, Chokling asked Guru Rinpoché at that time and received very many verses in reply; however, I did not write them down on that occasion. It seemed that the point [of the advice was that since the texts in question] had developed from the source treasures and were composed with the force of positive aspirations, I received the permission to collect and to organize the treasure texts as I wished.

On the morning of the third day of the lunar month, I offered Chokling gifts and a long-life ceremony based on *The Inner Essence of Immortality*. Then, after having performed a lengthy fragrant smoke offering and an impressive ritual for binding [the local deities] under his command, Chokling introduced us to the sacred ground of Tsadra Rinchen Drak. As he walked, he repeatedly fainted due to visions of Mantra Protectress [Ékajati]. Finally, I placed on his forehead a letter symbolizing the hand-implement of the master from Oddiyana. This revived him and he introduced us to the main self-formed caves, which were ideal for meditation practice.

The next day, when we entered the sacred ground, signs of great agitation arose, such as a great, violent wind. We went to the main residence of the lamas at the monastery and transcribed *The Location List of the Twenty-Five Major Sacred Sites of Amdo and Kham*. (*Autobiography*, pp. 85a-86b)

It is apparent that Chokling knew that Kongtrul's home surroundings stood on sacred ground before the treasure text was found and transcribed. Yet he did not precipitate events. Kyentsé also knew:

> [In 1856, Kyentsé, in the course of a teaching,] declared that this excellent place is the third Dévikotri, an external expression of the eye of wisdom at the highest extremity of the central channel. I wondered about that statement since that name for this place was unknown. Later I asked him why he had said it. He replied that, at that time, he had had a clear meditative experience of hearing it in a secret song of the wisdom *dakinis*. (*Autobiography*, p. 82a)

Yet Kyentsé had done nothing apart from making that passing comment. Kongtrul as well admits that he knew. In one passage (translated in full in the section "Jamgon Kongtrul at Home" below), he is coy:

> In my dreams and in my discursive thoughts I had wondered whether this place was an area of sacred ground.

But in another text he allows himself more credit:

> Although at first I had vivid experiences of both Tsadra Rinchen Drak and Dzong-shö Déshek Dupa Palace[13] as sacred ground, yet the time [for their unveiling] had not come. Later, in answer to my encouragement that he write a guide to the sacred place and to open it, Chokling retrieved *The Location List of the Twenty-Five Major Sacred Sites of Amdo and Kham* from Powerful Hero Cliff, and opened the area of sacred ground. (*My Past Lives*, pp. 39b-40a)

For most modern persons, these are examples of inexplicable behavior: why not just go ahead and publicize these special places, especially if one is convinced that it will do some good? This attitude, so reflexive to us, was not theirs. Even after the first treasure text confirmed their impressions, Chokling waited two years before retrieving the specific text for Tsadra and actually "opening" the area of sacred ground. I cannot second-guess these masters, but I suspect that their reluctance to rush had to do with their sensitivity to the correct confluence of positive conditions. This seems to be part of a treasure revealer's discipline: every aspect of the treasure's return to the world must be attended to—the time, the place, the revealer, the disciples or persons for whom the treasure is destined, and many other factors. These three masters, among the greatest Tibet had ever produced, waited. Whether they liked it or not, they had to wait until the conditions were right, whatever they may be.

In the case of the unveiling of Tsadra, all the necessary conditions converged at an auspicious time: a few months after the young Tai Situpa returned and was enthroned in Palpung, and while the head of the Kagyu lineage, Karmapa (the Fourteenth, Tegchok Dorjé), remained in the area, Chokling finally opened Tsadra. Kyentsé and Kongtrul together wrote the following short account of the event in their invitation to pilgrims to gather at Tsadra for the first twelfth-year anniversary of that opening event. These words were written in 1871; Chokling had died the year before, at the age of forty-one:

> The second buddha, Padmakara's [Lotus-Born Master's] three mysteries of enlightenment [i.e., his body, speech, and mind], his noble qualities, and his enlightened activity consecrated an inconceivable number of adamantine sacred places. Those that are well known include the especially holy twenty-one meditation places of Ü and Tsang and the twenty-five sacred areas of Kham, all primordially renowned locations. Among the twenty-five sacred areas of Kham, this sublime sacred place represents the heart of enlightened qualities.
>
> [Concerning its history], to begin with, in the Fire Dragon Year of the fourteenth cycle [1856], the full ritual of the practice and empowerment of *The Spiritual Master's Quintessential Vision* was performed in Palpung Monastery's [Palpung Toub-ten Chökor Ling's] Hall of Pure Fragrance, which contains the shrine of new statues, Gloriously Flaming Blessing. On that occasion, I heard in a vision the *dakinis'* secret instruction, "This sacred place is a third Dévikotri!" Later that same year, as the beginning of the Fire Snake Year [1857] approached, Terchen Chok-gyur Déchen Lingpa retrieved before a crowd of people the treasure text *The Location List of the Twenty-Five Major Sacred Sites of Amdo and Kham* from Powerful Hero Cliff. On the thirteenth day of the waxing moon of the first lunar month, he introduced us to the paths of circumambulation around this essence of the major regions of sacred ground, Tsadra Rinchen Drak.
>
> On the tenth day of the fifth lunar month of the Sheep Year [1859], at the time the victorious one and his spiritual heir [Karmapa and

Tai Situpa] of the Oral Instruction Lineage appeared, Terchen Rinpoché retrieved from Tsadra Rinchen Drak profound treasures of outstanding spiritual teachings and consecrated objects. On the same occasion, he unveiled this sacred area and gave a detailed and definitive description of its features. This proclamation of its magnificent qualities marked the beginning of this area's enlightened activity. Therefore the effects of virtuous acts performed here at any time—meditation practice, vajra feast or other offerings, prostrations, and circumambulations—are multiplied one hundred thousand times. This is stated firmly in texts of the adamantine speech [of Guru Rinpoché].[14]

Here and elsewhere we read the words "to open" used in relation to areas of sacred ground. Here we read the significance of the event: "This proclamation of its magnificent qualities marked *the beginning of this area's enlightened activity*." Areas of sacred ground blessed by Guru Rinpoché lie as if spiritually or energetically dormant until the time for them to aid others arrives. In this case, the signal that the switch has been turned on was the retrieval of the treasure text at the site. As Chokling's treasure text of 1859, *The Treasure-Text Guide to Tsadra*, states:

When this catalogue appears on the earth,
The body, speech, and mind of the *Héruka*
Will arrive here from the Highest Pure Land.

This was not an event that these masters took lightly. Kongtrul has described above the powerful events that occurred when Chokling first began to introduce him and others to Tsadra. Kongtrul had lived there for years and Chokling had often been his guest, yet his intention to present Tsadra, even semi-officially, triggered a violent reaction. We read below, in the next section, Matthieu Ricard's brief account of lamas' inaugural visits to Tsari, how different masters opened that land through different directional gates and how Yeshé Dorjé succeeded only on his third attempt. His difficulties were not only encountered on an outer level—inhospitable natives, wild animals, or impenetrable vegetation. As in Kongtrul's place and time, the way was completely open and traversed regularly by anyone else, yet Yeshé Dorjé could not enter.

This dilemma is similar to that of a bank: anyone can pass through and perform a normal transaction without any problem. But if a person asks to withdraw a million dollars, left in his/her name by someone else long before, chances are that such a transaction will draw more attention. In fact, even the person who makes such a withdrawal will probably consider the whole situation very carefully. Any treasure—a text, a statue, etc., or even an area of sacred ground—belongs to Guru Rinpoché. He and Yeshé Tsogyal left the treasure with the name of a specific recipient attached. The treasure revealer makes the withdrawal in his or her own name and the treasure guardians ensure that the destined person has come at exactly the right time and that all the conditions are correct. The larger the withdrawal, the stricter the control. In his *Pilgrimage Guide* below, Kongtrul gives this more explicit version of Chokling's first introduction of Tsadra:

> During the days of the waxing moon of the first month, the miracle month, of the new year of the Fire Snake, Chokling first performed a vajra feast on the plain in front of the sacred ground. At the highest point of the area, he conducted an extensive ritual to bind gods and spirits under oath; the ceremony began with smoke and *serkyem* offerings. After this was completed, he began walking, intending to introduce us to the features of the heart of the sacred ground. However the protector of the area, Mantra Protectress [Ékajati], appeared clearly before him; to others he appeared to have fainted.
>
> Even on the following day, vajra feast and *tormas* were offered, but a dark wind from the sky to the ground appeared along with other awesome signs of tremendous turmoil. Chokling had lengthy visions that convinced him that the time for the opening was not propitious and that we should delay our attempts. These events were reminiscent of the circumstances surrounding the opening of the sacred ground at Tsari by the three accomplished masters, Nyö [Chenpo Gyalwa Lhanangpa], Gar [Dampa], and [Palchen] Chö[yé].[15] This showed us that particularly powerful sacred places cannot be opened easily!

These kinds of accounts of missed or incomplete connections are common in stories of treasure revealers. In the list of treasures he himself revealed, Kongtrul includes this, without further comment:

> From Marong Drugu Auspicious Treasure Fortress, the main treasure I discovered was a box that contains the perfect Buddha's tooth and blood; however since one essential connection did not appear, the treasure guardians took it back. (*My Past Lives*, p. 35a)

Outside the domain of treasures, I have found the attitude of Tibetan masters toward taking initiative to be very different from our own. For example, my teacher Kalu Rinpoché told me shortly before he died that he had always wanted to pass on to a new generation the reading transmission for the entire Canon of the Buddha's teaching (the *Kangyur*, as that collection is known in Tibetan). In particular, he had hoped that the young Kagyu tulkus would ask him, as they had done for many other major key empowerments, reading transmissions, and instructions. Yet they never did, and Rinpoché, in spite of his seniority, his personal wishes, and the possible good such an important transmission might have done, never took that initiative, nor even hinted of his thoughts. I witnessed this same approach continually over the years with Rinpoché and other Tibetan lamas; judging by the written record left to us, these past masters displayed the same self-restraint and humility on a grand scale.

During the nineteenth century in eastern Tibet, three spiritual masters whose lives had been foretold by Guru Rinpoché collaborated for a brief period. Together they changed the spiritual consciousness of a country and opened the sacred sites of Kham and Amdo. They did so not as patriots or as politicians, but as living representatives of Guru Rinpoché's timeless wisdom, as revealed in treasure texts he had written expressly for a place that is foreign to us, but for a time that now includes our own: as of late 1998, Chinese authorities have declared most of these sites open to visits by foreigners. For the first time, travel there can be relatively hassle-free for modern, non-Tibetan tantric Buddhists.

TSARI, MOTHER OF TSADRA

Kongtrul's pilgrimage guide invites the reader to Tsadra Rinchen Drak. The name means Jewel Cliff Like Tsari; the last two words are abbreviated in Tibetan – Tsari becomes *Tsa*, and is joined to *dra* "to be like." In his *Pilgrimage Guide to Tsadra*, Kongtrul explains the origin of this pilgrimage site as related to the history of Tsari, a place he names as Tibet's only full-fledged primordial site where "*dakinis* are sure to gather."

The *dakini* population must surely outnumber that of humans, as Tsari can be found in modern Nang County, southeast of Lhasa.

It covers 6,477 square kilometers and holds just 5,637 inhabitants! However, according to the *Tibet Handbook*, pilgrimage could swell the number of persons to as many as one hundred thousand. Here is part of what Gyurmé Dorjé reports about Tsari:

> Mount Dakpa Shelri (5,735m) and its environs in Tsari form one of Tibet's most revered pilgrimage circuits—generally ranking alongside those of Mt Kailash and Mt Amnye Machen. For the Kagyu school in particular, Tsari is classed along with Mt Kailash and Lapchi Gang as one of the three essential power places of the meditational deity Cakrasamvara. Two of Cakrasamvara's 24 power-places mentioned in the *Root Tantra of Cakrasamvara* are said to be within Tsari, Caritra and Devikota.[16] (*Tibet Handbook*, p. 224)

Another book that will be treasured for generations, Matthieu Ricard's *The Life of Shabkar*, contains an account of Shabkar's pilgrimage to Tsari in Chapter 10, "The Ravines of Tsari." In the first note at the end of the chapter, the translator recounts its historical background:

> Tsari is identified as both *Caritra* and *Devikota*, two of the twenty-four great sacred places described in the tantras. . . .
>
> There are four main gateways to the Pure Crystal Mountain of Tsari [called by its Tibetan name, Dakpa Shelri, in the quote above]: the eastern one is that of Manjushri; the southern, of Vajrapani; the western, of Tara; and the northern, of Avalokiteshvara. According to Kunkhyen Pema Karpo, the general sequence of human entry into the Tsari mandala is as follows:
>
> Guru Padmasambhava entered through the southern door and remained seven years in the Magnificent Secret Cave. Vimalamitra, too, traveled miraculously to Tsari.
>
> Lawapa (or Kambalapada, tenth century), a teacher of Atisha, entered through the eastern door with his disciple Bhusuku, and later departed to the Buddhafield of Khechara without leaving his physical body behind.
>
> Kyebu Yeshe Dorje (twelfth century), an incarnation of Nyang Ben Tingdzin Zangpo, tried thrice to enter Tsari according to the prediction of Gampopa, his teacher. The third time, Yeshe Dorje was able to enter through the western door and reached the Turquoise Lake. He also opened the door to the Lake of the Black Mandala in Dagpo; there, together with Gampopa, he concealed as terma the *Teaching on Mind, the Wish-Fulfilling Gem*.

Tsangpa Gyare Yeshe Dorje (1161-1211, not to be confused with Kyebu Yeshe Dorje) went to Tsari, following a prediction given to him in a vision by Gyalwa Lorepa (1187-1250). After Tsangpa Gyare had opened the door of the sacred place he had a vision at the Turquoise Lake Palace in which Chakrasamvara told him, "You will become the Buddha known as The Young Aspirant, the youngest of the 1002 Buddhas of this kalpa, and your teachings will spread far and wide from here, to the distance of eighteen days of a vulture's flight."

Drigung Jikten Gonpo (1143-1217) sent to Tsari first three of his main disciples, headed by Nyö Gyalwa Lhanangpa, and then a great number of hermits.

Finally, Sonam Gyaltsen, from Ralung, entered through the northern door. (p. 267)

Kongtrul's praise to Tsari follows. In it, he identifies the location as one of the primordial areas of sacred ground, recounts some of its history, and relates the benefits of pilgrimage and spiritual practice there.

The yogi Yeshé Wongchuk, mentioned by Kongtrul as the originator of New Tsari, is not mentioned above because these masters' activity related to Old Tsari. Gyurmé Dorjé states that New Tsari "was founded by Rigdzin Kumaradza (1266-1343), a lineage-holder of the Nyingmapa school and the principal teacher of Longchen Rabjampa." (*Tibet Handbook*, p. 227) Further study may prove that the Yeshé Wongchuk named by Kongtrul is either one of Rigdzin Kumaradza's names or a copying error for his more common name, Yeshé Zhonnu. In his case and for the other masters' activity in Tsari, Kongtrul uses the verb "to open," an indication that by entering an area, they revealed or inaugurated it as a sacred place.

The Song of the Messenger of Spring
A short poem in praise of glorious Charitra[17]

Namo Guru Déva Dakini Houng

Innumerable major and minor sacred places,
Lie throughout the world and the Tibetan Himalayan land.
Connection to any of them is meaningful to spiritual life:
They have been consecrated by the Buddha and reflect his
    enlightened activity.

Nonetheless, from the principal great sacred places, others
   diffuse,
Growing and spreading like a tree's trunk, branches, leaves, etc.
In most, accomplished masters, awareness-holders, and yogis
Have practiced: the sites have been blessed by these individuals.
Many persons, both bad and good, later lived there.

Primordial, self-arisen places—the twenty-four great regions of
   sacred ground
And the thirty-two major sacred sites—are superior to all others.
Among these is the higher drink-severer, Charitra.[18]
On an inner level it represents the eyes. The natural radiance of
   the two eyes' channels
Appears in the world: one location of Charitra can be found in
   the exalted land of India,
Said to be situated on the shore of the southern ocean.[19]
The other is located in Tibet, on the border between Lho and
   Mön,
A site mentioned briefly by Lord Marpa.

In particular, the master foretold by the Buddha, the venerable
   Tsojé,
The incomparable master from Dagpo, Da'o Zhonnu [Gampopa],
In the midst of five hundred disciples, great individuals who had
   attained a stage of awakening,
Made a prediction in a fearless lion's roar
Of the topography and the qualities of Tsari.
Kyégom Yeshé Dorjé, an emanation of [Guru Rinpoché's
   disciple] Namké Nyingpo,
Followed his master's command and became the first to enter
   the sacred place,
Now known as Old Tsari.
A disciple of Dagpo, the Buddha Destroyer of Cyclic Existence in
   person,
The illustrious Pamo Drupa,
Had among his disciples of the Oral Instruction [Kagyu] Lineage,
   the four pairs and the eight equals,
One of whom was Kyobpa Jikten Soumgon [1143-1217].
Three disciples of his disciples, the accomplished masters Nyö
   [Chenpo Gyalwa Lhanangpa], Gar [Dampa], and [Palchen]
   Chö[yé],

Described in brief the characteristics of this sacred place [after
    having entered it].

In particular, the erudite and accomplished master from the holy
    land of India, Naropa,
Took intentional rebirth in the world as Tsangpa Gyaré.
He traveled through the amazing miraculous power of his tantric
    discipline
And opened the celestial realm of Charitra.
He pointed out the self-formed images there and showed the
    outer and inner paths for circumambulation.
He encountered no obstacles and made an infinite number of
    auspicious connections.
His reincarnation line, the omniscient Drukchen Rinpochés,
Have, in their series of lives, been the main residents of this
    place.
They were not impeded by obstacles, but have increased their
    benefit to others.

The king of all accomplished masters, [the Second Karmapa]
    Karma Pakshi [1204-1283],
Gave a command to the yogi Yeshé Wongchuk
To open anew the self-formed deep cave and other features:
This is known as New Tsari.

The fourth powerful victor [Karmapa], Rolpé Dorjé [1340-1383],
Traveled here with miraculous powers like those of Lotus-Born
    Master
And unveiled the sacred place of White Lake [Tso-kar].
Later, the Ninth Karmapa, Wongchuk Dorjé, [1556-1603],
And the other powerful victors of the series treated this place
    with great respect:
The Karma, Drukpa, and Drigung Kagyus
Constructed way-stations where faithful pilgrims
Could easily find provisions and rest.
Since the share of each entailed a great expense,
They initiated the custom of collecting donations for this purpose
    throughout upper and lower Tibet.

Charitra, supreme among the sacred places of Tibet,
Is not an ordinary place but a celestial pure realm.
The *Héruka*, the glorious honored one, Wheel of Supreme Bliss,

With his assembly of spiritual heroes and *dakinis*, actually resides
   here.
Guardians of the doctrine and guardians of the treasures wander
   throughout this place.
There are an inconceivable number of amazing signs of this.

This is the place for yogis' tantric discipline;
The ground for meditators' experience and realization to
   increase;
The field for the rich to cultivate merit;
And the region where evil persons' obscurations are forcefully
   purified.

Seven days of meditation in Tsari bring one closer to attainment
Than many months or years spent meditating elsewhere.
It is more useful to create auspicious connections here
Than to spend one hundred years exerting oneself in physical
   and verbal virtuous practice elsewhere .

By having done meditation and spiritual practice here, one will
   reach attainment during this lifetime;
Whatever prayers one makes will be effortlessly fulfilled.
Each circumambulation multiplies the virtue done during it
   many hundred million times.
All connections made here, such as through vajra feasts and
   offerings,
Dispel all obstacles and lead to ordinary and supreme
   accomplishments.

Even if one doesn't meditate or practice here as one should,
One will be reborn in the celestial realms after leaving one's
   body:
That even animals who have died here leave relics is a sign of
   this!
If with faith one takes seven steps in the direction of this place,
The door to miserable existences will be shut at death.

If one sees the supreme supports of Tsari,
Such as the precious central antler and the skull,[20]
This has the same blessing as actually seeing Tsari,
And if one cultivates merit before them, one gains the same
   merit.
This is not just my opinion: it is well-known from long before

As the excellent speech of the Oral Instruction Lineage's
   accomplished masters.

To encourage faithful persons to virtuous practice,
The learned practitioner of virtue, Lodrö Tayé
Has composed this poem: May it lead all those who read it to the
   celestial realms!

May virtue and well-being increase![21]

This marks the first mention in this book of claims Kongtrul made
of the benefits of meditation or spiritual practice in a sacred place:
seven days spent there equal months or years elsewhere; spiritual
practice there leads to attainment in one's lifetime, and even a visit
made without correct practice is a ticket to celestial realms after
death. Kongtrul repeats these kinds of strong claims in his pilgrimage guide for Tsadra and he justifies his confidence with references
to the relationship between Tsari and Tsadra.

   In his *Pilgrimage Guide to Tsadra*, Kongtrul takes pains to draw
parallels between Tsadra and Tsari, including giving the same
names to the main hills and many features of the land. Spatially,
this was like comparing Luxembourg (Tsadra) to Germany (Tsari),
but to Kongtrul, size did not matter, blessing did, particularly that
of Guru Rinpoché. Further, Tsari, for all its impressive size, did not
have the undeniable attraction Tsadra exercised for half of Tibet's
pilgrims: Tsadra was open to women. Inexplicably, most of the main
routes in Tsari were prohibited to female pilgrims, whereas
Kongtrul announces no such restriction at Tsadra. Of the five pilgrimage routes he describes, two are indeed "closed," but to *all*
"ordinary" persons, male or female, and open only to accomplished
tantric practitioners of either gender.

   Kongtrul did not live in Tsadra with monk attendants but with
his mother and, after her death, his niece. His *Autobiography* relates
that in her final days he went to accompany the woman who had
accompanied Chokling on the occasion of Tsadra's successful initial opening years before. Tsadra was sacred ground but it was also
shared ground, unlike Tsari, where the separation of the sexes,
understandable in the context of personal liberation vows or periods of intense retreat, seems to have been wrongfully transposed
on to what should have been a region of open, tantric practice.

For a more complete look at Tsari, interested readers can turn to *The Cult of Pure Crystal Mountain* by Toni Huber. Professor Huber translates the full accounts of Tsari's openings by the masters mentioned above and does an astounding job of reconstituting the life of the region during and after pilgrimage seasons. The book is relatively slim, but it has the feel of a monumental undertaking on the scale of the pilgrimage circuit it describes. As one who is incapable of such long and painstaking work, I find myself in an uncomfortable position, that of expressing a single but important reservation concerning Huber's view on pilgrimage.

Professor Huber appears to be very sympathetic toward pilgrimage as a general religious exercise, but hesitates to place it within its context as tantric practice. He acknowledges the visionary experience of great masters who opened or meditated at Tsari, but he gives us the impression that the vast majority of Tsari's pilgrims had nothing more than a sense of history and strong motivation to purify sins or cultivate merit. He does not give the reader a sense that another dimension to pilgrimage existed or can exist for any but "elite pilgrims," i.e., lamas or full-time meditators.

This does not do justice to common Tibetans and it is interesting to speculate why Professor Huber arrived at his conclusions. Perhaps most of his sources for accounts of the last major pilgrimage gathering in Tsari, held in 1956, were too young at the time to have matured in their personal practice. Their reports would reflect their own state of mind at the time, their youth, but not that of their elders, whose voices are now silent.

In general, the Tibetan tantric landscape was populated by an elite class of clergy, the visible professional guild of lamas, scholars, and meditators, of which there were few, and by informed, competent pilgrims or spiritual practitioners, of which there were many. To suggest that there was a level of pilgrimage that was inaccessible to all but a restricted elite is to posit the existence of a gaping gulf between a tiny group of enlightened pilgrims and a mass of well-intentioned but benighted spiritual plebes who circled Tsari like so many head of two-legged cattle. The professionals who exited from three-year retreats or monastic colleges were the equivalent of our automotive engineers, driving instructors, or car mechanics: they knew the inner workings of the spiritual path of Buddhism and could be called upon to help when necessary. Their numbers were dwarfed, as they should be, by informed and conscientious practitioners, the equivalent of our licensed drivers.

There is no need for an ordinary individual who treads the tantric Buddhist path all the way to enlightenment to be a member of the clergy. Movement along the path, from the initial path of cultivation to the paths of application or seeing, etc., does not have to be accompanied by any form of formal acknowledgement, such as a title or a role. The pursuit and attainment of knowledge within the Buddhist tradition extraneous to one's immediate needs on the path neither qualify an individual for further progress nor disqualify him or her. The most esteemed, eloquent, learned scholar and the most obscure, inarticulate, simple pilgrim can find themselves at exactly the same point on the path; the yogi proficient in inner heat meditation can be equaled by a humble layperson who scrupulously follows the advice of his or her chosen qualified tantric master.

To suggest that tantric pilgrimage is the domain of professional Buddhists does no justice to the depth of the Tibetan people's experience and realization, nor does it help new non-Tibetan tantric Buddhists situate themselves with self-confidence in relation to the path. Some beginners' eager enthusiasm at the outset of the path is relatively harmless and can be channeled to a student's advantage by a qualified spiritual mentor. The other extreme, becoming disheartened because one has set, or thinks others have set, the bar too high, is much more problematic. Those who don't believe in the power of mantras, should try this one: "I can't possibly do that, it's way beyond me." Repeated regularly enough, with feeling, it is sure to produce sure signs of accomplishment, guaranteed.

Further, perhaps Professor Huber believed his Tibetan sources told him the truth concerning their inner spiritual lives or would have confided their experience to him. I do not believe this is the case, and this has nothing to do with Professor Huber. I would never expect a Tibetan tantric practitioner, even long-time trusted companions, to confide their personal experiences to me. Most Tibetans have a deeply ingrained resistance to sharing the least detail of their meditative experiences, visions, or dreams with anyone but their most trusted spiritual guides. Ordained persons or laypersons alike never let their guard down. For them it is much

less reprehensible to lie and mislead concerning their experience –
"I saw nothing, I don't understand a thing, I'm a hopeless sinner"
– than to whisper the truth, even to close friends and family. Modern persons might ask, "Why not share?" to which a Tibetan practitioner might reply, "Why share?" They question what good ver-
balizing experience on the path does for the speaker or listener
alike. They feel it leads easily to pride on the one hand, jealousy on
the other, and heavy reification on both. "Still water runs deep"
would be their motto, if they knew it.

I am appalled that Tsari was effectively closed to women and,
while I admire his scholarship, I read Professor Huber's book with
the impression that he felt true pilgrimage was closed to most of
the rest of us. I find no justification for either restriction.

AN INVITATION AND A SUPPLICATION

This final section of "The Outer Journey" contains two translations: an invitation Kongtrul and Kyentsé extended to pilgrims
to visit Tsadra and a supplication Kongtrul wrote to evoke Tsadra's
majesty.

The Invitation

This invitation is one of three that Kongtrul wrote; the first two
were co-authored with Kyentsé. Each was written for the anniversary of the opening of Tsadra, Sheep Years in the twelve-year cycle
of Tibetan-Chinese astrology. Passages of the first were included in
sections above; the complete texts of the first and third can be found
in the Appendix. Each of the three invitations covers the same
material but in slightly different and interesting ways. The following invitation was the second, written in the Water Sheep Year, 1883.

A Letter of Sunshine to Encourage Virtue
The Second Notice of Gathering at the Sacred Place [1883]

Here in the Himalayan region, the holy bodhisattva All-Seeing Eyes
has shown remarkable kindness greater than that of all victorious
buddhas. He was first responsible for the appearance of human
beings and nutritious food in this land and then consecrated its
earth, rocks, mountains, and cliffs. His manifestations in the guise

of kings fostered the construction of sacred representations of the
Three Jewels: through the sovereigns' acts, this outlying border-
land came to equal the exalted land of India. All-Seeing Eyes himself took the form of a vajra master, the second buddha, Padmakara,
who came to Tibet. He traveled all over the central region and out-
skirts of the Tibetan land: there was no area of soil larger than a
horse's hoof that his feet did not touch. He bound under oath all
gods and malevolent demons and made all snowy cliffs and mountain lakes places for meditation, consecrating them as inseparable
from primordially existing areas of sacred ground. Their enlightened activity creates a beneficial influence in one's spiritual life
through any connection with them.

The Amdo and Kham regions contain an inconceivable number
of major and minor sacred places, principally the areas renowned
as the twenty-five major sacred places. Among these this notice
concerns one of the five areas of the qualities of enlightenment
which grace this kingdom of the four kinds of magnificence and
the ten virtues of a piece of land.[22] This area of sacred ground,
Dévikotri Tsadra Rinchen Drak, represents the heart of the qualities of enlightenment and is inseparable from glorious Charitra. It
was known in the past as a great sacred location but remained concealed. As the time has now come for it to aid the world, an excellent auspicious confluence of place and time led the indisputably
great treasure revealer, Orgyen Chok-gyur Déchen Lingpa, to retrieve the treasure texts of a general declaration [of the sacred areas of Amdo and Kham] and the guide to this area in particular,
and to inaugurate this area of sacred ground.

This sacred place has been praised in unison by the illustrious
powerful victor, Karmapa, his spiritual heirs, and by other holy
persons. Persons with pure vision see that a palace of wisdom filled
with an ocean-like assembly of the Three Sources [master, meditation deity, and *dakini*] remains here permanently. Therefore this land
is always blessed. Virtuous practices done here, such as prostrations and circumambulations, reap benefits as described in the
source treasure texts. Nevertheless, the special occasion for pilgrimage is stated in the same treasure texts:

> Especially, in the Year of the Sheep, during the Monkey
>   Month,
> A congregation of awareness-holders, meditation deities,
>   and *dakinis*
> Gathers from the ten directions and appears in this place.

As stated here, the beginning of the Sheep Year, and in particular the Monkey Month, mark the definite time for a special gathering [of the deities at this place]. Therefore, during this year's Monkey Month (as calculated by three different traditions)—the fifth, sixth, or seventh lunar month—and specifically during the sixth month, the palace and the deities of the supreme sacred place of Charitra will actually come and remain here. During that time, the effect of seven circumambulations of the summit, three intermediate circumambulations, or one circumambulation of the extremity is amplified seven hundred million times. The treasure text [*The Treasure-Text Guide to Tsadra*] states the general [benefits of cultivating merit here]:

> At all times, ordinary or special,
> One is protected from the *dukka* [suffering] of miserable
>   existences
> By just reaching this sacred place
> With stable faith and devotion.

> By making offerings of outer, inner, and secret vajra feasts,
> One completes a great cultivation of merit and wisdom.
> Whoever makes prostrations and circumambulations here
> Purifies all negative acts and obscurations.

> One session of meditation here is more profound
> Than a year of meditation done elsewhere.
> Whoever meditates single-mindedly
> Will attain ordinary and supreme accomplishments by the
>   blessing of this place.

> Whoever makes offerings at this sacred place
> Will experience the full increase of longevity and merit.

The Additional Declaration states:

> A prostration done once
> Or one complete circumambulation purifies the body's
>   obscurations.
> Whoever lauds this place's great qualities
> Purifies the obscurations of speech.
> That great faith and certainty toward this place lead to
>   supreme accomplishment
> Goes without saying.

These and other passages record the repeated praise of this sacred place given in the adamantine speech of the master from Oddiyana, Guru Rinpoché. Have faith and confidence in it, untroubled by any doubt, and while visiting this sacred place, avoid all forms of unvirtuous action, such as killing birds and deer, cutting grass and trees, breaking rocks or causing landslides, stealing, arguments, and anger. Do whatever virtuous acts you can, such as offering vajra feasts, making offerings, releasing animals to the wild, putting up prayer flags and banners, reciting mantras, and doing prostrations and circumambulations. Since the benefits of each of these acts will be multiplied as mentioned above, all persons, high or low, should keep this occasion in mind. In a very short time [spent in practice here], one can accomplish one's wishes for this and all future lives: act accordingly and don't apathetically waste this opportunity!

This notice, A Letter of Sunshine to Encourage Virtue, *was written on the Excellent Day [the second] of the waxing moon of the fourth lunar month during the female Water Sheep Year [1883], by both [Kyentsé Wongpo], Péma Ösel Do-ngak Lingpa; and [Jamgon Kongtrul], Chimé Tennyi Yung-drung Lingpa. Sarva Daka Laya Nam Mangalam Bhavantu*

The Supplication

The following supplication by Kongtrul provides another example of the connection he makes between the two places, Tsari and Tsadra, separated by hundreds of miles. Kongtrul begins by recalling Buddhist sacred geography, by listing some sacred places in the Tibetan Himalayan region, and then identifies Charitra as the foremost among all. Kongtrul lists here some masters intimately connected with Tsadra Rinchen Drak, and deities and protectors whose influence there is strong. Close to the end, he devotes four lines to each of the three main institutions in the area: his own retreat center, Kunzang Déchen Ösel Ling; an older retreat center, Samten Chökor Ling (the history of which he tells in the next section); and the main monastery, headquarters of the Tai Situpas, Palpung Toub-ten Chökor Ling. The long version of this evocation of the spiritual influence of sacred ground is followed by a short version. Both are used to help the pilgrim bring to mind the full majesty of the sacred environment.

Music of the Celestial Realms

*A Long Supplication to Tsadra Rinchen Drak, the Sublime Sacred Place of the Heart
of Enlightened Qualities*[23]

É Ma Ho! [How wonderful!]

From the expanse of space, [where you are Buddhas] Ever-
   Excellent and Boundless Light,
You appear as enlightenment's perfect rapture, Buddha
   Illuminator and [the bodhisattva] powerful All-Seeing Eyes.
You are manifest enlightenment who guides beings in infinite
   pure lands:
To you, Lotus Skull-Garlanded Adept [Guru Rinpoché], I pray.

In the realm of this world, source of the Vajra Way,
The victors' subjugation of those difficult to tame
Created spontaneous sacred places, regions, and charnel
   grounds:
To the assemblies of deities who reside there, I pray.

The realm blessed by Lord of the World,
The Himalayas, has five valleys, three provinces,
Large and small secret regions, major and minor sacred places:
To their temples and deities, I pray.

The meditation places of Vajra Skull-Garlanded Adept —
The supreme locations of his body, speech, mind, qualities, and
   activities' influence;
Four snowy peaks, eight great caves,
Cliffs in four directions, etc.—cover the surface of the earth:
To the circle of wisdom of these treasures, sacred places, I pray.

In the three circles of Ngari stand twenty snowy cliffs;
In upper and lower Ü-Tsang, sixty-five meditation places;
In Do-Kham, twenty-five major sacred places:
To these places that help beings in appropriate ways, I pray.

The lord and chief of them all is glorious Charitra;
From its celestial city to the vajra enclosure,
It contains one thousand and two subsidiary sacred places:
To its every configuration of deities, I pray.

The second Tsari is Tsadra Rinchen Drak,
The majestic castle of Great Glorious *Héruka*,

The three-year retreat center at Tsadra Rinchen Drak, originally built by Jamgon Kongtrul, enlarged by Kalu Rinpoché, and rebuilt after the Cultural Revolution.

Within the retreat center, these upper buildings were Jamgon Kongtrul's residence, where he meditated, painted, and wrote.

The retreat center's temple, still very much in use by the retreatants, who pray and meditate together there daily.

This view of Tsadra Rinchen Drak and the retreat center faces west. The path to the left leads toward Palpung Monastery, a very steep mile or two away.

Dergé: A high mountain village (3,292 meters), but on the 31st parallel—it is located further south than San Diego, California or the city of Algiers in northern Africa.

A woman from Dergé. The ring of gold that holds a large turquoise informs the viewer that she is married.

The center of Dergé: The lower large building dates from 1729, Dergé's printing press. The upper building is Dergé Monastery, first constructed in 1448, rebuilt after the Cultural Revolution.

Palpung Monastery, jewel in the center of a lotus-ring of hills.

The main temple of Palpung Monastery, built in 1727 by the Eighth Tai Situpa, and spared during the Cultural Revolution.

Looking northwest, toward Dergé, from a stupa that marks the birthplace of Kalu Rinpoché (1905-1989) at Rongpatsa, near Ganzé, eastern Tibet.

Kalu Rinpoché's birthplace, seen from close by the birthplace of his illustrious ancestor, the First Karmapa (1110-1193).

Pilgrims on the trails behind the Tsadra retreat center. The high trees on the right were planted by Kalu Rinpoché and Jamgon Kongtrul the Second where they used to meditate.

Along the pilgrimage route, a meditator's shelter, first used by the great Indian master Humkara.

Mount Zhara Lhatsé (5,820 meters), seen from the road between Lhagang and Gathar. Among Kham and Amdo's twenty-five sacred sites, it represents the body of the mind of enlightenment.

The Divine Lake of Yi-lhung, where Kalu Rinpoché meditated in a cave above the snow line. The highest peak here rises above 6,000 meters. Dergé is 110 miles away, over a 4,916 meter pass

The remaining traces of Tai Situpa's residence, where Jamgon Kongtrul and Chok-gyur Déchen Lingpa opened and translated Tsadra's treasure texts.

Another ruin above Palpung Monastery, the residence of Palpung Kyentsé Rinpoché, where those who had finished a three-year retreat could continue retreat for one year.

The last dance: Kalu Rinpoché watching his lamas perform dances for the last time in his life; Bodhgaya, India, 1988.

A matchless sublime sacred place of the heart of enlightened
   qualities:
To it and to its subsidiary sacred places, I pray.

This place, foretold by Joyous Vajra [*Hévajra*] incarnate, Marpa
   the Translator,
Is the third Dévikotri, the eye of wisdom,
Known as the palace of the vajra heart of enlightenment:
To this place, to which any connection is meaningful, I pray.

One session of resting in meditative absorption here is more
   profound
Than one year of meditation elsewhere.
"Single-minded practice here leads to the celestial realms!":
To this prophecy by the master from Oddiyana, I pray.

The earth, rocks, hills, and cliffs are rainbow-colored, the shape
   of circles;
There are an inconceivable number of sure, symbolic marks of
   the Buddha's doctrine;
There are streams of longevity, and medicinal pools for washing:
To these many marvelous adornments, I pray.

Here, the Three Sources and an ocean of committed protectors
   always gather;
Here, spiritual heroes and *dakinis* dwell in various forms.
Those who keep tantric commitments attain supreme
   accomplishment; those who break them are destroyed:
To this active, wrathful blessing, I pray.

Seen from without, this place naturally has all the ten virtues of a
   piece of land;
From within, it is a gathering place of infinite numbers of the
   Three Sources;
Secretly, it is a celestial palace of indestructible design:
To this supreme Highest Pure Land appearing on earth, I pray.

Here reside Humkara, Vimalamitra,
The master from Oddiyana and his consort, Bérotsana, Namké
   Nyingpo,
Jangchub Lingpa, Karmapa and his spiritual heirs, and other
   masters:
To these spiritual masters of the instruction lineages, I pray.

Here reside Vajrasattva, Yangdak Héruka, Wheel of Supreme
    Bliss, Joyous Vajra, Wheel of Time,
Powerful All-Seeing Eyes, Horse-Neck, Mother Tara,
Vajra Radiance, Co-Emergent Woman, and other deities:
To the assemblies of meditation deities and *dakinis*, I pray.

Here reside the Six-Armed Wisdom-Protector; Four-Armed
    Protector;
Black Caped-One and his consort; Action Protector; Son of
    Renown;
Mantra Protectress; Field Protector; Black and Red Blacksmiths,
    and others:
To these guardians of the sacred place and its treasures, I pray.

On the upper level, Kunzang Déchen Ösel Ling
Stands on the focal point for bringing happiness and benefit to
    the region.
It contains the sacred supports of the *Héruka's* body, speech, and
    mind:
To this place that fulfilled the prophecy, I pray.

On the middle level stands the retreat center, Samten Chökor
    Ling,
The foundation for the vitality of the doctrine of the practice
    lineage:
To this place surrounded by clouds of blessings
Of the master from Oddiyana's spokesman, named Péma [Tai
    Situpa], I pray.

At the base stands Palpung Toub-ten Chökor Ling,
Source of all instruction lineages, respected throughout the
    Himalayan region,
The place that brings joy to the bodhisattva Loving-Kindness:
To its buildings and their sacred contents, I pray.

By the power of my homage, offerings, praises, and prayers,
May all illness, famine, and disputes be pacified throughout the
    world;
May happiness swell like lakes in the summer;
And may spiritual wishes come spontaneously to fruition.

May the victors' doctrine in general and that of the practice
    lineage in particular
Shine brilliantly throughout the world;

May the lives of all who preserve the teachings long be secure;
And may the enlightened activity of the two cycles [scholarship
and practice] increase!

During our lifetimes, may I and others accomplish our wishes in
harmony with the teachings;
May we encounter no obstacles on the path to freedom;
May we travel to the celestial realm of Blissful, or to other pure
realms,
And there fully attain great awakening!

The Short Supplication

Hri!

The source of all qualities, the place of the radiant heart of
enlightenment
Is the second Tsari, Tsadra Rinchen Drak,
Vajra Dévikotra.
To all who reside there: awareness-holders of all lineages,
accomplished masters,
Spiritual masters of the instruction lineages, assemblies of
peaceful and wrathful deities,
Spiritual heroes, *dakinis*, committed protectors, and guardians,
I bow, offer gifts and praises, and pray:
May all obstructive forces be pacified and conducive
circumstances quickly accomplished;
May I travel to the celestial realm of Blissful
And be blessed with the attainment of ordinary and supreme
accomplishments!

[Kongtrul's colophon:] *In answer to the request of the diligent practitioner Lama Tashi Gélek, Karma Ngawang Yonten Gyatso wrote this
prayer at the eastern gate, the wheel of wisdom, of this sublime sacred
place. May virtue and well-being increase!*

NOTES

[1] By far the best work on the subject of Tibetan sacred architecture-as-acupuncture
remains unpublished: a master's thesis by Cyrus Stearns entitled "The Life and
Teaching of the Tibetan Saint Thang-stong rgyalpo, King of the Empty Plain." How
very unfortunate that this wonderful work is not available to a wider audience!

[2] In Tibetan, Four Rivers-Six Ranges is pronounced *Chu-zhi Gang-drouk;* in Chinese, the name of the province where Dergé is now situated, Sichuan, also means Four Rivers.

[3] Kongtrul wrote this catalogue for a temple within the town of Dergé.

[4] Both Kongtrul and the Eighth Tai Situpa Chökyi Jungné state that Déchen Sonam Zangpo followed the Seventh Karmapa's advice in going to the region that became known as Dergé, but the founding of Lhundrup Teng Monastery is situated in 1448 (before the Seventh Karmapa's birth), according to two sources: *The Great Tibetan-Chinese Dictionary* (pp. 1471-1472) and the editor of Tang-Tong Gyalpo's biography, who states that he was eighty-six years old at the time.

[5] The full text of Kongtrul's genealogy of the Dergé kings can be found in the Appendix.

[6] The view from close by as one approaches Palpung Monastery has been captured by Matthieu Ricard in *Journey to Enlightenment,* pp. 122-123. The first photo of the book, opposite the title page, shows Kyentse Rinpoché setting off toward Palpung, along the "White-Hair" Pass.

[7] I am sorry to report that I received word of Omdzé Zopa's death just before this book went to press.

[8] The correct name for this text is *The Location List of the Major Sacred Places of Tibet, Composed by the Scholar from Oddiyana, Padmasambhava* (*Bod kyi gnas chen rnams kyi mdo byang dkar chags o rgyan gyi mkhas pa padma 'byung gnas kyis bkos pa*); however, since its content is heavily weighted toward Kham, it is most often referred to by this other name.

[9] My copy of this text was handwritten and my scholar-lama friends are as puzzled as I concerning the word that appears here—*bing.* We fear it is a scribe's error, and regret that no plausible guess as to the correct spelling is forthcoming.

[10] The complete list of sites can be found in the Appendix.

[11] Jamgon Kongtrul Lodrö Tayé, *Enthronement: The Recognition of the Reincarnate Masters of Tibet and the Himalayas,* trans. and ed. Ngawang Zangpo, pp. 97-154.

[12] As in this case, a treasure revealer could sometimes unearth or reveal treasures that were destined for another treasure revealer. Here, Chokling unearths the statue, but since it is not intended for him, he functions as a postman to deliver the statue to Kongtrul.

For more on this statue, see the letter from Chokling to Kongtrul, included in the section below, "Life on Sacred Ground," under the heading "The Best of Times and the Worst of Times."

[13] An exquisite photograph of this site can be found in Matthieu Ricard's *Journey to Enlightenment,* p. 35.

[14] The complete text of this invitation can be found in the Appendix.

[15] See Huber, pp. 66-68 for this story, and note 33 for their identity.

[16] Sensitive readers may note that we see Caritra here and in other quotes from other sources; Charitra elsewhere. Gyurmé Dorjé notes at the beginning of his guide

that in such Sanskrit words as Caritra and Cakrasamvara, "*palatal c* is rendered as *c* (but to be pronounced as in *Italian ch*)" [italics his]. It seems that, in writing Sanskrit words, pleasing both the eye and ear is impossible: my preference is for a rendering of these words closer to their pronunciation.

We read Devikota here and either Dévikotra or Dévikotri elsewhere, wherever we conform to Kongtrul's spelling. I am at a loss to explain the difference; I suspect there is none.

Finally, Kongtrul uses the names Charitra and Tsari interchangeably: throughout this work, I have left each as he has written them, although the difference between them may only signal the constraint of Tibetan poetic form, in which the number of syllables in a line is strictly limited.

[17] *dPal gyi tsa ri tra'i bsngags brjod mdor bsdus dpyid kyi pho nya'i mgrin dbyangs,* Collected Works, vol. 11, pp. 461-476—pp. 1b-3b.

[18] "Drink-severer" has been explained above, in the section "Sacred Regions for Tantric Conduct."

[19] Huber gives the location: "In the ancient geography of India, the site of Charitra was a southern port city on the Orissan (Udra) coast." (p. 83)

[20] Huber (p. 148) states that every Monkey Year, a female deer would grow a central antler. The same deer would die as the year came to a close. I have found no further information concerning the skull Kongtrul mentions here, "*thod pa smug chung*" in Tibetan.

[21] Unfortunately, Kongtrul wrote no colophon at the end of this prayer.

[22] As we will see in the *Pilgrimage Guide*, this is an oft-repeated play on words to suggest Dergé, an abbreviation of "four *kinds* ("dé") of magnificence and the ten *virtues* ("gé") of a piece of land."

[23] *Yon tan thugs kyi gnas mchog tsa 'dra rin chen brak gi gsol 'debs rgyas pa mkha' spyod rol mo,* Collected Works, vol. 1, pp. 206-210.

Life on Sacred Ground

This section has four parts. First, "Jamgon Kongtrul at Home" consists mainly of a translation of Kongtrul's own story of how his life's outer and inner journeys led him to Tsadra. He writes of Tsadra's history, long before it was unveiled, and of his own life, long before he imagined himself a spiritual master. Kongtrul makes it clear that, from the outset, Tsadra's discovery and inauguration made his life more complicated. He had not planned to build an institution: Chokling insisted that it had to be done, and done right away, not with a meditator's customary procrastination. Kongtrul was yanked off his meditation cushion, forced to put pens, paper, and paintbrushes aside, and thrust into the whirl of monastic politics and building projects. It was not as if he had been asked to build the Potala, but Kongtrul's life took an important new turn with Tsadra's birth.

Second, "Sacred Supports and Consecration" tells the inner story of the construction of buildings at Tsadra. It is not enough for land to be cleared, materials collected, structures erected, and the completed project blessed. Kongtrul describes why and how he took infinite care with each element of the building and its contents, particularly with the sacred statues and images. I find this section a reminder of what I see as a major theme of Kongtrul's life: impeccable stewardship. He never tried to amass land, wealth, students

and renown. He devoted his life to putting the teachings he received into practice and trying to further their preservation. The
honor that was thrust upon him, as the founder of Tsadra, enlarged
the scope of his stewardship; it changed the field of his activity, not
his character. A reader can glimpse in this section the selfless attention he brought to all aspects of his spiritual work.

Third, "The Best of Times and the Worst of Times" attempts to
situate Kongtrul in the events of his day and age. He lived during
immense upheavals in China and in Kham (eastern Tibet); Tibetans may not be careful with historical objects, but they are impas-
sioned oral historians. This is perhaps due to their never having
been sedated by modern sensory overloading, through magazines,
newspapers, radio, television, telephones, and the internet, all dedicated to disposable culture and commentary. Modern meditators
might be eager to flee such input and to cultivate detachment from
the world's ephemeral fashions, as have generations of Buddhists
for thousands of years. Yet, while most lamas I have met seem vac-
cinated against fads, they have a profound grasp of history and,
paradoxically, of the present. They may not be up on the latest,
newest wave, but they are fully engaged in the present, in making
a perduring contribution to the world's living beings and to hon-
oring those of the past. We will see in this section how Kongtrul
and Tsadra's lives intersected with mid-1800 current events.

Finally, "Life in the Land beyond Sacred Ground" points to a
destination beyond the subject of this book—the goal of all pilgrimage and spiritual practice on sacred ground. Kongtrul sometimes used the subject of sacred sites and pilgrimage to point to
another level of sacred vision. I have translated here two excerpts
from praises he wrote to areas of sacred ground. Kongtrul indicates that we eventually reach the destination of our sacred journey and, once there, we must discard our identity as a wanderer in
a sacred world, lest our attachment to sacred ground transform it
to the quicksand of dualistic clinging. After all, as mentioned above
in "The Inner Journey," this is tantric Buddhist practice situated at
the path of application, only the second of the five Buddhist paths.
Kongtrul reminds us that many more splendid journeys await us
after we've made this one.

JAMGON KONGTRUL AT HOME

Any description of Tsadra's sacred ground would ideally include an account of Jamgon Kongtrul's years there. Fortunately, he wrote a short outline of his life in relation to this place, which is included in full below. He relates how Tsadra began as his personal meditation center, where he evaded the world to retreat happily into private peace and quiet. Later, the world beat a path to his door when Tsadra was discovered as a place sacred to the followers of Guru Rinpoché. Kongtrul's humility prevents him from mentioning that it was also due to his long residence there that Tsadra became a magnet for pilgrims, meditators, and spiritual VIPs. Although Kongtrul took obvious pride in what he had built, his temple and retreat center remained tiny by any standards, including those of his day. In his youth, he was too poor to contemplate major building projects, but later in life, his rising fame undoubtedly would have allowed him to surround himself with more material ease and splendor, had he chosen to upgrade his living quarters. But such was not his choice: a renunciate he remained. His lifestyle was reflected in the outer simplicity of his home, which was filled to overflowing with the spiritual wealth he found in books, in consecrated statues and paintings, and in the profound peace of meditation.

In the following passage, Jamgon Kongtrul begins with his family history, that of the Kyung (Garuda) clan. He then speaks disparagingly of himself and allows us to read a little of his personal history before he changes the subject to the past history of Tsadra as a retreat place related to the Karma Kagyu monastic system. He then describes the events leading to the recognition of Tsadra as an area of sacred ground, to his undertaking of the construction of a temple at the site, and to the furnishing of the temple and retreat center as a semi-public facility for meditation.

Jamgon Kongtrul does not portray himself as ambitious or as an independent, willful man. At every step of the way, he sought the permission and encouragement of his spiritual guides, even when they were younger than he (as in the case of both Kyentsé and Chokling). Unlike so many other great masters, before and during his time, Kongtrul's life had been foretold by no less than the Buddha

Shakyamuni and Guru Rinpoché, yet he clung to a humility that seems incredible and unimaginable in our day and age. What's more, the retreat center he gave birth to was not as imposing as we might imagine from the care we read in his words: in fact, there were rooms for only five retreatants in his three-year retreat. I suspect that Kongtrul was not attached to the smallness of his center, but that he wished to make every project, regardless of its size, lastingly worthwhile.x

Here is Kongtrul in his own words, with titles added:

Life Before Tsadra

> It is appropriate to begin with a description of the identity of the virtuous practitioner [at this retreat center]. Those who recount such stories start with the details of the mother's and father's family background and elaborate the story from there. In my own case, I have heard that I am definitely a descendant of the White Garuda family.[1] This line originates with one of the six [ignorance]-destroying awareness-holders, the teacher of the upper direction, [Buddha] Ever-Excellent, Awareness-Illumination, Radiant King. To help all beings, he transformed himself into manifestations of enlightenment: four emanated children born from four eggs—white, yellow, turquoise, and black—of the celestial hawk, the great garuda. The last child, called Exalted Multi-Colored Garuda, rode a turquoise dragon, his feet supported by four miraculous medicine goddesses, and arrived in Gyalmo Rong,[2] the principal place where he worked for the good of others. Specifically, this branch of the family is called Den-chung. Amazing, supremely accomplished persons, such as Drakpa Gyaltsen of Nangchen, have appeared continually within this family up to the present day.
>
> Although I would like to claim, "I was born in that family!," the Honored Buddha's doctrine is not based on family, nor is it based on clan: it is based entirely on an individual's training and qualities. From that perspective, whatever I have gained materially in my life amounts to wrong livelihood and undeserved offerings [Tibetan: *kor nak*]; all I think about is the eight worldly concerns[3] and negative emotions; all I have done has been committed due to overpowering mistaken perceptions and the force of arrogance. I haven't managed put into practice even the slightest fraction of the genuine view or conduct as taught by the Buddha. My whole

life has been spent in contrived study, contrived behavior, and contrived meditation practice so that now, in old age, my qualities that are in harmony with spiritual life are like flowers in the sky or horns on a rabbit: there are none whatsoever to talk about.

Nevertheless, since this is not the right occasion to dwell on my faults and character failings, I will put the subject aside for now.

In spite of these faults, from the time I became self-conscious, my mind has been entirely inclined to virtue. With an attitude of disillusionment toward the state of the world, I have yearned to live in a fine, isolated place, in a grove of juniper trees where the sweet sounds of divine birds[4] resound, and to absorb myself in meditation. In particular, I have felt undivided faith in he who embodies all buddhas, Guru Rinpoché. That faith's spontaneous force and its auspicious connections have ensured that from childhood I have not had to concern myself with a home or its affairs: I have always been independent. Until the age of twenty, I exerted myself in training in the arts and sciences, and after that age, I decided to devote myself entirely to a life of simple renunciation. However, after I entered the community of this great Buddhist center, I was obliged to teach some of the arts and sciences here due to the constraints of [the monastery's] regulations and because my noble spiritual master refused to grant me permission [to leave the monastery]. Concurrently, I performed some intensive meditation practices at the great [lower] retreat center and elsewhere.

At the age of thirty, I was afflicted by some sicknesses, which proved to be blessings in disguise [lit., helpful adverse circumstances]. I totally renounced [in this context, this means to sell] whatever few material possessions I owned in order to commission in my own name for the first time in my life sacred supports of the Buddha's body, speech, and mind: a series of eleven fine paintings of The Spiritual Master's Quintessential Vision [meditation practice], each painting framed above, below, etc. with rich brocade; a volume of *The Perfection of Wisdom in Eight Thousand Lines*, written in silver and gold; and one hundred thousand miniature stupas [*sa-tsa*]. I then asked my refuge and protector, the Buddha Vajra Bearer incarnate [Tai Situpa], for permission to stay at this hermitage for three years of intensive meditation practice. In the beginning it seemed very difficult [for him to agree], but in the end he gladly gave his assent and I dedicated myself to living here.

Past History of Tsadra

Concerning this place, it is beyond question that during the time of the illustrious Jangchub Lingpa [late twelfth-early thirteenth centuries] and many other masters, powerful practitioners of tantric meditation, have claimed this place as a site for meditation. Even now, some ruins of their habitations can be seen in the shelters of cliffs. Further, in texts written in the past for smoke-offering to local deities, we can recognize a reference to this place in the line, "The palace of spiritual life, the isolated hermitage."

Later, when the great omniscient one, Dharmakara [the Eighth Tai Situpa, Chökyi Jungné], with a lion's fierce, incontrovertible roar, turned the wheel of the instructions of the definitive meaning, beginning with the subject of buddha-nature, he saw in this direction the exalted [Indian master] Asanga, wearing clothing of the gods.[5] Further, it is said that Black-Caped One and his consort, and the glorious Powerful Field Guardian, have showed their forms [to meditators] in visions here; thus, sacred supports representing them have been made.

For these general and specific reasons, and because the life-force of the Buddha's doctrine depends entirely upon the lineage of meditation practice, Tai Situpa himself first practiced here for some time to bless this place. He then gave a command to the great, accomplished master, Kagyu Tenzin (known as Satsa Lodrö) to meditate here for three years on the Six Doctrines of Niguma, Great Seal, and other practices.[6] Later, the younger brother of Tok-den Ö-chung, named Lama Ten-gyé, was installed as chief lama of the area, and lodging for ten meditators was built. The retreatants were asked by Tai Situpa to remain here for the rest of their lives. He cared for this retreat center and it thrived until he gave his attention to the benefit of others elsewhere [i.e., he passed away].

The one named Yoru Nyonpa, who departed to the celestial realms from Tsurphu Monastery's Lotus Garuda Fort [Péma Kyudzong], attained accomplishment in meditation here before going to upper [Tibet]. He is one example of the many who lived here, gained realization, were pure renunciates, and lived long lives. "Even if one doesn't stay in the retreat center until reaching the goal, no one has left without completing one hundred million mantras in intensive practice"—this saying is well-known, even these days, among all the elderly of this region. However, after Tenpa Nyin-jé [another name for Chökyi Jungné] departed for the Joyful heaven, the monastic administration's decreasing wealth made the distribution of food to the meditators here a rare event, so their numbers decreased.

Foundation of the Main Retreat Center at Palpung

Moreover, when Öntrul Rinpoché, Wang-gyal Dorjé, preserved the doctrine [as Tai Situpa's regent], his position obliged him to concentrate on the cycle of activity and to somewhat forget the cycle of renunciate meditation.[7] Therefore, to replace this center, he saw that the founding of a special center for renunciates would be of incomparable, lasting service to the precious doctrine of the practice lineage. In trying to divine which site to use for the construction, three proposed pieces of land (including one on White Conch Ridge) were submitted to the Thirteenth [Karmapa, Dudul Dorjé, (1733-1797)] for divination. [This place was not among the three] since earth and stone for building were scarce here and simple earthen buildings make for far from comfortable housing. Thus, construction here of such high, spacious, solid, straight, complete, and clean buildings as a temple and monastic quarters would prove difficult.

[Karmapa's] divination fell on the site above the monastery. After the awareness-holder Rikzin Dorjé Drakpo performed the land-taming ritual, the structure and contents of the great meditation retreat center, Drubgyu Dargyé Ling [The Place of the Flowering of the Practice Lineage], were constructed there. Fifteen meditators entered three-year, three-fortnight retreat at that center and arrangements were made to provide continual material support and service for their meditation practice. From that point, the structure and contents at this place naturally dissolved into the sphere of totality.

Although my refuge and protector, Buddha Vajra Bearer [the Ninth Tai Situpa, Péma Nyin-jé Wongpo] himself repeatedly said that it was wrong to let this place deteriorate, the situation followed the will of the monastic officials and [Tai Situpa's] intentions were as if left by the wayside: this became a deserted place.

Kongtrul's Early Life at Tsadra

I had the habit of keeping in my heart the wish to go to an isolated mountain hermitage; so, one day at the beginning of summer during my twenty-eighth year, I came here to make smoke-offerings. At that time, no traces of paths existed; but in spite of the fact that my companions and I did not know the way, we set off at sunrise, singing *The Seven-Line Invocation to Guru Rinpoché* as we went. A vulture landed on the roof of the great retreat center: it looked at us, nodded its head, then went uphill. I said, "Let's go wherever that vulture goes!," so we chased it. The bird went hopping to the top of the hill behind this hermitage, then flew off toward the east. It looked around, saw the ruins of the mountain hermitage, and descended. We went there and performed an extensive smoke-offering to the gods. It was a very good day: auspicious signs occurred, like mixed snow and flower-petal rainfall, increasing my delight. The vulture's foot-path became called "Vulture-Face Path," the very same path of descent used these days. After that day, whenever I would come here, positive signs and portents appeared.

In particular, in the autumn of my thirtieth year, I fashioned a symbolic semblance of a retreat house. As provisions, I had a broken piece of a block of tea; as clothes, my ragged monk's robes; as sacred supports, just symbolic representations of the Buddha's body, speech, and mind. Apart from those things, I owned no material possessions whatsoever, but I managed to gradually acquire enough food that I did not have to go begging.

Once I had received the empowerment and reading transmission from the lord of refuge [Tai Situpa], I first spent three years meditating on the entire range of preliminary and main practices of The Gathering of the Jewels. [During that retreat,] my mind was clear and my virtuous practice increased. Following it, I performed various practices from the New and Old Treasures of the Ancient Instruction Lineage, such as the Quintessential Secret [meditation on the spiritual master], Quintessential Vision, and The Gathering of the Joyful Ones of the Eight Great Configurations of Deities; and practices from the lower and higher tantras of the Later Translations, such as Wheel of Supreme Bliss, Joyous Vajra, and Ocean of Victors. I performed the intensive practice of each of these, along with their corresponding completion phase meditations. In particular, while resting in the nature of mind, the heart of Great Seal meditation, I borrowed [from the works of others] to compose whatever treatises were appropriate.

It has now been twenty-one years since I moved here. During this time, whatever harmful sicknesses I have experienced due to the effects of my past negative acts or to the obscuring contact with those who have broken their tantric commitments, etc., have been completely healed through the compassion of the spiritual master and the Three Jewels. Apart from [sickness], no misfortunes what-soever have occurred; on the contrary, the positive side of my prac-tice has increased.

In particular, I've felt devotion toward Guru Rinpoché since my childhood, and faith toward those practices that contain the es-sence of the million meditations [which he taught]. My diligent practice of these has produced believable and visible signs of suc-cess: the omniscient Dorjé Ziji Tsal [Jamyang Kyentsé Wongpo], who is Vimalamitra appearing in the form of a spiritual friend, and Orgyen Chok-gyur Déchen Lingpa, the representative of the great master from Oddiyana, his emanated messenger of peace to the world, have both come to this place often, in the past and re-cently, to open the secret treasury of an ocean of tantric teachings. They have given me many consecrated substances and very sa-cred objects, such as statues, yellow parchment [of the treasure texts], etc., and they have created a boundless number of positive auspicious connections.

In my dreams and in my discursive thoughts I had wondered whether this place was an area of sacred ground. As well, when I was performing offering ceremonies for the practices of the origi-nal and later tantras, such as Quintessential Vision, I wondered if a small temple should be built here since the usable space in my house was too small. However I knew that after my period of residence here, whatever construction was done now would be wasted. I therefore accepted the discipline of simplicity.

Later, our refuge and protector, Buddha Vajra Bearer [Tai Situpa] said, "The former noble master [Tai Situpa] was intently concerned about this retreat place, but it has since deteriorated. Now it would be very good if it were restored by the construction of a temple and a retreat center. This project must be vigorously undertaken!" In spite of this command, I did nothing specific to fulfill it because, among other reasons, the master was close to passing away.

Tsadra as Sacred Ground

In the Fire Dragon Year [1856], during the great empowerment-practice of the Quintessential Vision of the Spiritual Master, held in the great center [Palpung Monastery], before Blazing Auspicious Glory, the shrine of new statues, the omniscient spiritual master, Jamyang Kyentsé Wongpo heard a vajra song of the wisdom *dakinis*, saying, "This place is the third Dévikotri!" Similarly, at the end of that year, the reincarnate great treasure revealer, Chok-gyur Déchen

Lingpa, came from the great monastic center of Ok-min Karma [to Palpung], to kindly bestow to us our share of instructions related to meditations on Guru Rinpoché, *The Seven Profound Cycles*. During this period, he opened major areas of sacred ground, principally Lotus Crystal Cave [Péma Shel-pouk] in Men-shö Jam-nang, and he unsealed the profound secret treasure of three lineages hitherto unknown in the world, including *Three Classes of Great Completion's Sacred Instructions*. In response to my prayer that he open this area of sacred ground, he retrieved from Powerful Hero Cliff *The Location List of the Twenty-Five Major Sacred Sites of Amdo and Kham*, which contains a reference to this area. Further, he translated some of the yellow parchment [i.e., treasure] texts of the Three Sources, White Buddha of Boundless Life, and the cycle of Wrathful Spiritual Master at this retreat place, an extremely virtuous positive connection.

Later, in the female Earth Sheep Year [1859], the leaders of the three worlds, the bearers of the black and red crowns, the Victor and his spiritual son [Karmapa and Tai Situpa] appeared here. For my own part, I vowed that no matter what else I did, I would be sure to construct a small temple at this place. The master, the great treasure revealer Chokling, arrived at that time and here translated the yellow parchment text of *The Heart Practice, Union of All Visions*. His adamantine words were, "If a temple and retreat center are built at each of the twenty-five great areas of sacred ground in Do-Kham [eastern Tibet], this will pacify all troubles, especially border wars, in the Himalayan region in general, in Amdo and Kham in particular, and specifically within each temple's respective district. These [areas of sacred ground] are locations of this pacifying power.[8] A person to construct these buildings will appear in connection with each area of sacred ground. In this place, it's you. To begin with, it's essential that you make a statue of glorious Yangdak Héruka. The material for the statue itself and the objects to put within it [for its consecration] are probably [concealed] as treasures in this vicinity." Although I had no wealth with which to make large buildings, I appreciated the special circumstances and promised to do exactly as he commanded.

Together with Öntrul Rinpoché, I again requested Chokling to unveil the treasure of this sacred ground. We received the following letter in reply, affixed with his personal seal:

"In answer to your request that the area of sacred ground at Palpung, Tsadra Rinchen Drak, be unveiled, I ask that you do as is explained in *The Prophecy of the Dakinis of the Three Sources*:

> This sublime sacred area called Tsadra represents the mind
> of enlightenment
> And has a form resembling the eight petals of the channel
> at the heart.
> Once the construction of a temple of the glorious *Héruka*
> At the eastern gate has begun,
> And a shrine and statue of the area's guardian have been
> completed,
> The sacred area can be unveiled. These preliminaries are
> extremely important!

and in *The Proclamation of the Prophecies*:

> A temple made by this embodiment of enlightenment will
> appear in the valley of Uk.[9]
> After his death [he will be reborn] in the East. [passage
> unclear]
> There will be a temple built at Tsadra, the mound of jewels.
> An emanation of Bérotsana and Shakya Lodrö
> Will construct a statue of the glorious *Héruka* appearing on
> the earth,
> Which can liberate through being seen, heard,
> remembered, or touched.
> He will found a meditation place for the practice of the
> three classes of inner tantras,
> Where diligent persons will surely attain freedom.

and in *The Secret Transmission of the Dakinis*:

> The monastery will definitely be destroyed by fire:
> Construct a temple of the glorious *Héruka* in the north!

As is said in these texts, a spiritually advanced person will appear at the center of each of the twenty-five areas of sacred
ground, the main sacred areas [of this region]. If each of these
persons constructs a temple, nothing further needs to be done
to ensure the happiness of Tibet and Kham.

In this specific case, a temple of the *Héruka* must be constructed on the eastern side of the sacred area, symbolizing the
eastern entrance to the channel of wisdom. The base of the wish-
fulfilling tree is the support for Mantra Protectress. In connection to this, a shrine for this protectress should be made at the
eastern entrance. Since [these preparations] are important for
the actual unveiling of the sacred area, please discuss with the
spiritual brothers [of Tai Situpa], and the treasurers and directors

[of the monastic administration], to see if these wouldn't be possible. Please send me a clear reply to this."

He also declared that both the yellow parchment [treasure texts] and the secret prophecies clearly stated that this monastic center [Palpung] was in great danger of being destroyed by fire [or] by enemies. The solution to this was to build a temple dedicated to the great glorious one [Yangdak Héruka] on the northern side of the hill. If this were done, no harm would befall [Palpung]. He warned that if the auspicious circumstances of this moment were not seized and if work was delayed, it would be of no use whatsoever: the temple had to be finished this year!

I hadn't previously collected wood and other materials that could be used for the construction and my livelihood came from begging in the region: I had nothing on hand with which to build a temple. Therefore, I asked Öntrul Rinpoché, a pillar of the doctrine of the practice lineage, to request the monastic administration to sponsor the construction of the outer temple. If it did so, I would sell whatever objects of value I owned to gradually complete the other buildings and the large and small statues for the interior. He agreed because of his expansive concern for Buddhism. Once he gave his permission by issuing an explanatory directive to the members of the administration, it was decided that the temple would be built.

My thought at the time was that even though a temple itself might be completed, if it had no specific owner, it would be difficult for the general owner, the monastic administration, to preserve the place over a long period. Therefore, I wondered if it was a good idea to establish a small retreat center connected to the temple here. I requested a divination on this subject from the very erudite master, Dabzang Rinpoché. He reported having extremely positive dream signs which indicated that such a center would be helpful to Buddhism. I also asked the omniscient master, Dorjé Ziji Tsal [Kyentsé]: he reported that he had had a special vision that foretold success. Based on his reassurance, I undertook the construction of the retreat houses and surrounding buildings. (*Tsadra Catalogue*, pp. 8a-14a)

This concludes the first passage, Kongtrul's account of the prelude to the construction of his retreat center. He continues with mention of the consecration of the ground of the temple, for such a building project was not left only to builders. Kongtrul counts three occasions when the land itself was the subject of preparation: First, Chokling performed a ritual to subdue unfriendly gods and demons nine times. Second, a reincarnate master from the mother institution, Palpung Monastery, led a group in a ritual to request the use of the land from its owner, the local gods, then the lamas purified it. Finally, Kongtrul joined another group, led by another reincarnate master, in two such rituals, culminating in the burying of "treasure vases." These are planted in the ground where the Goddess of the Earth is drawn in sand or other material. A lama digs a hole in her belly with a gold-painted shovel and buries the vase, a process said to symbolize that the construction above that location is intended to enrich, rather than to pollute, the earth. Kongtrul continues with his story:

> In the beginning, one or two semblances of rooms remained in the ruins of the old retreat center. After I rebuilt these a little, I was able to meditate here for some years, increasing my virtuous practice. Gradually, in response to the unavoidable housing needs for those who wished to recite prayers and meditate, and for those who copied texts, the lower rooms were constructed around this main middle level, my retreat place. During the spring and summer of the female Earth Sheep Year [1859], before the unveiling of the sacred ground, I made statues of the protector and his consort, as well as built the protector temple, according to the command of Terchen Rinpoché [Chokling]. This marked the beginning of the new construction of the temple and retreat center.
>
> Later, Terchen Rinpoché made a statue of [Guru Rinpoché, in his form called] He Who Overpowers All Appearing Phenomena With His Brilliance. Then he repeated nine times [the ritual] of binding under oath and his forceful command the [local] gods and malevolent spirits. At the same time, he consecrated the ground where the temple would be built by scattering auspicious flowers in a great rain over the whole area.
>
> On the tenth day of the rising moon of the [third] lunar month [of the constellation] Caitra, a day of exceedingly propitious aspects of planets and constellations, the vajra master of the great retreat center [of Palpung Monastery], a treasury of the volumes of the three collections of the Buddha's teaching, Karma Ngédön, first led a group of fully-ordained lamas who had completed the three-year retreat in the auspicious ceremony to purify and restore the vows of renunciate ordination. They continued with impeccably

performed rituals of request for the land from the local deities, purification of the ground, holding and guarding it. Their rituals were based on the practice of the deity, the Honored One, Wheel of Supreme Bliss. On the full moon [of the same month], the vajra master of the large gathering [i.e., Palpung Monastery], a living treasury of the qualities of scripture and realization, Karma Ratna, a few fully-ordained persons, and I performed the ground-ritual and the extensive version of the offering-practice of the glorious Kalachakra. Further, we performed the ground-ritual from the practice of The Spiritual Master's Quintessential Vision and, in the course of that ritual, buried many special treasure vases.

The pillar of the Buddha's teaching, Öntrul Rinpoché, then went to the trouble to arrange for the monastic administration to provide the beams and other materials necessary for the outer structure of the temple. Following this, I myself requested and received from the monastic administration the favorable circumstances [i.e., the building materials] for the middle-level circle of renunciants' rooms designed on the model of my own meditation room.[10] The gilded copper ornament for the roof [of the temple], nine paintings of [the Buddha and his eight] great spiritual sons, and a design of Yangdak Héruka were all given by my relative Yung-drung Tsultrim. As for the rest, briefly, apart from some statues, paintings, offering implements, and musical instruments, the entire structure and contents of this place—the details of the design of the buildings; the major and minor carpentry work, such as the "joyous enclosure" and the shrine for offerings; the major and minor metalwork, such as the metal locks for the doors; and the painting and sculpture—were all gradually completed through my own exertion. (*Ibid.*, pp. 14b-15b)

Later in the same text, Kongtrul speaks again of his attention to every detail of his center:

[As I have explained above,] I have collected for the retreatants every necessary support for their meditation practice and requisite article for their survival. These include their seats and cushions in their rooms and the temple; the images, paintings, mandala plates, offering bowls, etc. in each retreatant's room; all the large and small cooking utensils in the kitchen—such as cast iron pot and pans, water buckets, lids, and platters; and all the necessary things for the storeroom. I have gathered everything and not overlooked a single detail. (*Ibid.*, p. 98a)

We see here, and we will see in the next section, how Kongtrul took enormous care to create a sacred environment on his sacred ground. These passages have been taken from Kongtrul's catalogue of his home/retreat center's contents. That book, 354 Tibetan folios long, dwarfs the seventy folios of *Kongtrul's Pilgrimage Guide to Tsadra,*the main text in this volume!

SACRED SUPPORTS AND CONSECRATION

In the above section, Jamgon Kongtrul relates how he found himself living in an area of sacred ground, Tsadra, and how he came to construct a temple and retreat center there. He portrays himself as initially a somewhat passive participant in the events, his choice of retreat location just one of many positive elements that converged to unite the appropriate place, time, and individuals. Nevertheless, once Chokling made it clear to Kongtrul that he could not afford to procrastinate any longer, that the temple had to be built immediately, he gave it his full attention.

A Buddhist temple dedicated to tantric practice comprises both structure and contents; both must be constructed according to specific guidelines and both must be consecrated. Consecration of the ground prior to construction has been mentioned above. This preliminary step is no different from the process that follows: at every juncture, the construction of sacred structures and the fabrication of sacred supports are accompanied by consecration. This section will define sacred supports and the consecration process, and relate how Jamgon Kongtrul consecrated his sacred environment.

First, what is a "sacred support"? Technically, a support is a representation of the body, the voice, or the mind of enlightenment and acts as a receptacle for its blessing. However, such supports for the Buddha's blessing must inspire faith to be effective. Kongtrul states here that although anything and everything can be a sacred support, since the buddhas' and bodhisattvas' blessings pervade the universe, it is an individual's faith that identifies an object as a support, which in turn blesses the individual. Kongtrul then supplies a more textbook definition of the "three supports":

> [On the subject of] supports for the body, speech, and mind of the
> victorious Buddha and his regents, the blessings of these skillful,

compassionate ones' physical, verbal, and mental wisdom-vajras pervade the entire animate and inanimate universe. The object of someone's faith will bless that individual. Therefore any object of faith is a sacred support.

Nevertheless, the supreme receptacle for the blessing of the body of enlightenment's great merit is an image, be it painted or sculpted, etc. The supreme receptacle for the blessing of ever-present enlightened speech is the words and terms rendered in written letters in a volume of scripture. The supreme receptacle for the blessing of enlightened mind endowed with the two understandings is a *stupa* of one of the eight models, or others. These three are known as the three precious supports.[11] (*Dergé Temple Catalogue*, pp. 12b-13a)

According to the tantric tradition, construction or fabrication of any sacred support is not sufficient in itself: it must be consecrated. For example, a statue of Buddha bought in the marketplace must be filled with substances, such as mantras printed or written on paper which is tightly coiled. Then it must be consecrated, ideally in the course of a specific ritual for such blessing. In the two following passages, Kongtrul explains the logic behind this:

Once the virtuous activity of constructing the three precious supports has been completed, it is appropriate that they be consecrated. Pandit Rong-zom Chökyi Zangpo considered that bestowal of empowerment to a human being and consecration of a deity's image were essentially the same process. For example, although the human body of the six elements has the original, primordial nature of the deities, until the purifying influences of the profound instructions for maturation [i.e., empowerment] and liberation [i.e., instruction] have been received, an individual cannot practice meditation on the phases of creation and completion. However, reception of these instructions plants the seeds that actually produce results.

Similarly, although these supports for remembering the Three Jewels might ultimately [be receptacles for] blessing by virtue of their form and features alone, their excellent consecration (*supra-titra* in Sanskrit) is effected by having the wisdom deities merge with the commitment deities [i.e., the specific object that constitutes the consecrated support, whether or not this has the outer shape of a deity]. Until a qualified vajra master has performed such an authentic ritual of consecration, the object does not contain that blessing. (*Ibid.*, pp. 59a-b)

On the subject of the meaning of consecration, Rong-zom Pandit stated that the meaning of the act of bestowal of empowerment to human beings and of consecration of deities is in fact the same. In the bestowal of empowerment, the basis of purification is the natural body and mind; what is to be purified are incidental impurities; what effects this purification are the four empowerments, with all their supplementary aspects; and once these have effected the purification, the seeds of the result, the four bodies of enlightenment, are planted.

Similarly, in a consecration, the basis for purification is the inert image; what is to be purified are the impurities of the maker and the owner; what effects this purification is the flawless performance of the stages of the consecration ritual by which the wisdom deities enter the commitment deity and remain there; and the result of the purification is the spontaneous performance [by the consecrated image] of activity that benefits others within the essence of the vajra body, speech, and mind of enlightenment. (*Encyclopedia of Buddhism*, vol. 2, p. 713)

Thus, Kongtrul maintains that consecration is an essential element in the preparation of the three supports and that a vajra master should perform the ritual. In the following passage, we return to his narrative of his temple construction at Tsadra. He describes in detail his and others' efforts to ensure that what he had so painstakingly built be carefully consecrated. Here, Kongtrul overloads his reader with names of spiritual masters and rituals, but perhaps in so doing he underlines the importance he placed both on the consecration process and on Tsadra itself.

In relation to the three representations of the Buddha's body, speech, and mind in general, regardless of the quality of the workmanship, their size, or their quantity, their benefits will not be effective without their having been consecrated. Instead, the lack of consecration will create a number of negative influences. To begin with, one must have a pure motivation; one must follow this with pure substance used in the fabrication of the support; and one must finish with performance of a pure consecration. Supports produced in this way, large or small, etc., provide continual, far-reaching benefits and blessings.

Therefore, in the beginning, my motivation was not mixed with mistaken desires, such as to selfishly increase my own longevity, merit, power, wealth, or renown, or to compete with others. Following this, the substance of the supports made was not mixed with anything impure, i.e., objects acquired through theft, forceful acquisition, deceit, dishonesty, trade in butchered animals, or the sale of Buddhist images. To conclude, the consecration was undertaken with the utmost care and six excellent substances,[12] and not casually done in relation to its place, time, necessary articles, the persons performing the consecration, or the rituals used.

Since consecration of these objects is so vital, past masters dedicated to spiritual teachings would bless each support with consecration rituals from the major tantras a minimum of seven times. At their conclusion, reassuring signs that inspire belief [in the efficacy of the rituals] would appear. They followed the rituals with vajra feasts and celebrations during which they would make vast offerings of many hundred measures of silver. The blessing of sacred supports thus consecrated has not diminished to the present day and they manifestly provide auspicious circumstances for the region where they are kept. The example of such supports illustrates the vital importance of consecration above all else. In my case, because of my modest circumstances, I had no hope of making significant offerings, but my deeply respectful requests to noble, illustrious spiritual masters [met with a positive response]: masters replete with every positive characteristic performed impeccable, confidence-inspiring rituals for consecration a number of times. The account of their consecration follows:

[Consecration of the Outer Building]

When the temple's exterior was complete, Terchen Chok-gyur Lingpa and the manifestation of Nyak-chen Yeshé Zhonnu, the very erudite spiritual master Dawa Zangpo [Dabzang Rinpoché], performed rituals to create auspicious connections to ensure the pacification of obstacles and the increase of all positive conditions. Using the Heart Practice of Vajrasattva, they blessed the environment and all beings, and recited the appropriate number of mantras as they performed a burnt offering ritual for pacification. They then performed the extensive burnt offering ritual of Wish-Fulfilling Wheel [White Tara] and offered a vajra feast and fulfillment offerings based on the practice of Union of the Jewels. The consecration complete, they scattered a rain of auspicious flowers.

[Consecration of Structure and Contents]

Most of the structure and contents of the temple were complete by the fifth lunar month of the wrathful Iron Monkey Year [1860] (the fifth month is Monkey Month, according to the unmistaken calculations of Ngari Penchen Rinpoché; [Lochen Dharmashri], brother of [the first] Minling Terchen; and other great erudite and accomplished masters of the Original Tradition). On the first day of that month, this place was visited by the guide of the three worlds, protector of the Himalayan region, the fourteenth in the series of holders of the crown which is the characteristic mark of the sapphire-blue [Buddha] Unmoving, whose name is famous throughout existence and the realm of perfect peace, the omniscient powerful victor Fourteenth Karmapa, Tekpa Chok-gi Dorjé. Once his lotus feet, marked with lines of auspicious design, had reached this hermitage, he blessed it by turning the wheel of special spiritual instructions. This teacher was accompanied by fifty persons, including some particularly outstanding individuals, including the cousin of Karmapa, supreme manifestation of the incarnate master and treasure-retriever, Chökyi Wongchuk; a reincarnation of the personal attendant [presumably of a Karmapa] Karma Sidral, the play of the enlightened activity of the noble Eighth Karmapa; noble Ön Sampel Chok-trul, emanation of Landro Translator; the master of accomplishment, Péma Sang-ngak Tenzin; and Ripa Chok-trul Darjé Gyatso.

On the second day of the month, they began seven nights and eight days of rituals, including demarcation of boundaries [i.e., closing the retreat]. This retreat for the manufacture of nectar medicine, which culminated on the tenth of the lunar month, was based on our recitation of one hundred thousand mantras of the mandala of The Spiritual Master's Quintessential Vision. Of all the treasures hidden in Tibetan soil, the profound, forceful blessing of this meditation makes it clearly superior to all others; moreover, the transmission of this golden teaching is the domain of the Kamtsang's [i.e., Karmapa's] lineage. Accompanied by virtuous signs, the session was completed without interruptions. At its conclusion, the lamas performed a ritual of consecration, complete in every detail: the wisdom deities entered the structure and contents of the temple, and flowers of virtue and well-being were scattered like rain. I made extensive offerings at the end, during a celebration and an excellent mandala offering.

[Consecration of the Contents]

When the three supports were completed, in the ninth month, on the celebration date of the victor's descent from the gods' realm, [a further consecration was performed] by ten vajra masters, each a master of the three trainings [in ethics, meditation, and transcendent knowledge] who had completed intensive practices; plus five other lamas. They included Péma Kunzang [the young Tenth Tai Situpa] Chökyi Gyalpo, whose appearance has been repeatedly prophesied in old and new treasure texts as an emanation and representative of the second buddha, Padmakara [Guru Rinpoché], the guide Loving-Kindness [*Maitreya*] incarnate, the supreme manifestation of the enlightenment of the omniscient Tai Situpa; Karma Drub-gyu Tenzin Trinlé, the supreme manifestation of the enlightenment of the noble Ön Sampel, himself the reincarnation of the great trea-sure retriever Long-sal Nyingpo; and the supreme manifestation, noble Ön Samten, embodiment of the magical web of wisdom of the incomparable doctor from Dawkpo [Gampopa], noble Yu-tok-pa, and others. This group performed the consecration ritual con-nected to the practice of the configuration of deities of the Hon-ored One, glorious Wheel of Supreme Bliss. This ritual included a burning and pouring ritual for [the enlightened activity of] en-hancement, and the making of *cha-ru* food, both done strictly ac-cording to the instructions written by the ninth lord [Karmapa]. The preliminaries, main part, and conclusion of the rituals were all performed flawlessly in their entirety. On the second day, a celebration of the successful completion of the ritual was held, ending with mandala and other offerings which I presented to the participants.

[Subsequent Consecrations]

In the new year of the female Iron Bird Year [1861], the eighth day of the [third] lunar month [of the constellation] Caitra marked a conjunction of the victorious star and the planet Mercury. On that day, the wisdom of all buddhas in a single form, the masters Manjushri-mitra and Vimalamitra incarnate as a holy spiritual guide, the second omniscient Dorjé Ziji Tsal, the all-knowing and all-seeing Jamyang Kyentsé Wongpo assumed the form of the chief of all buddha-families and configurations of deities, the Honored Buddha, glorious Vajrasattva. Following the Minling tradition meditation text *The Wish-Fulfilling Cow of Virtue and Well-Being*, he kindly performed a three-day ceremony (including both prepara-tory and main rituals), during which the preparatory, main, and concluding stages of the ritual of having the wisdom deities merge with the commitment deities were done fully and in their exten-sive forms. Then he performed complete consecration ceremonies based on the practices of the nine-deity configuration of Yangdak

Héruka in the So tradition, Wheel of Supreme Bliss in the Luhipa tradition, glorious Kalachakra, and The Spiritual Master's Quintessential Vision. After he had scattered a rain of blessing flowers, he unveiled the great configuration of the Honored One, Joyous Vajra, in four traditions, and bestowed seven [empowerments], with all their parts, to bring disciples to spiritual maturity. He then turned the wheel of profound and extensive spiritual teaching, including the main text that describes Path and Result, the mind-essence instructions of the very illustrious master Virupa; and the blessing-empowerments and instructions for the Vajra Noble Woman's oral transmission, the Intensive Practice of the Three Vajras from the great, accomplished master Orgyenpa. He thus blessed the temple and its contents as the configuration of the five certainties,[13] the spontaneous adamantine design in the Highest Pure Land. I then offered him a mandala and a celebration with presentation of gifts as I was able, in thanks for his kindness.

Again, during the [third] lunar month [of the constellation] Caitra of the female Water Pig Year [1863], I led a gathering of excellent awareness-holders, who had completed the full amount of intensive practices, in a ten-day profound and extensive ceremony of group retreat, based on the Heart Practice of Buddha Vajrasattva, chief of all families of enlightenment. Through this and other ceremonies, I have done as much as possible to consecrate the sacred supports by resting naturally within the simple, changeless nature of reality, the absolute expanse, the intrinsic, primordial inseparability of the commitment and wisdom deities. I have repeatedly formulated aspirations of true words that this consecration will create the radiance of the auspicious interconnections within conventional reality to ensure that these wisdom deities remain here for one hundred aeons.

[Conclusion]

Holy persons, who have attained supreme wisdom, consecrate objects spontaneously through just seeing or giving their attention to them: such consecration does not depend on symbols or rituals. Those who have attained some degree of heat in the practice of the two phases of tantric meditation,[14] or fully qualified vajra masters who have perfected the ten ultimate qualities,[15] perform long or short authentic consecration rituals by which the wisdom deities enter the support when they throw consecrated flowers [at the conclusion of the ceremony].

The tantras and the excellent pith instructions of accomplished masters affirm that a region where the wisdom deities remain firmly [in the supports] over a long period enjoys the wealth of an ocean of auspicious events. In this case, that these masters have attained supreme wisdom is beyond any doubt or suspicion. Not just one of them, but each and every one is a channel for excellence and has mastered the infinite enlightened activity of the ten ultimate qualities, etc. of a vajra master. Therefore, their repeated blessing of [the temple and its contents] in the course of authentically performed consecration rituals based on the great tantras has made these supreme supports particularly sacred: by being seen, heard, remembered, or touched, they will continually produce the enlightened activity of the buddhas until the end of time. (*Tsadra Catalogue*, pp. 98b-102a)

Kongtrul devoted years of time and energy to Tsadra, with the intention that it help others long after his death. Certainly it has, in the person of Kalu Rinpoché and so many other great masters who learned meditation or taught there. However, the sacred supports that Kongtrul refers to can no longer be seen, heard, or touched; they can only be remembered. Tsadra has been rebuilt from the Cultural Revolution's total devastation, some old statues have found their way back home, and new sacred supports have replaced those that were irretrievably lost. The three-year retreat continues there, under the direction of an elderly nephew of the lama who taught Kalu Rinpoché when he was a young man in the same retreat.

THE BEST OF TIMES AND THE WORST OF TIMES

It was the best of times, it was the worst of times, it was the age of wisdom, it was the age of foolishness, it was the epoch of belief, it was the epoch of incredulity, it was the season of Light, it was the season of Darkness, it was the spring of hope, it was the winter of despair, we had everything before us, we had nothing before us, we were all going direct to Heaven, we were all going direct the other way—in short, the period was so far like the present period, that some of its noisiest authorities insisted on its being received, for good or for evil, in the superlative degree of comparison only.

A Tale of Two Cities

There is no relationship whatsoever between Charles Dickens and Jamgon Kongtrul, except that Dickens's prose captures well the atmosphere of life at any period of crisis and for a simple coincidence—the book that began with these lines was first published in 1859, the year Tsadra was opened.

Jamgon Kongtrul never wrote a book on political history or current affairs and we might be forgiven for imagining that he lived in a never-never land far from the dreary world of wars, famines, and social upheavals. In fact, he lived in a very turbulent time.

During Kongtrul's lifetime (eighty-seven years, 1813-1899), five Dalai Lamas sat on the throne in Lhasa. In some countries (Italy, for example), this might be heralded as remarkable stability, but the fact that the supreme authority in Tibet was consistently unable to live until his majority was a sign of Tibet's political ill health. The Ninth Dalai Lama lived from 1805-1815; the Tenth, 1816-1837; the Eleventh, 1838-1855; and the Twelfth, 1856-1875. Once again these dates represent lifespan, not periods of reign. Although the Thirteenth Dalai Lama, born in 1876, was to prove exceptional in that he lived to the age of fifty-seven, it must have seemed to Kongtrul and others that the odds were against such longevity in high places. Lhasa must have seemed a sorry place during Kongtrul's time and the Chinese could not be blamed entirely for this state of affairs, as Gyurmé Dorjé notes: "It is important to note that the Tibetans still controlled their own affairs and that apart from a diplomatic legation in Lhasa there was virtually no Chinese presence on the Tibetan plateau, even in those supposedly partitioned eastern regions." (*Tibet Handbook*, p. 680)

If the untimely demise of the Dalai Lamas was the doing of the Manchurian delegation in Lhasa, as some suggest, one has to wonder how independent Tibet really was or, if it was a state apart, how competent the Tibetans were if they so consistently failed to protect their most important living national treasure. In any event, Khampas of Kongtrul's time could not look west toward Lhasa with much optimism and those of the Karma Kagyu tradition had even more reason to turn away.

In the late 1700s, one of the main disciples of the Karmapa, the Zhamarpa, had lost his life, crown, title, holdings, and right to formal recognition of subsequent reincarnations from having been, or having given the appearance of being, on the wrong side in a dispute between Nepal and Tibet. Kongtrul never overtly commented on the events that led to Zhamarpa's demise, but even if he had supported the Lhasa government in this affair, one has to doubt that he felt the punishment fitted the crime. This was, after all, the Zhamarpa, very close spiritual son to the Karmapa for many generations, and moreover, this reincarnation, Mipom Chödrup Gyatso, had been a master of Kongtrul's principal master, the Ninth Tai Situpa. Regardless of their opinion, if any, regarding the dispute in question, no Karma Kagyu follower could accept the severity of the sentence: death to the spiritual leader in question and the abrupt end of a line of reincarnate masters that had served as a main pillar to their lineage for hundreds of years. After that incident, no Kagyu could look to Lhasa and imagine that the government's decisions reflected their long-term best interests. And in the end, while Lhasa's suppression of the Zhamarpas did rid the central government of his apparently meddlesome presence, the wars with Nepal continued during the 1800s without him.

Yet, for all that Lhasa was mired in troubles, so was Beijing, and to a much greater degree. By the mid-1800s, the mandate of heaven had been resting on the shoulders of Manchurian emperors for two centuries. While all Chinese emperors might look alike to foreigners, the Manchurians were not Han Chinese. Upon their conquest of China (the Ching Dynasty was established in 1644), the Manchus had imposed their ways on the Han people and had earned the sincere hatred of their subjects. That a tiny minority was able to rule China and destabilize Tibet for over two and a half centuries is a credit to their will, intelligence, and discipline, as well as to the lack of natural cohesion and solidarity in the huge Han majority. The tide began to turn against the Manchurians rulers in the 1800s, first in their relations with another group of foreigners as proud, willful, arrogant, and universally despised as themselves, the English. These bearers of the white man's burden to bring civilization to the world fought a war with China from 1839 to 1842 over the struggle to open China's markets to trade, specifically the opium trade. The Opium War, as it is called, ended in a victory for free enterprise and in defeat for the Chinese throne.

The Manchurian ruling minority had been able to stem popular dissent but seemed incapable of holding its own against foreign incursions that started with the opium trade and became more and more outlandish. The honor of the Hans had been crushed by the Manchurians; China's honor, by the white ghosts. With a mixture of patriotism, both Han and Chinese, and religion, of a grotesque, home-grown version of messianic Christianity, a popular revolt shook China for nineteen years, from 1845-1864. Called the Taiping Rebellion, it left at least twenty million persons dead in its wake.

Although ultimately victorious over the Taiping, the Manchu Dynasty was irreparably weakened. Its success in internal repression stood in stark contrast to its weakness against the foreigners who had once again humiliated China. In September, 1860, the English attacked Beijing and burned the emperor's summer palace to the ground. This and many other affronts to Chinese dignity led to the anti-foreign "Boxer Rebellion" and the eventual end to the Manchurian mandate of heaven.

Jamgon Kongtrul never mentioned these events in his writing, but he lived closer to China than to Lhasa and it is hard to imagine that he was unaware of such major human disasters so close by. All Tibetans knew for centuries what Mao later said: "Political power grows from the barrel of a gun." Tibetans also knew that the gun or sword that created political power in Tibet was "Made in China." After the line of Tibetan kings ended in the ninth century in a remarkable series of assassinations, beginning with that of Trisong Dé'u-tsen (the king who had invited Guru Rinpoché to Tibet), Tibet's religious rulers, such as the Dalai Lamas, had ascended the throne with the help of China's rulers' military might. Tibetans could not afford to ignore what was happening in China. During Kongtrul's time, the news was not encouraging.

The turmoil to the east and west of Kham in the mid-1800s did not signal a period of peace for the region. Quite the contrary. In 1837, a Khampa chieftain by the name of Gonpo Namgyal began to fight his neighbors. For almost the next thirty years, his campaigns continued throughout Kham and he managed to conquer the entire territory, including Dergé, which he defeated in 1863. That victory represented the summit of his power. Kongtrul reports that he himself became very troubled by the occupation of

Dergé, particularly because Gonpo Namgyal kidnapped the queen mother, Kongtrul's patron and disciple, and the princes.[16] When an army arrived from Lhasa to do battle with the Khampa rebels in 1864, Kongtrul was called as a physician for the commander and ended up as a strategist for a major battle. Kongtrul was not asked for his opinion on military matters, but for his divinations. He remarks that he was asked impossible questions, such as the time and the direction of the rebels' attack, and that he replied with whatever came into his mind. "By the blessings of the Three Jewels" his predictions all proved accurate and the Lhasa forces won the battle and, eventually, the war. Gonpo Namgyal withdrew to his home-base further east in Kham (a district known as Nyarong) and died in 1865, in a fire he himself set to consume his fort rather than surrender.

This period of upheaval swirling around Kongtrul did not prevent him from continuing his work. During the Nyarong rebellion years, he worked on some of his monumental collections, alluded to in the following letter from Chokling. Kongtrul had written him, asking Chokling to explain the importance of a statue of Six-Armed Protector that the treasure revealer had unearthed and given to Kongtrul. He told him it had belonged to the great Indian master Nagarjuna and had traveled to Tibet with Guru Rinpoché, who had concealed it as a treasure. What was its special significance? Kongtrul wondered, why had it appeared now?

Chokling writes of the general importance of Tsadra's temple, that its establishment would bring peace and happiness to the region. He names Kongtrul as the reincarnation of Bérotsana, a realized master of Guru Rinpoché's era, states that the statue was meant for him, and claims that its appearance would prove beneficial. He goes on to mention Kongtrul's work in compiling the masterworks of the Marpa Instruction Lineage and the treasures of Guru Rinpoché, compendiums that would become known as *The Treasury of Oral Instruction Lineage Tantras* and *The Treasury of Rediscovered Teachings*, two of Kongtrul's Five Treasuries. He refers to what he considers a vital project, the construction of temples at specific power points throughout Kham, work that Kongtrul and Kyentsé had undertaken. Chokling credits the construction and consecration of Tsadra for assuring the protection of Kagyu and Nyingma monasteries in the Dergé region during Gonpo Namgyal's attacks. He ends with predictions of future misfortunes that could be prevented by similar constructions at other locations and by meditations, rituals, and prayers in Tsadra, the implication being that practices done at that charged and significantly situated site would be more effective than practices done elsewhere.

Here is the letter, bracketed by Kongtrul's introduction and comments:

> Later, I asked the great treasure revealer Chok-gyur Déchen Lingpa to explain the specific importance of the secret protector's image. I received his reply from Karma Monastery:
>
> *É Ma Ho!* [How Wonderful!]
> From the isolated hermitage of Palpung to the East,
> I received a request from the noble spiritual master, Kongtrul
>   Rinpoché,
> Concerning the image of the protector retrieved as a treasure,
>   which I offered him,
> And which has been placed as the main support within the
>   protector temple
> In the temple of the *Héruka*.
> Although I have already given him the account from the
>   treasure texts,
> He asks now for the specific importance of this image.
> The secret, general, and other transmissions of Guru
>   Padmakara
> Are all in accord: If this temple of the blood-drinker [the
>   *Héruka*] is constructed,
> It will become a major focal point for the land of Tibet
> And will become the life-force for the essential teachings in
>   particular.
> It has been very explicitly stated in the texts
> That, since the all-seeing Kongtrul Péma Garwang [his tantric
>   initiation name]
> Is really an emanation of the great translator Bérotsana,
> The essential teachings will become like an iron mountain
> If the cycle of the instructions of the glorious protector and the
>   protector's image are given to him.
> Therefore, following the texts' instruction, I offered them to
>   the holy spiritual master.

Whoever holds this support and instructions must guard
     them with care:
Don't forget them; they are very important!
This is not just my opinion but the instructions of Padmakara:
     They are really important!
In this evil time of degeneration,
When the old sacred places, sacred supports, and monasteries
     are neglected,
It is meaningless to trouble oneself to build new ones.
Moreover, the noble spiritual master Gar-gyi Wongchuk
     [Kongtrul]
Has collected into jeweled boxes
All the profound teachings, heart-jewels of the new and old
     doctrines, to prevent them from becoming scattered and
     lost.
He has done a great work of composing the rituals,
     empowerments, transmissions, explanatory texts, and
     meditation manuals
For the configurations of deities in the tradition of Marpa and
     Ngok-pa, and for the treasure teachings.
He has no leisure time to construct a temple,
And because he lives as a renunciant in a hermitage,
He has no great wealth of material goods with which to make
     supports.
However, he sincerely received the transmissions of my
     treasure texts
And due to his belief in them and to his diligent application,
He accepted various hardships and constructed the temple
     and its contents.
The pillar of the doctrine, Öntrul Rinpoché, gave his
     assistance;
Thus the temple's marvelous structure and contents were
     completed.
All-seeing Kyentsé Wongpo and I
Offered him the best-available images for the interior:
This is a particularly holy temple of the *Héruka*.
On all the vital points of the land of Tibet in general
And on all those in the Dergé region in particular,
Temples, colleges, meditation centers, stupas, etc.
Are needed, but no one is making them.
Therefore, the gentle protector, all-seeing Kyentsé Wongpo,

Has constructed special buildings at the sovereign meditation
place, Lotus Crystal Cave [Péma Shel-pouk],
And at Lotus Power Cave [Péma Wong-pouk]:
These have become sources of benefit and happiness.
In the Monkey Year, following instructions from *The
Quintessential Vision Medicine Preparation Prophecy*,
The powerful victor, the great Fourteenth [Karmapa], holder
of the black crown;
The supreme manifest form of enlightenment, Péma Kunzang
[Tai Situpa]; and others
Performed the great preparation of medicine of the
Quintessential Vision
In the temple of the *Héruka*
Of Palpung's hermitage, Tsadra Rinchen Drak.
Through the enlightened activity of the awakened protector,
Vajra Six-Armed Protector,
And the guardian of the doctrine Lu-tsen Barwa,
Important persons—rulers and ministers—and patrons
attended.
Recently, the uprising of the peasant army in this region
Left no one with an avenue of escape:
At that time of suffering, the food and lodging of all the
upholders of the Kagyu and Nyingma traditions were left
undisturbed.
This as well was due to the kindness of this temple.
These days, due to evil policies, both the center and the
border regions [of Tibet] are in turmoil;
In Tibet and Kham, various misfortunes will happen.
The stages of practice to reverse these events should be
performed in this temple
According to the prophecies, to bring happiness to Tibet and
Kham.
In future times, this temple
And the essential instructions of the stream of meditation
practice should not be allowed to diminish:
This is very important, you of future generations!
This is not for one [lineage's] individual benefit,
But will surely be a source of benefit and happiness for
impartial practitioners of the Buddha's doctrine.
This letter has been written in the southern hermitage of
Karma Monastery

> By Chok-gyur Lingpa during a three-year retreat
> In time between periods of meditation, in answer to the
>   master's command.
> I offer it to him: May it be music pleasing to his ears!

As is stated here, this temple is of vital importance. Those alive today and those of the future who are concerned about the Buddhist doctrine in general and its specific lineages should not forget the significance of this letter: this is important above all else! (*Tsadra Catalogue*, pp. 121b-123b)

This letter is not dated, but it was obviously written after the threat of Gonpo Namgyal's forces fully subsided in 1865. Chokling is obviously intent that his work to protect Tibet and Kham from future disasters continue, however it was not he who would do it. He died in 1870, at the age of 41. As he had predicted, trouble for Tibet was not far behind: as the Ching Dynasty waned, Sichuan warlords began to move into Kham (from 1894) and the irrepressible English invaded Tibet, arriving in Lhasa in 1904. This in turn heightened Chinese interest in the region and led to aggressive military campaigns in Kham in 1909-18 and 1928-33. The Thirteenth Dalai Lama died in 1933.

As a footnote to this mention of the troubles of the mid-1800s, it is interesting that the memory and reputations of both leaders of the rebellions mentioned above, Hong Xiuquan of the Taiping and Gonpo Namgyal in Kham, have been somewhat rehabilitated in recent years. Despite the Taiping leader's extravagant brand of Christianity (read, for example, *God's Chinese Son* by Jonathan D. Spence for a detailed picture of the incredible man and his movement), the Communist Party has reexamined Hong's life and declared him a pre-communist patriot.

Gonpo Namgyal, too, is better regarded now that he is safely off the scene. Any elderly Khampa can tell the story of this notorious rebel. They recount his exploits much as Tashi Tsering does in "A Khams-pa Warrior" (included in *Soundings in Tibetan Civilization*, pp. 196-214). His attitude is clearly as ambivalent as any loyal Khampa's, as if to say, "Yes, he was a scourge and a scoundrel, but he was *our* scourge and scoundrel." After attributing the most horrible character flaws imaginable to Gonpo Namgyal, Tashi Tsering ends his article with this remarkable paragraph, leaving the reader with the impression that Gonpo Namgyal's defeat spelled the end of the final chance Kham had to unite: (brackets added)

> After the betrayal of [Gonpo Namgyal] by the Tibetan Government and his subsequent death, the people of Khams lost faith in the Central Tibetans. [Nyarong Gonpo Namgyal's] rule had had the positive effect of uniting many provinces of Khams, including [Gyaltang], to resist any invader. Unfortunately that unity was lost after his death, leaving Tibet open to the last incursions of the dying Manchu dynasty which ultimately reached even Lhasa. (p. 214)

LIFE IN THE LAND BEYOND SACRED GROUND

Kongtrul encouraged pilgrimage and spiritual practice at areas of sacred ground and he did his utmost to renew and preserve the spiritual vitality of Tsadra. Yet he also led faithful pilgrims to a destination beyond tantric pilgrimage. Throughout his *Pilgrimage Guide*, translated as the main text below, he keeps his feet firmly planted on his own sacred ground, but he sometimes hints broadly at a wider perspective:

> In general, no place lies outside the pervasive influence of pure lands and the play of enlightenment's manifestations. Therefore, those engaged in meditation practice and those whose vision is pure can witness the infinite miraculous powers of buddhas even in inanimate objects. As is said,
>
>> Who brings the Buddha to his mind
>> Will before him Shakyamuni find.
>
> This means that for those who have faith in and devotion toward the Buddha, all form and sounds appear as the play of the body, speech, and mind of enlightenment. Therefore the thoughts, "This *is* a sacred place" or "This *is not* a sacred place" amount to the erroneous discursive thoughts of an impure mind.

He devotes part of his *Pilgrimage Guide* to a description of how the same environment can appear differently to an ordinary person, to a tantric practitioner, and to a spiritually advanced person. He later leads the reader on a careful guided tour of Tsadra, but precedes it by situating his perspective, that of a tantric practitioner:

The vision of spiritually advanced persons exceeds the experiential domain of ordinary individuals. The perception of ordinary, conventional persons, however, resembles the defective sight of a person with a liver ailment who sees a white conch as yellow. Reality as it appears is continually experienced in a distorted fashion. Therefore, neither of these modes of experience provides a useful basis for a description of this place. Here we will examine this place according to how it appears to tantric practitioners and is confirmed by the perception of spiritually advanced individuals.

Kongtrul invites his reader, a present or future pilgrim, to progress from poor vision to pure vision. He counsels pilgrims to maintain this attitude:

Don't place imaginary limits on the miraculous manifestations of spiritual heroes and *dakinis* in this place: regard everything you see, good or bad—human beings, animals, birds, mice, deer, or carnivorous animals—with faith and pure vision.[17]

At the end of his guide, Kongtrul remarks

Those who have eyes free from obscurations
Find right beside themselves the array of the buddhas' pure
    lands.

Here Kongtrul still uses the language of a reporter or of a teacher who guides others on the tantric path. Elsewhere we hear him speak live, as it were, direct from the destination. Two such passages[18] translated here were written as praises to areas of sacred ground in Kham, close to Dzongsar, the main residence of Jamyang Kyentsé Wongpo. The first place, Tiger Den at Rongmé Karmo, is sacred to Dorjé Drolö, one of the eight main forms of Guru Rinpoché. Both these passages form part of longer, more descriptive prayers to these areas of sacred ground.

Kyé Ma Ho!

To those of aberrant minds, this place is just earth, stone, water, and trees.
To mistaken intellects, it appears as solid, inanimate objects.
To practitioners, appearances have no intrinsic nature;
To those of pure vision, it is a celestial palace full of deities.
To those with realization, it is the radiant luminosity of innate awareness.

In the all-pervasive body and pure land of the Buddha Ever-
  Excellent,
The all-inclusive expanse is primordially pure.

"Impurity" is just a mistaken term and designation.
Its use reflects the limited thinking of an immature mind —
In fact, nothing whatsoever exists, like space.
Cyclic existence and its transcendence are just the intellect's
  ideas;
Purity and impurity, just the use of terms;
Buddha and sentient being, just the mind's limited posture.

In the primordial basis, nothing at all exists;
From this non-existence, various appearances arise.
Once one recognizes them as the display of innate awareness, the
  nature of the three bodies of enlightenment,
One doesn't avoid or entertain, reject or accept.

This is a special instruction of the lords of spiritual practice —
Whatever fraction of this inner nature I have understood
I could relate but there would be no end to it,
And to speak of the appearance of what does not exist is like shit
  or lies.
I have some more such false teachings to explain:

Kyé! Kyé!

If some intelligent persons
Want happiness in this world and in the next,
They should abandon negative acts in this sacred place and
  cultivate a great amount of merit and wisdom;
Meditate on the meaning of the phases of creation and
  completion; do mantra practice and enlightened activity
  meditations diligently;
And at least make a positive connection to this place.

He who always visits sacred places without faith or respect,
With the idea that they only contain ordinary earth and stone,
Is a beast in the body of a man.
Think of this and please exert yourself to cultivate as much merit
  as you can!

Whatever connection you can make, large or small,

Will now and ultimately lead to attainment of ordinary and
    supreme accomplishments.
Guru Rinpoché's benevolent wishes and acts are inconceivable
And in particular, his enlightened activity to guide those
    disinclined to spiritual life
Is superior to that of all buddhas of the past, present, and future.

Therefore, the human beings and even the animals born here
Are disciples of the great, glorious Dorjé Drolö,
Fortunate ones on the secret path.
Having seen the excellent qualities of this sacred place, I have
    written this poem:
May it cause this place's enlightened activity to endure and
    spread everywhere.

May virtue and well-being increase![19]

The second passage relates to Lotus Crystal Cave (Péma Shel-
pouk), the center for the speech of the qualities of enlightenment.
Kongtrul mentions three names at the finish of these verses: Péma
Garwang, Lodrö Tayé, and Ten-nyi Lingpa. These three are Kongtrul
himself: his tantric name, his bodhisattva name, and his name as a
revealer of treasures.

Those born close to this supreme sacred place, or to ones similar
    to it,
But have no faith and do not cultivate merit in them,
Are human beings with minds of beasts of wretched fortune:
Like paupers unaware of gold buried beneath their hearth, they
    don't accomplish what is necessary.
Therefore, I beg you to exert yourself to develop faith and belief
And to make aspirations to awaken your enlightened potential.

Those who have faith and belief in their hearts, by small
    cultivation of merit and wisdom here,
Will accomplish something very meaningful for this life and
    forever. With belief and devotion toward this,
Our commonly owned jewel bestowed by Guru
    Padmasambhava,
Do prostrations and circumambulations, and cultivate merit and
    wisdom connected to your meditation practice.
Since you have obtained life as a human being,

Use these activities to seize the essential value of meeting this
sacred place.

Ah Ho!

The phenomena of the wheel of life and of transcendence of
suffering arise from the creative display of awareness:
If one realizes this, phenomena are pure lands; without such
realization, they are ordinary reality.
Practitioners neither accept nor reject; they have no reference
points—
Wherever they look, the sun of radiant awareness dawns on the
horizon.

This absolute expanse that pervades all space does not need to be
created:
It is a great spaciousness that surpasses all grasping thoughts.
Regardless of what designs the clouds of mind may take,
gathering or separating,
The sky of unceasing innate awareness cannot be obscured.
The great exaltation of the body of ultimate enlightenment is the
changeless, great pervasive sphere.

The two—the person and the place—merge as one.
There is nothing to see: the viewer is at the very basis empty.
Meditation is impossible: the meditator has vanished into the
absolute expanse.
There is no activity: the calculation of artificial styles of conduct
has been destroyed.
One is free from hope or fear that one can find the result
elsewhere
Than empty awareness, the body of ultimate enlightenment, to
which we are never joined and from which we are never
separated.

Péma Garwang seems to be very fortunate, very fortunate.
The old monk Lodrö Tayé seems to be crazy, crazy.
Ten-nyi Lingpa seems to have no happiness, no sadness, nothing.
May auspiciousness without hope and without fear blaze in
glorious splendor![20]

In the context of our spiritual path, pilgrimage is an opportunity
for tantric practice, but such practice, however sublime, is nothing

more than a path. Tantric pilgrims are not meant to make the path of sacred ground their resting place, their home. A spiritual path is an opportunity to rid oneself of attachment, including attachment to the path itself. Kongtrul here speaks to us from his true residence, the non-localized, non-material, pervasive, timeless destination that lies beyond the bounds of conceptual, dualistic maps, even those that purport to identify sacred ground.

NOTES

[1] Kongtrul's *Autobiography* makes it clear why he must affirm his paternity here: his biological father was not the man his mother lived with, who became Kongtrul's "karmic" father.

[2] Gyarong, as this area is more commonly called, comprises many districts of far-eastern Kham.

[3] The concerns that dominate worldly life are pleasure and pain, loss and gain, fame and ignominy, praise and blame.

[4] According to Sarat Chandra Das, these birds are called in Western classification systems *Crossoptilon tibetanum*.

[5] Tai Situpa is renowned as an incarnation of the Bodhisattva Maitreya/Loving-Kindness. In the heaven called Joyful, the Indian master Asanga received instruction from this bodhisattva and later recorded those teachings as the *Five Treatises of Maitreya*. The subject of buddha-nature is one of the central themes of those treatises. Thus, Tai Situpa's vision in the course of that teaching constitutes a renewal of his past life's connections.

[6] Kongtrul would continue the practice and teaching of Niguma's doctrines at Tsadra; Satsa Lodrö, the lama mentioned here, returned to the monastery he headed, Satsa (or Tsatsha), 150 miles northwest of Manigenko, and founded a three-year retreat center of his own, based entirely on Niguma's teaching. That retreat center still functions today; the latest reincarnation of Satsa Lodrö now lives in Dartsendo and leads Kalu Rinpoché's home monastery in Rongpatsa, as well as his own. He helped me with difficult passages in the pilgrimage guide's translation.

[7] The three cycles, ideally done in sequence, are the cycle of education, meditation, and activity.

[8] In this case, the word used in Tibetan for location is *mé-tsa (me btsa')*, the geographical equivalent of an acupuncture point on the body.

[9] This is a reference to Shakya Jungné (1002-1062), a great master of the Ancient Instruction Lineage, who constructed a temple in the Uk Valley. Kongtrul was considered to be an incarnation of this master as well as Bérotsana, and many others.

[10] This account features repeated requests for help from the monastic administrators. The late Dézhung Rinpoché remarked that in Tibet he often found the administrators

of the monastery he led to be highly unsympathetic to his requests for money to purchase more books: "You already have so many!," they would complain, and refuse. Reincarnate lamas were often prisoners to the bureaucracy they inherited from their past life.

[11] The monuments known as stupas can be constructed in innumerable styles; the eight models mentioned here commemorate significant events in Buddha Shakyamuni's life.

[12] The six excellent substances are different spices.

[13] The environment of the bodies of enlightenment's perfect splendor is character-ized by five certain elements: place, time, central figure, surrounding individuals, and the instruction.

[14] Heat here is used as a technical term to indicate positive signs of spiritual prac-tice, not what is sometimes called "inner heat" in Tibetan yogas.

[15] Kongtrul lists these ten in *Buddhist Ethics*, p. 48, in a quote from a tantric text: vajra, bell, wisdom, deity, mandala, fire offering, mantra, colored sands, food offer-ing, and empowerment.

[16] We read in Kongtrul's genealogy of the Dergé kings (in the Appendix) of the esteem and hopes he had for the princes.

[17] One can find any conceivable idea echoed in the Bible and this is no exception: "Be not forgetful to entertain strangers: for thereby some have entertained angels unawares." (Hebrews 13: 2)

[18] Both these passages are from the same text in Volume 11 of *Kongtrul's Collected Works*. The first is found on pp. 474-476; the second, pp. 469-470. Neither bears a title.

[19] This text has no colophon.

[20] Colophon to this prayer: "The one named Guna [Sanskrit for Yonten, part of an-other of Kongtrul's names] wrote this according to the command of the Mahaguru lord of truth [Kyentsé Wongpo] while making a connection with this, the sovereign of practice places, Lotus Crystal Cave."

Jamgon Kongtrul's
PILGRIMAGE GUIDE TO
TSADRA RINCHEN DRAK

Table of Contents

Music From the Ocean of the Mind

The Story of the Sublime Sacred Ground of the Heart of Enlightenment, Dévikotri, Tsadra Rinchen Drak

INVOCATION

Namo Guru Padmakara-ya

The lotus flower of the heart of enlightenment, sweetened with
    the honey of great bliss,
Takes an eternal form, the intrinsic vase body of enlightenment,
And binds the web of distorted appearances within the secret
    heart of awakening.
I have faith in this inconceivable, secret sacred subject.

Bodhisattva Bearer of the White Lotus, you compassionately
    nurture those attached to the extreme of existence.
Skull-Garlanded Adept [Tötreng Tsal; i.e., Guru Rinpoché], you
    appear as a dancer who guides beings in a multitude of forms,
Now known as Karmaka and Tai Situpa.[1]
I bow to the appearing forms of these incomparable spiritual
    masters.

No one in the past, no one now, and no one in the future
Has your mastery of the precious treasuries of Padmakara:
Chief of all accomplished masters, you are known as Chok-gyur
　　Déchen Lingpa.
Your brilliant kindness fills the world: may you be victorious!

Within the sacred places and regions, the spiritual heroes' and
　　yoginis' chief
Is Vajra Varahi, sovereign queen of the absolute expanse.
May she, the committed protectors, lords of the treasures, and
　　guardians of the sacred places
Look upon this work with pleasure and grant their permission
　　for its completion.

The city of the *Héruka*, the supreme "other" level,
Appears on the inner level as channels, vital essence, and
　　circulatory energy.
Their natural radiance appears outwardly as sacred places and
　　higher sacred places.
I will now describe a small portion of their amazing story.

This work describes the qualities of the great, sublime sacred place
of accomplishment, Tsadra Rinchen Drak, under eight headings,
the number of the auspicious signs:

1. A general description of the origin of sacred places
2. Categories of the different kinds of sacred place
3. Proof of the existence of sacred places
4. A description of this great sacred place in particular
5. How this place was blessed and how the door to this place
   was opened
6. A guide to the features of this place
7. How to perform pilgrimage at this place
8. A description of the benefits of such pilgrimage

PART ONE: THE ORIGIN OF SACRED PLACES

This section has two parts:

1. A general description, the pure lands of the three bodies of
   enlightenment
2. The main explanation, the origin of sacred places

1. The Pure Lands of the Three Bodies of Enlightenment

In general, the sphere of purity, the body of ultimate enlightenment's pure land, can be defined as the absolute expanse, the fundamental nature that pervades all animate life and every environment throughout the wheel of life [*samsara*] and states of transcendence [*nirvana*]. Although this pure land, neither measurable nor localized, appears differently to different perceivers, its essential nature remains unchanging: radiant luminosity within the great, primordially existent sphere of vital essence.

The pure land of enlightenment's body of perfect rapture constitutes an inner self-manifestation: on these pure lands' every atom appear an infinite expanse of pure lands and forms of enlightenment, equal in number to the total of all atoms in the land.

Furthermore, on this same, single basis [two dimensions of pure lands can arise]:

1. configurations of deities and mantras in any form arise as the pure, infinite expanse of the spontaneously present body of the complete and perfect rapture of enlightenment
2. the outwardly-appearing pure lands of the manifest body of enlightenment.

Persons with supreme spiritual acumen experience these as pure lands; persons of moderate acumen, as sacred places; and those of ordinary acumen, as impure, inert forms, such as earth, rocks, and hills. Although these pure lands rest within all beings' experiential domain, they exist naturally or innately within the music made by the buddhas to benefit beings. These pure lands are self-arisen due to the blessing of the truth of the nature of reality and of the transcendent ones' compassion; they are sublime and amazing.

2. The Origin of Sacred Places

This section has two parts:
   a. The origin of primordial sacred places
   b. The origin of later sacred places

a. The Origin of Primordial Sacred Places

According to *The Great Discourse of Enlightened Vision* and other scriptures of the Original Translations, in the past there lived a person

named Rudra Evil Freedom, who persisted in an aberrant understanding of his spiritual master, of the view, and of conduct. He,
his wife, and their followers took control of the entire world and
oppressed beings with perverse behavior. Therefore all buddhas'
compassion united in the form of a blood-drinking *héruka*, whose
overt dance of great, fiery wrath liberated[2] the male Rudra and
scattered pieces of his corpse over the Land of Jambu. The locations where these fell to the ground became palaces of Secret Mantra practice, such as the eight great charnel grounds, sacred places,
sacred regions, etc., pure manifestations of naturally existent primordial sites.[3] The women in Rudra's entourage became the
Héruka's sexual partners and were installed as the major female
guardians of the sacred places and charnel grounds. Rudra's consciousness became the glorious Mahakala, whose presence, in person or through emanations, pervades all sacred places, regions, and
charnel grounds and there guards the Buddha's teaching. From
Rudra's bodily fluids, such as semen and blood, grew wish-fulfilling sandalwood trees and *rasayana* [extracted essence, mercury],
which have the properties of the eight principal [medicinal] substances. Impure matter scattered from his body became the thousand secondary medicinal substances, of the nature of ambrosia,
spontaneously consecrated as the essential material that fulfills
tantric commitments.

According to the account transmitted in such tantras of the Later
Translations as *The Utmost Secret: The Tantra That Binds the Net of the
Dakinis*, after the formation of the universe at the beginning of this
age of illumination, Wrathful Terrifier [*Bhairava*], his wife Sign of
the Times, and their entourage took control of the three existences
and began to act perversely. Among their entourage, arrogant gods
and *ghandarvas* in the sky; harmful spirits and cannibal demons on
the earth; *nagas* and demi-gods under the ground; *mamos, tramen,*
and other spirits took possession of the sacred places, sacred regions, and the charnel grounds. The whole world became a fearful
place. To subdue these hateful beings, the Honored One, great Vajra
Bearer [Buddha *Vajradhara*], assumed the form of a *héruka* and manifested a full configuration of deities on the summit of Supreme
Mountain, the central mountain of this world-system. He overpow-
ered Wrathful Terrifier and his army by authority and tamed them

by enjoyment and dissolution.[4] Vajra Bearer then taught *The Root Tantra of Supreme Bliss* [*Chakrasamvara*] and an infinite number of other tantras. All the places, regions, and charnel grounds that the arrogant spirits had controlled, above, on, and below the ground, were consecrated as manifestations of the three circles of deities surrounding Supreme Bliss, and thus became an inconceivable number of major and minor natural sacred places, domains of spiritual warriors and *yoginis*.

These primordial sacred places can bless the individuals who visit them; any connection to them through sight, sound, recollection, or touch is spiritually meaningful. Such sites include the twenty-four sacred places.

b. The Origin of Later Sacred Places

Although later sacred places do not number among these primordial, supreme places, they have been consecrated as places for meditation practice by spiritually evolved individuals and by accomplished yogis. Their blessing has many positive effects, such as ensuring that future meditators at these locations will be able to meditate without impediments and can quickly attain results in their practice. Most [consecrated] meditation sites in India and Tibet belong to this category of sacred places blessed by individuals.

PART TWO: CATEGORIES OF SACRED PLACES

This section has two parts:

1. General categories of sacred places
2. The reason for these categories—how sacred places are grouped according to inner and outer

1. General Categories of Sacred Places

The renowned thirty-two major sacred regions—the twenty-four major sacred places (such as Jalandhara) and the eight drink-severers[5] (such as Dala)—are considered, by virtue of their pure outer and inner correspondence, to be the principal, the source, or the standard for all sacred places. An inconceivable number of sacred places throughout the world have spread from these thirty-two.

According to Vimalamitra's *Guide to Charitra,* in general, one hundred and thirteen major charnel grounds, places where all *dakinis* are sure to gather, exist in the world.

Among them, thirty-two are found in India:

6 places to perform tantric conduct
14 places to preserve meditative experience
8 places to fulfill tantric commitments
4 places that incite intense yearning

Among these, the supreme places are those that contain the eight great charnel grounds where *dakinis* naturally dwell. [The remaining] places where the *dakinis* are sure to gather are the following:

8 in Oddiyana
10 in Kashmir
5 in Turkestan and Mongolia
5 in Tsab-mar Tak and Zhang-zhung
10 in Asha and Zahor
10 in Ton-mi and Gar-lok
30 in China
1 and 1/2 in Tibet.[6] (The half refers to Dro Drak-kar in Sho-tö, where *dakinis* sometimes gather; and the one, to the great self-arisen stupa at Charitra [Tsari] in southern Tibet.)

These sites are considered the principal sacred places because each features a primordial, naturally appearing celestial palace in which resides an assembly of emanated deities.

Of the secondary sacred places that spread from these principal ones, the profound treasure texts of the great master from Oddiyana list in Tibet alone [the following sacred sites]:

5 supreme places for meditation practice
5 supreme places of the body, speech, and mind of enlightenment
25 wondrous great places
5 valleys, three provinces, and one park
8 major meditation places
4 snow-mountain enclosures
21 hidden regions
21 snow-mountains
108 major sacred places

1,002 minor sacred places

The Location List of the Twenty-Five Major Sacred Sites of Amdo and Kham from the New Treasures lists the following:

20 great sacred places in India

20 Himalayan cliffs, the main sacred places in the Ngari Korsum area

65 places for meditation in the four districts of Ü and Tsang [central and western Tibet]

42 supreme great sacred places in the six ranges of Do-Kham [eastern Tibet]—

25 great sacred places

5 central sacred places[7]

4 special places

8 places that are emanations of enlightened activity to tame beings

2. The Correspondence Between Outer and Inner Sacred Places

Why are sacred places categorized into principal and subsidiary places? The locations of the deities within the "other" supreme, ultimate, essential configuration (the result of purification) correspond to the elements of the true nature of reality (the basis of purification). The impure channels, circulatory energy, and vital essence of the inner vajra body (that which is purified), arranged in a pattern of structure and contents, appear in the outside world in the form of sacred places, sacred regions and *dakinis*.

To illustrate this, the moon, sun, and Rahu circulatory energies descend through the major channels that have the nature of enlightened body, speech, and mind. These are twenty-four channels (in three groups of eight) that branch off from the main right, left, and central channels. The twenty-four major channels (including one called Undivided at the forehead, for example) appear in the outer world as the twenty-four great sacred places (including Jalendhara). The spring [vital essence] and the circle vital essence, etc., based in these channels at the forehead, appear outwardly within the sacred grounds as the twenty-four male spiritual warriors (such as the one named Piece of Skull) and female spiritual warriors (such as the one named Very Fierce). Each of the twenty-four channels is further subdivided by dissolution, enjoyment, and authority, to produce seventy-two subsidiary channels. In the outer world these appear as the three sets of twenty-four places—actual, subsidiary, and hidden—bearing similar names. Further, [when outer sacred places that correspond to] the supports for the five subsidiary circulatory energies and the three main channels are added [to the twenty-four sites], thirty-two great sacred regions appear externally. Such subdivisions are limitless.

In conclusion, on the "other," pure, level, in the pure lands, abide twenty-four male and female spiritual warriors, each surrounded by seventy-two thousand spiritual warriors and *dakinis*. On an inner level, in the vajra body, there are twenty-four main channels, surrounded by seventy-two thousand subsidiary channels. In the outer world there are twenty-four main sacred places, each having seventy-two thousand subsidiary places. On the ultimate level, all of these are bound together within the single equanimity of inseparable bliss and emptiness, the natural, innate essence of the masculine and feminine principles in union. Therefore, all sacred areas exist as symbols of the union of skillful means and transcendent knowledge.

PART THREE: PROOF OF THE EXISTENCE OF SACRED PLACES

In general, ultimately no place lies outside the pervasive display of the pure lands and forms of enlightenment. Therefore, those who are engaged in tantric practice and those whose vision is pure can witness the buddhas' infinite miraculous powers even in inanimate objects. As is said,

> Who brings the Buddha to his mind
> Will before him Shakyamuni find.

This means that for those who have faith and devotion toward the Buddha, all forms and sounds appear as the display of the body, speech, and mind of enlightenment. Therefore, the thoughts, This is a sacred place or This is not a sacred place, amount to the distorted discursive thoughts of an impure mind.

In particular, that the primordially existent sacred places constitute sublime sites for engaging in the conduct that leads quickly to awakening is stated in the precious tantras: their existence is therefore undeniable. The existence of the other places [mentioned above], such as subsidiary sacred places, is proved logically by the correspondence between the inner and outer levels, as explained. The existence of sacred places is also proved by scriptural references. *The Tantra of the Original Buddha* [i.e., Kalachakra] categorizes areas of sacred ground, such as the sacred places, by size—large, medium, and small. The large sacred area includes the four continents of this world-system and everything that lies between [the surface of] this world-system and [its foundation,] the configuration of wind. Medium-sized sacred areas include the individual regions comprising this lesser Land of Jambu. According to *Pure Light* [commentary to the Kalachakra Tantra], small sacred areas are defined as follows:

> These are said to be areas to which ordinary, spiritually immature persons can travel, such as the sacred place Jalandhara. On an ultimate level, sacred places eternally encompass everything; therefore the thirty-six classes of *yoginis* can reside in the same city. What has created these places? They appear because this supreme, original Buddha pervades all things. Therefore, areas of sacred ground, such as sacred places, exist in all regions, such as at locations within Tibet and China.

The collection of teachings on monastic discipline [*Vinaya*] states:

> O monks! To the north, within the enclosure of the Himalayas, even the earth, rocks, and inanimate nature work for the benefit of others!

The following quote appears in treasure texts retrieved by both Ratna Lingpa [1403-1479] and Jatson Nyingpo [1585-1656]:

> Beginning with his stay in Samyé-Chimpu, [Guru Rinpoché's] feet touched all areas of Tibetan soil, blessing them. He consecrated places for meditation practice including the regions of Mount Kailash [Gangkar Ti-sé], Kham Tsang-kha, Gen, Jang, Hu, Ményak, Hor, Li-yul, Gugu, Kong Gyal, Chim, Nyang-kha, Long Drak, Mön Tak-go, Boum-tang, and Paro. In each place, he ripened others spiritually and placed them on the path to liberation. Persons of the future will attain accomplishment and achievements by the sight, sound, recollection, or touch of his five sublime sacred places for meditation practice and of any of these areas he consecrated.

Further, clear details of the sacred places in Tibet are given in *The Testament of the King*. *The Guide to Tsari* by [the Third Karmapa]

omniscient Rangjung Dorjé, a jewel among men, states that the sacred area of Tsari extends to the white pillar at Rong Tsen in the
east, to the great sacred places of Nepal in the west, and to
Kamarupa in the south. Within these boundaries of Tsari alone he
counts a thousand subsidiary sacred places, both sacred places and
higher sacred places.

This sublime place [Tsadra] is truly genuine. Specifically, when
the spiritual refuge Jikten Soum-gyi Gonpo [1143-1217] turned the
wheel of spiritual teachings, Tsadra's local deity, a great Buddhist
genyen god, went to meet him. He invited the master by saying,
"I have a unique meditation place on my property; would the
precious spiritual master be so kind as to visit it?" Jikten
Soumgon sent Jangchub Lingpa as his representative to this place
and he taught Buddhism here. This account serves to illustrate
the fact that this sublime place has been known to exist since time
immemorial.

PART FOUR: A DESCRIPTION OF THIS MAJOR AREA OF SACRED
GROUND

This section has five parts:

1. The essence of this area of sacred ground
2. The literal meaning of its names
3. The wonderful prediction of it
4. Signs that confer confidence in it
5. Its characteristics

1. The Essence of This Area of Sacred Ground

What is the essence of this area of sacred ground? Among pure
lands of enlightenment's three bodies, it forms part of the pure
land of the material manifestation of enlightenment.

Among the twenty-four sacred places, it is a higher sacred place,
the embodiment of the eyes' channels. Among [the five forms of]
Dévikotri [Palace of the Goddesses] [related to the five families of
enlightenment], it is Vajrakotri [the Vajra Palace].

Among the thirty-two sacred regions, it is a branch of the sacred
place Charitra, which has the nature of the Awadhuti [i.e., central]
channel; it is called Tsadra Rinchen Drak.

Among the three circles of the pure three worlds, it belongs to the celestial realm of the circle of enlightened mind.

Among the great and lesser sacred places, it is the sublime place of the heart of enlightened qualities, one of Amdo and Kham's [eastern Tibet's] twenty-five great sacred places. Together, they represent the qualities of the spiritual path's fruition, free from all incidental impurities, the nature of the twenty-five circles of the inexhaustible ornaments of the body, speech, mind, qualities, and activity of enlightenment.

In essence, it is a primordially existent place because it numbers among major sacred places and regions. In its manifest aspect, it is a later sacred place, as it was consecrated as a major sacred place of the Himalayas by the embodiment of all victorious ones, Vajra Tötreng Tsal [Guru Rinpoché] and other spiritual masters. It is a fortress of great liberation and a majestic celestial palace of all buddhas.

2. The Literal Meaning of Its Names

The name "higher sacred place" derives from the occasional presence of *dakinis* in certain places. In the body, these places correspond to the occasional presence of the body's white vital essence within the channel called *gompa-mo*, through which the liver's element descends. The name "drink-severer" refers, on a physical level, to the merging of the body's white and red vital essences in the Awadhuti channel to produce co-emergent bliss. To drink this bliss severs all obscurations. Places in the outside world that correspond to this and have an identical effect on the visitor are called drink-severer.

Dévikotri means Palace of the Goddesses: many of the cliffs here have boulders shaped like hearts and clefts that resemble vaginas. These symbolize that here, for someone not on the spiritual path, groups of worldly female gods and demons display mirages that increase the visitor's impure passion. For someone on the path, these same spirits assume the form of the four *mudras* and generate the wisdom of bliss and emptiness. At the stage of fruition of the spiritual path, this place appears as the basis of all positive qualities, emptiness endowed with all sublime qualities, and aids in its attainment.

According to the basic treasure text that provides a guide to this place, this area is one of the [five] Dévikotri, called Vajra Chitta Kotri—The Palace of Vajra Mind. In other words, this place is a fortress that provides a unique home for the buddhas who have the nature of the vajra mind: the Honored One Vajrasattva, in both peaceful and wrathful forms; and the *hérukas* and their retinue who belong to the vajra family of deities, such as the glorious Wheel of Supreme Bliss.

In the name Tsadra Rinchen Drak [in English, Jewel Cliff That Resembles Charitra], Charitra (a Sanskrit word) means union of everything. On an inner level, this refers to the central channel and on an outer level, to the southern sublime sacred place of glorious Charitra. This place is a branch of Charitra and resembles it. Rinchen [jewel] in the name refers to the family of the qualities of enlightenment and indicates that this place belongs to that family. The outer forms of most of the cliffs and hills here are shaped like blazing jewels.

That this place is called both Dévikotri and Tsadra is not contradictory. The central channel pervades the twenty-four main physical channels; similarly, Charitra pervades all sacred places. Dévikotri and Charitra are the pure expressions of the channels that lie in the center of the eyes and the heart, and moreover, the heart and eyes are connected to one another. Therefore, the Dévikotri situated at Karchu in Lhodrak is a branch of Charitra, as has been stated in the past by those who have the vision of wisdom. The statement by the spiritual master, gentle protector Jamgon Kyentsé Wongpo, that this place has the nature of the middle eye of wisdom also arose in a vision of wisdom. The middle eye of wisdom represents the pure wisdom of emptiness at the upper extremity of the central channel, the gate for the arising of wisdom from the middle of the heart. This [relation between the heart and eyes] corresponds exactly to the content of the treasure text that states, "Dévikotri, Tsadra Rinchen Drak."

3. The Wonderful Prediction of This Sacred Place

When the noble Milarepa departed for [retreat in] Tsang [western Tibet], Lord Marpa the Translator gave a prediction that confirms this sacred place. At that time, he offered a fine feast and gave extensive predictions concerning Milarepa's future enlightened activity. Marpa said,

> To the east lies a great sacred place related to both Dévikotri and Tsari, but the time to open it has not come. In the future, someone who preserves your children's spiritual lineage will appear there.

These words provide a very clear prediction of this sacred place by mentioning the direction, its name, its nature, and its lineage of meditation practice.

4. The Signs That Confer Confidence in This Sacred Place

In the past, when the *Héruka* subdued Wrathful Terrifier and Sign of the Times, who had taken control of the world, the signs of his consecration of a location as a sublime, sacred place appeared as marks of skillful means and transcendent knowledge. Wherever these appear, they are universally recognized as indications of a special, major sacred place. Here we see such marks: self-arisen *linga* [male sexual organ] and vaginas. On the upper part of this land, special springs of *chu-gang* flow; from the lower flank, vermilion.[8] In the four directions, unchanging tree-spikes grow and, as the tantras state:

> The goddess, who in that region stays,
> Within the cliffs her home she makes.

This place has a self-arisen, heart-shaped stone palace with a secret cave where dwells the protectress of Tibet, Co-Emergent Woman. These are all the characteristic marks of the sacred place Dévikotri.

Further, a *bhatra* tree grows at the center of this sacred place, exactly the same species, color, and shape as similar trees in Charitra and Karchu Rongtsen. This is a clear sign that this place is Charitra. Signs of the doctrine of enlightened body, speech, and mind; impressions of hands or feet left in stone; and other signs are evident to the viewer's senses and provide manifest proof [that this place is authentic].

5. The Characteristics of This Place

This section has three parts:

a. The characteristics of this place as they appear to all ordinary persons in common
b. How they appear to the minds of special practitioners
c. How they appear within the vision of extraordinary, exalted, great individuals

a. How This Place Appears to Ordinary Persons

All persons, high or low, can see here every rare feature of positive geomancy, exactly as described in Indian and Chinese texts on that subject. The land here is gentle; there are no canyons or precipices, and few stones or thorns. This place lies far from potential harm by inhuman spirits and fierce animals. In particular, snakes and other malicious animals do not even inhabit the surrounding areas. Its altitude is moderate and one is not troubled here by extremes in temperature. The air is always clear in winter and summer, making one's spirits high. The very beautiful cliffs and hills are covered with garlands of white, red, and blue flowers and decorated with various trees in fine forests and attractive dense carpets of grass in meadows. A number of types of medicinal plants of outstanding taste and potency grow here. The wall of the mountains is open and its connecting area is indistinct. Clear, cool water flows with a delightful sound from the right and left of the land and meets at its center. The hills form part of the Himalayan range and the streams eventually flow into rivers that reach the sea. Many persons of different languages and races gather here and we enjoy the abundant splendor and wealth of the four kinds of magnificence.[9] Further, as is said,

> The virtues of the land are land for homes and land for
>   cultivation.
> The virtues of wood are wood for construction and wood for
>   fuel.
> The virtues of stone are stone for construction and stone for
>   grinding.
> The virtues of water are water for drinking and water for
>   irrigation.
> The virtues of grass are close pastures and distant pastures.

These ten virtues of a region are all immediately available here. Thus on an outer level, this place is praiseworthy; its many glorious qualities form a great mound.[10]

b. How This Place Appears to Practitioners

Within the domain of experience of those who delight in inner meditation, this sacred place has all the qualities of an ideal meditation site as described in the Buddha's discourses on discipline [*Vinaya*]: it is filled with forests that belong to no one and with shelters in the cliffs that are suitable places for cultivating meditation. It has the qualities described in the collection of the Buddha's teachings on knowledge [*Abhidharma*]: this area is pleasant and located well beyond an ear-shot from a village. This place has every characteristic mentioned in the main texts of the Original and Later Traditions of mantra for places of meditation practice: it slopes toward the east and is mounded in the south, rises in the west and peaks in the north; the streams flow from the direction of power; a park of flowers grows in front; spiritual heroes and *dakinis* gather here and countless accomplished masters of the past have visited this place. Here one finds a thick forest, the place to develop mental tranquillity; high areas where one's awareness is clear, places to develop insight; and meditation sites of awareness-holders of the past, places for realization to arise. The mountain behind resembles a meditator; the lower meadow, crossed legs. Hollows in the cliffs provide a place for cultivation of the experience of the bliss and emptiness produced through inner heat meditation. The fearful charnel ground is the site for maintaining conduct that enriches meditation experience. In brief, this sacred place manifests every outer and inner auspicious connection necessary for meditation. Thus, on an inner level, this jeweled cliff [Rinchen Drak] of precious qualities is a spontaneously appearing treasure.

c. How This Place Appears to Exalted Individuals

Within the vision of exalted, accomplished individuals, each feature of this sacred place—land, rocks, cliffs, and even its shrubs and stones—are structures of celestial palaces in which reside the past and present spiritual masters, assemblies of deities, spiritual heroes and *dakinis*, groups of protectors and guardians of the spiritual teachings. Signs of their actual presence can been seen in the self-arisen representations of the body, speech, and mind of enlightenment that fill every part of this area. To these persons the streams resound continually with the sound of mantras, various accomplished awareness-holders rest in meditation within the shelter of the cliffs, and many realm-protectors endowed with miraculous powers play within the charnel grounds. At times of accomplishment and on special occasions, countless accomplished ones, spiritual heroes, and *yoginis* gather to enjoy vajra feasts and to bestow accomplishment on fortunate persons. In particular, on auspicious occasions, the two kings who achieved immortality—our sole refuge, Mahaguru Padmakara [Guru Rinpoché] and he who attained an indestructible body, Vimalamitra—come here in their dance of vajra wisdom and nurture meditators, bless the minds of the faithful, and accept offerings, such as vajra feasts, thus aiding in the completion of the cultivation of merit. Thus, on a secret level this place, Vajrakotri, resembles Charitra to the point of being identical to it.[11]

PART FIVE: HOW THIS PLACE WAS BLESSED AND HOW IT WAS OPENED

1. How This Place Was Blessed

Initially, the Honored Ones, the *Héruka* with his vajra queens, blessed this place to spontaneously appear as a great self-arisen charnel ground. In the interim period, our teacher Lord of the Shakyas [Buddha Shakyamuni] filled this area with a great radiant light of countless signs of perfection. The wisdom bodies of the bodhisattva All-Seeing Eyes [Tibetan: *Chenrézi*] and his manifestation, the Buddhist king Song-tsen Gampo, consecrated this place by entering into its [natural] representations of the Buddha's body, speech, and mind, that they should spontaneously aid beings until the end of cyclic existence.

This area was visited and used as a meditation place by the masters of accomplishment, Humkara and Vimalamitra; and particularly, by the leader of all awareness-holders and accomplished ones, the great master from Oddiyana, Padma Tötreng Tsal [Lotus Adept Garlanded in Skulls (i.e., Guru Rinpoché)], his consort, the seven disciples who had a karmic connection [to this place][12], and other masters. Here, Guru Rinpoché bound all wild malevolent spirits under oath, gave the transmission of definitive, profound tantras, discussed the teachings of Secret Mantra, and compiled the genuine instructions on definitive meaning. Thus, he consecrated the earth, rocks, and cliffs here. Guru Rinpoché concealed many large and small treasures in this area and entrusted them to *dakinis* and protectors with the understanding that, at a future time, they would be of infinite benefit for the world. Since the intended time had not arrived, this place remained hidden, an area so wild and forbidding that people were unable even to travel through it: it became known as a region of demons.

Later, during these dark times, the illustrious master Jangchub Lingpa came here. He was the heart-son disciple of Kyob-pa Jikten Soumgon, an emanation of the illustrious guide, exalted Nagarjuna. Jangchub Lingpa forcibly liberated a wild *naga* of Rétso Lake by squashing it under his staff (see footnote 2). As a result, the lake almost entirely dried up. On the summit of the mountain lived a cliff-dwelling *tsen* spirit, Ma-chö Gapa. Jangchub Lingpa miraculously bound the spirit with a lasso around its neck and led it down the mountain. The spirit offered the teacher his talismanic turquoise,[13] took refuge, accepted the vows of a layperson, and was thereby bound under oath. He was given the name Dorjé Dzongmar. Jangchub Lingpa blessed the entire area and made miraculous impressions of his hands and feet in stone at the top, middle, and lowest levels of this area: these can still be seen today.

Jangchub Lingpa made the plain of Palpung his principal residence. Branches of this center, such as Drak-nak [Black Cliff] Monastery, functioned mainly as monastic colleges. He also founded a hermitage for renunciants on the side of Big-Head Hill [U-ché]. The number of members of the monastic community gathered in these institutions reached several tens of thousands. In the vicinity of these centers, he constructed a throne for spiritual instruction where he gave various teachings on the subject of action, cause and result, and where he gave empowerments and liberating instructions to many people. This is the origin of the current name for this meadow, Plain of the Throne of Spiritual Teachings [Chötri Tang]. In other places as well, Jangchub Lingpa turned extensively the Great Way's wheel of spiritual teachings: for the precious teachings of the practice lineage, his influence was like that of sunlight heralding the dawn.

As this noble master said:

This place, in the general area of Amdo and Kham, is located at a high elevation and is pristine. The doctrine of the Transcendent One has spread here and flourishes. The land itself is excellent and is the homeland of those who have cultivated merit. Specifically, it is situated east of the wealth of the true instructions at Dri-lung, west of the source of the Three Jewels at Tréga Cliff, east of the lamp of teachings at Denlang Plain, south of the northern sacred place of Putsur Galo, and north of the envoy of Jam-kyong of Or-ngu.

This monastery was bestowed by my precious spiritual master. It has been blessed by the noble woman, Parna Shawari, so that the first letter of her name appears [on the hillside, thus it is called] Pa-pang Monastery. Ultimately, this signifies that this place gathers those who subdue all negative emotions; therefore, it is called Pa-pung [Army of Spiritual Heroes] Hill. This is a land where the rain of precious devotion falls; where various deliciously perfumed incense scents rise; and where many musical sounds originate.

This place has been consecrated by the authentic spiritual master, the Honored One, Great Glorious *Héruka*, whose body is adorned with the signs and marks of perfection, surrounded by an assembly of spiritual heroes and *dakinis*. It has been blessed by the enlightened intention of past Buddhist kings, emanations of the bodhisattva-guides of the three classes of beings. The *genyen* spirits here offered the great master Lotus-Born their essential life-force [mantras] that included their own name. The great master Lotus-Born gave these spirits empowerment, placed his vajra in their hands, gave them secret names, and entrusted them to guard the doctrine. They include great *genyen* gods related to the encircling Himalayan peaks, such as Ngadra, Dorjé Purbu of Powa, Dorjé Lodrö of Nyen-dang, Dorjé Zhonnu of Trozil Trom.

Since I have come from Dri-gung Jangchub Ling, I am called Pol Jangchub Lingpa: my monastery's name will be Pol Jangchub Ling, the Place of Glorious Awakening, Place of the Vision of Stable Attainment, Sacred Ground of Vajrasattva, Treasury of Auspicious Portents.

This passage gives a clear description of the features of this place. Its explicit account of the consecration of this place by the *Héruka*, the Buddhist kings who were emanations of bodhisattvas, and others, serves as convincing testimony that this is a great primordial sacred ground. The signs of the blessing of Parna Shawari can be seen on the flat grassy plain on the facing hill: the first [Tibetan] letter of her name, *Pa* in its printed form, is clearly visible there.

Many years after the time of Jangchub Lingpa, this place became the residence of a great holder of the illustrious Sakya lineage, the fully erudite scholar from Ngari, Tsultrim Özer. He turned the wheel of profound and extensive instructions, including the Path and Result teachings of Secret Mantra. He spread the Buddha's teachings far and wide through lectures, debate, and writing. This activity continued here until the time of the abbot Palden Lhundrup. Then, for a variety of reasons, all the institutions here were abandoned.[14]

As predicted in a number of infallible treasure texts by the great master from Oddiyana [Guru Rinpoché], an omniscient master during this age of conflict, [the Eighth] Tai Situpa, Chökyi Jungné, emanation of Buddha's regent, Protector Loving-Kindness [*Maitreya*], Lord Marpa the Translator intentionally reborn in the human world, came to this place. He established his main residence here: The Glory of Every Precious Quality Without Exception, Gathered from Every Source [i.e., Palpung Monastery]. His widespread activity in both the scholastic and meditative fields rekindled the fire of the practice lineage teachings from their dying embers. He meditated extensively in all the upper and lower retreat caves in this area: infinite numbers of the three sources in general and the male and female protectors, glorious Powerful Realm-Protector [Tib: *Shing Kyong Wongpo*], and others showed themselves to him. Based on these visions, he identified such sites as the cliffs where Realm-Protector resides, places known to all today.

In particular, while Tai Situpa Chökyi Jungné [1700-1774] taught *The Unsurpassable Continuity*, he had a vision of the venerable master Asanga: his body was enormous and he wore the clothes of a king of the gods. Tai Situpa saw Asanga here in the center of Tsadra Rinchen Drak; Asanga looked at him from this place. For this and many other reasons, Chökyi Jungné would sign his books, "This was written by a servant of the scholar from Oddiyana at the home of the *Héruka*." This provides undeniable proof [of the sacredness of this place].

One of this master's students, the supreme child of accomplishment, Vam-teng Tulku, Tsok-nyi Lek-drup, meditated in complete simplicity throughout this area. He clearly recalled his past life as an accomplished meditator who wore dog-skins and who had meditated over a long period in and close to this area. He is known to have shown clearly his [past life's] caves for meditation practice and the signs of his attainment [at those locations].[15]

Similarly, Karma Dudul Gyalpo, the magical reincarnated form of Rikzin Rolpé Dorjé; and Rikzin Dorjé Drakpo, manifestation of the sovereign Tsangpa Lha'i Métok [i.e., King Tri-song Dé'u-tsen], have both publicly affirmed that the large central white cliff is a place sacred to [the form of the bodhisattva] Great Compassion, [known as] Ocean of Victors. In later times, the display of the wisdom of Nyak Jnana [Kumara], the great scholar and high bodhisattva Karma Tenpa Rab-gyé, had visions that confirmed their statements. This master climbed to the central summit of this place to bury a treasure vase to restore the vitality of the essence of the region's earth. All who participated at that event saw an amazing rainbow circle the rising sun and enter the ground where the treasure had been buried.

The Buddha Vajra Bearer who appeared during a dark age, protector of all beings, regent of Lotus-Born, [the Ninth Tai Situpa,] Péma Nyin-jé Wongpo [1774-1853], founded a retreat center here. As a sign of his experience of the equality of cyclic existence and perfect peace, by which he transformed beings and the environment into the three sacred configurations [of the body, speech, and mind of enlightenment], he left concealed imprints of his feet on the right slope of the mountain. Further, well-known great spiritually advanced individuals, such as the protector of the Himalayan region, the victorious Karmapa, Tai Situpa, and the mighty, illustrious Pawo Rinpoché, have all visited this place, led great practice sessions of Secret Mantra meditations, bound the gods and spirits under oath, and turned the wheel of spiritual teaching. Their careful consecration of this place, like polishing a sovereign gem, makes any connection to this sublime sacred place significant to one's spiritual life. As Bengar Kunkyen wrote in his praise of the Seventh Karmapa [Chödrak Gyatso(1454-1506)]:

> This place, endowed with signs of auspicious portent,
> Has atoms touched by the tips of your toenails,
> Which thus become supreme *stupas* for beings:
> I pray to you, incomparable lord of the teachings!

2. How the Gate to This Place Was Opened

When the great treasure retriever Ratna Lingpa made clear predictions concerning future regents who would become chief of the general transmission of his instructions, he foretold:

> One by the name of Norbu will appear in southern Kham.

Further, Drimé Kunga and several other revealers of past treasures similarly foretold the life of the indisputable, timely emanation, the great treasure revealer, Orgyen Chok-gyur Déchen Lingpa. During his youth, Chokling lived here for an extended period and saw clear evidence that this place was a supreme residence of the *Héruka*.

While the reincarnation of King Trisong Dé'u-tsen, the omniscient Jamyang Kyentsé Wongpo, was preparing a major empowerment of the Quintessential Vision of the Master at the main monastery [of Palpung], he heard the voice of a wisdom *dakini*, "This is the third Dévikotri!" I myself had wondered in my discursive thoughts, due to dreams before and after this event, whether this was a major sacred place. Therefore, when Terchen Rinpoché [Chokling] visited at the end of the Fire-Dragon Year [1856], Öntrul Rinpoché, the primordial emanation of the great Langdro Translator, and I offered this master an auspicious *mandala* and asked [him to open this place] for the good of the teachings and all beings. He then retrieved *The Location List of the Twenty-Five Major Sacred Sites of Amdo and Kham* from Powerful Hero Cliff.

During the days of the waxing moon of the first month, the miracle month, of the new year of the Fire-Snake [1857], he performed a vajra feast on the plain in front of the sacred area. At the highest point of the land, he conducted an extensive ritual to bind gods and spirits under oath; the ceremony began with smoke and *ser-kyem* offerings. At its completion, he began walking, intending to introduce us to the features of the heart of the sacred ground. However, the protector of the area, Mantra Protectress [Ekajati], appeared clearly before him; to others, he appeared to have fainted. Even on the following day, vajra feast and tormas were offered, but a dark wind from the sky to the ground appeared with other awesome signs of tremendous turmoil. He had lengthy visions that convinced him that the time for the opening was not propitious, and that we should delay our attempt. These events were reminiscent of the circumstances surrounding the opening of the sacred ground at Tsari by the three accomplished masters, Nyö [Chenpo Gyalwa Lhanangpa], Gar [Dampa], and [Palchen] Chö[yé].[16] This showed us that particularly powerful sacred places cannot be opened easily!

The great treasure revealer [Chokling] returned here at the beginning of the female Earth-Sheep Year [1859], called Accomplishment of Goals, at the time of the appearance of the victor Karmapa and his spiritual heir [the new incarnation of Tai Situpa]. He provided *The Prophecy of the Dakinis of the Three Sources*, which stated:

> This sublime sacred area called Tsadra represents the mind of
>   enlightenment
> And has a form resembling the eight petals of the channel at the
>   heart.
> After you begin the construction of a temple of the glorious
>   *Héruka*
> At the eastern gate,
> And you complete a shrine and statue of the area's guardian,
> The sacred area can be unveiled. These preliminaries are
>   extremely important!

Thus, this text foretold the correct time for the unveiling of this sacred place and the necessary procedure to be followed to facilitate this. In keeping with this advice, the pillar of the practice lineage teachings, Öntrul Rinpoché, in his expansive vision, initiated the construction of the Pal-chen Temple at the Kun-zang Déchen Ösel Ling hermitage. A statue of the glorious awakened protector, Vajra Six-Armed Protector [Tib: *Chak-drukpa*]; and special outer, inner, and secret supports for the presence of Mantra Protectress Ekajati were quickly made, as were general and specific shrines to honor the *naga* kings, including the Chief of Mantras and Kar-nak.

Once these preparations were completed, on the eighth day of the Monkey Month, the fifth lunar month according to the common system of the Ancient tradition, Chok-gyur Déchen Lingpa walked to the slope of the hill of the great local deity, Dorjé Pal-bar. There he offered a vajra feast to the ocean of the three sources, invoked the local deity to service, and performed a lengthy ritual of incense and *ser-kyem* offerings. This done, the master, accompanied by just a few disciples, walked along the *Héruka* path and indicated the general locations of the outer and inner routes for circumambulation. As previously, some specific events at this time were identical to the circumstances of the opening of the glorious sacred ground at Tsari. He told us to make sure to keep to the path and pointed out most of the self-arisen sacred features along the way.

The particular event which marked the opening occurred as specified in the declaration [retrieved as a treasure] from Burmo Cliff. On the tenth day of the Monkey Month, Chok-gyur Déchen Lingpa retrieved treasures from inside the secret cave of Guru Rinpoché located on the right side of the self-arisen Palchen deity. These included four groups of profound instructions, the guide to the sacred features of this area, and a small container made of earth from the eight great cemeteries and the sixty-four great sacred regions [of India] which held fourteen precious large pills, made from precious substances uniting the relics of all transcendent ones. Since responsibility for this hermitage had been vested in me, I opened the treasure container and translated the yellow parchment text. At that time, clouds of rainbows arose and at the site of the treasure a pair of ravens appeared who displayed attachment to and possession of the site. Everyone present witnessed these events.

PART SIX: THE GUIDE TO THE FEATURES OF THIS SACRED PLACE

This section has two parts:

1. A presentation of the source texts
2. A guide to the actual features of this place as described in the texts

1. A Presentation of the Source Texts

The Location List of the Twenty-Five Major Sacred Sites of Amdo and Kham states:

> To present the supreme sacred place of the heart of enlightened qualities,
> It is situated at Dri, within the Amdo and Kham regions of Tibet.

Its glorious mountain is shaped like the crest of an elephant's
    head
And it reflects the nature of the nine *hérukas*.
Lotus-Born's meditation cave, which resembles a blossoming
    lotus, is located there.
On the side of the cliff are self-arisen forms of the peaceful and
    wrathful deities.
There is also the half-moon shaped supreme meditation place
Of the heart awareness-holder, Namké Nyingpo:
Those who wish for supreme attainment should meditate single-
    mindedly there.

In particular, the supreme sacred place
Blessed by my crown [i.e., spiritual master], Vimalamitra, is
    hidden to one side.

A cave close to the *bhatra* tree, the place sacred to Mantra
    Protectress,
Is the site of the residence of myself, the master from Oddiyana.
While I was staying there, the heart awareness-holder, Humkara,
    arrived
And spent three days compiling the teachings.

The two masters [Vimalamitra and Humkara] left clear self-
    arisen forms of themselves
And impressions of their wisdom-bodies feet [in stone].
Such marvellous special features can be found in this place!

The Additional Declaration from Lion Cliff states:

Further, where the stream that flows from this northern hidden
cliff joins another, stands a hill that resembles the crest of an
elephant's head. The precious jewel on its crown, a white rock, sits
grandly, the palace of Great Compassion. At this site, make offerings to the guardian of this place, Dorjé Palbar.

Along the eastern face of this hill stands a high cliff that resembles
hands folded in prayer. In this secluded place grows a *bhatra* tree
with needles like silken thread. At a distance of nine *dom* [approxi-
mately eighteen meters or fifty-four feet] from the tree is the meditation cave of Humkara, who travelled here miraculously. At the
distance of an arrow shot along the plain in front of the cave rises
the cliff which resembles Great Glorious *Héruka*. On each side of
the cliff are hidden the five heart treasures to guide the world.

Indication of their concealment places can be found at the base of [rock formations that] resemble fingers.

In particular, the next section will provide a detailed description of the area according to the treasure texts' guides. This description has not been composed based on visions of the spiritually advanced nor on the records of an ordinary mind's fantasies: it is based entirely on the clear and precise details recorded in the adamantine speech [of Guru Rinpoché].

2. The Guide to the Actual Features of This Place as Described in the Treasure Texts

As mentioned above [in Part Four, under the heading "How This Place Appears To Exalted Individuals"], the vision of spiritually advanced persons exceeds the domain of experience of ordinary individuals. The perception of ordinary persons, however, resembles the defective sight of a person with a liver ailment who sees a white conch as yellow. Reality as it appears is continually experienced in a distorted fashion. Therefore, neither of these ways of experience provides a useful basis for a description of this place. Here we will examine this place according to how it appears to practitioners of tantra, a view confirmed by the perception of exalted individuals.

An Overview

In general, the sovereign realm of the Dergé monarch, protector of the Buddha's Way, includes the five sacred areas that represent the qualities of enlightenment and most of the sacred areas related to enlightened activity. The upper region of the kingdom—places such as Zil-trom, Munam, Ngadra, and Tsang-kar—extends along the range of eternally white and cool mountains that forms part of the Himalayas. It corresponds to skillful means, great bliss, and the syllable Vam; and is principally the residence of Great Glorious *Héruka*. The lower region of the kingdom—places such as Ata Rong, Pérong, Mérong, and Ter-rong—extends to densely forested and hot valleys, and dark, rugged ravines. It corresponds to transcendent knowledge, emptiness, and the syllable *É*; and is principally the residence of the Trodhi Sharima goddesses.

The middle region of the kingdom—places such as Tro-zhung, Zil-gyu, Alo, Palpung, Méshö, Rong-mé, Ter-lhung, and Dzing-tro—corresponds to the three main channels and five channel-circles within the body and is the gathering place of an ocean of spiritual heroes and *dakinis*. This sublime sacred place of Tsadra is included in this last category as the heart wheel. Its specific shape is mentioned in *The Treasure-Text Guide to Tsadra*:

> This place, Tsadra Rinchen Drak,
> Is shaped like the channel-spokes of the wheel of great bliss.

As a sign that this place is the castle of the vajra heart of enlightenment, the land is shaped like a human heart. The eight spokes of [the channel-wheel at the heart], "the wheel of spiritual teachings," represent the purification of the eight great time periods and cause the dawning of the experience of the luminous body of ultimate enlightenment. These [eight spokes] are symbolized by the ridges that diffuse from the center of this sacred place. As mentioned in the text cited above [*The Prophecy of the Dakinis of the Three Sources*], this retreat center is built upon the eastern ridge, the Great Vajra Spoke. Since the eastern spoke of the wheel [at the heart] is also considered to be the spoke of wisdom, meditation here stimulates supreme realization and can lead to primordial states, such as the highest, middle, or lesser pure existences, and the four modes of liberation.[17] This relationship [between the land and the inner channels] compelled us to construct sculptures of the deities of Great Glorious *Héruka* [in the retreat center temple].

Similarly, the Jewel Crown Spoke in the South is the ridge called Papang Ridge, upon which stands the great monastery, Palpung Toubten Chökor Ling [Mound of Glory, Place of Shakyamuni's Cycle of Spiritual Teachings]. This site creates ever-increasing renown; moreover, residents of this place will find that their positive qualities grow and flourish according to their respective capacities. The Great Lotus Spoke in the West is the Ra-chen Ridge. Clear self-arisen forms of the auspicious knot of eternity and of Buddha Eternal Life can be seen there. If one makes there a truly spiritual home and performs meditations for longevity, one will attain supreme accomplishment of the power of longevity. The Great Force Spoke in the North is the ridge face that runs in the direction of Pa-ok [Stream]. Persons of adept and forceful minds will come from this line of hills, and if one meditates there, one will succeed in producing wrathful enlightened activity. The spokes in the intermediate directions [southeast, etc.] are clearly evident in ridges between these main four. Meditation on each of them will result in the attainment of accomplishments corresponding to the respective spoke of the heart's channel-wheel.

The Specific Features of This Sacred Place

The description of this sacred place begins with the center of the land, as written in *The Treasure-Text Guide to Tsadra*:

> It is called Vajra Chitta Kotri.
> Its central cliff is the *Héruka*,
> Surrounded by the eight Gauri goddesses.

Vajra Chitta Kotri in Sanskrit means Vajra Heart Castle. Since this refers to the eastern vajra spoke, Vajra Heart Castle is another name for the site of the retreat center. The high cliffs to the right and left are the six arms of the *Héruka*; the cliff at the summit is his three heads; this retreat center lies at his heart; and the cliff faces below the retreat, which divide into two on each side, are his four spread legs. The arrangement of Gauri and other goddesses, arrayed in front [of the main cliff], will be explained below.

Scriptures praise the glorious sacred ground of Chikchar at Tsari as a site that brings happiness to this world because it gathers in a single site the three Vajra Sows [*Vajra Varahi*]—forms below the ground, upon it, and in space. Similarly, those of pure vision can clearly see here the palace of Great Glorious *Héruka* above in space, and below, under the ground. Between the two, on the earth, we have constructed the structure and the contents of the castle of Great Glorious *Héruka* [i.e., the retreat center temple]. This will provide a source for perfect happiness in the world.

In addition, this place has other features in common with the glorious sacred ground of Charitra:

> The line of hills to the right of the retreat center is the Skillful
> > Means Vajra Hill
> To the left stands the Transcendent Knowledge Bell Hill
> The center is the Union Middle Hill
> The summit is the Pure Celestial Hill.

Features of the Skillful Means Vajra Hill

The cliffs of the Skillful Means Vajra Hill to the right of the retreat center are splayed like fingers. On their front side lies Master Lotus-Born's meditation cave, which resembles a blossoming flower. Within it can be found the impression of the guru's footprint in stone, over a cubit in length; the impression of his staff; and the opening of the treasures' [concealment place], sealed with his personal insignia. The exterior of the cave is marked by many self-arisen features: the three syllables [*Om, Ah, Houng*] mark the door; images of the guides of the three kinds of beings[18] mark the left side of the cave; a form of White Tara is found below, in front; and the one hundred peaceful and wrathful sacred deities cover all sides.

Ascending to the right of the cave into a narrow dark gorge, one can see an impression of Guru Rinpoché's foot in stone, over a cubit in length. Immediately above this stands a self-arisen throne where he bound the gods and demons under oath and turned the wheel of spiritual teachings. Around the throne are self-arisen images of this master from Oddiyana, as well as similar images of Yeshé Tsogyal and Bérotsana. There is also an old juniper tree here which grew from the staff of Guru Rinpoché. Along the path up the ridge from this place, one can find two white *Hom* syllables and one white *Ah*, all in stone.

At the residence of Yeshé Tsogyal, one can find such special features as impressions of her hands and feet in stone where she made nectar, prostrations, and offerings; and a flat rock on which she sat during her experience of direct vision [*tö-gal*]. There was once a protruding formation on a rock formed by her having touched it with hands wet with nectar. That moisture became dark red forms of Vajra Sow and the four *dakinis*. Later, however, some pilgrims chipped it away: it has now been placed within the statue of Wheel of Supreme Bliss in the retreat center's temple.

Along the path which runs clockwise around the meditation cave of Lotus-Born Master, there is a jewel-like rock which faces it: there one can see the image of Red Jambhala.

If one looks up and to the left toward the east from the lower meditation cave of Bérotsana, one can find his higher meditation cave: both contain impressions of his hands and feet in stone. To their left is the secret cave of Guru Rinpoché, called Two Side-Entrances [*Do Nyi-ma*]. To its right, the syllable *Tom* protrudes in stone and there are visible impressions in stone of the hand implements of the master from Oddiyana, a vajra and skull-cup. In the cave on the left, one can see traces where profound treasures, such as the guide to the area, were retrieved. Below and to the right, at a short distance, is the meditation cave of Karchen Palgyi Wong-chuk. Directly below that is the half-moon shaped meditation cave of the great accomplished master, Namké Nyingpo. Forms of the nine deities of the configuration of Yangdak Héruka can be found within this cave and a self-formed vajra, symbol of enlightened mind, can be found on the lower left face of the cave. On the face of the rock above the cave, many marks in vermilion indicate treasures' concealment places.

The stream of Namké Nyingpo's [accomplishment of] longevity flows from a crevice in the rock below this cave. At Tsari, the water in the Precious Stone Stream on the Skillful Means Vajra Hill is very clear and has the qualities of nectar. It is said that if persons who have received the appropriate meditation instructions drink from it one evening, this alone results in an indestructible body and eternal life. This stream [here in Tsadra] is the equivalent [of that one in Tsari]: if one uses its water to make the nectar of longevity through meditation or if one always mixes this water with other water blessed by meditation, the benefits of drinking it equal those of the stream in Tsari.

The flat rock facing the meditation cave of Namké Nyingpo is a place of oath-bound protectors. One can see a form of [the protector] Dark-Red Blacksmith on the front side of the rock. Directly in front of this on the rock face are Green Tara and the three syllables. The spring that flows in front of this is known as Blacksmith's Stream. Many impressions of goats in stone can be found to the right and left of these features. Above the spring in a thicket of juniper trees is a cavern in the rock: this was the residence of Yeshé Tsogyal.

This side of the area of sacred ground is ideal for meditation focused mainly on skillful means, the creation phase of meditation.

Features of the Transcendent Knowledge Bell Hill

To the left of the crevice of the highest spring on this hill is a white syllable *Jo*. The spring of [the stream that flows with the sound of] the eight-syllable *Rulu* mantra is situated on the far side of the cliff from that spot. Along the path below the spring, one can see the three syllables above and the six-syllable mantra below. Further in an upward direction, one comes to a large cave known as the Gate to the Sacred Ground, where the great treasure retriever [Chokling] meditated on the spiritual master's body of ultimate enlightenment and experienced an infinite number of pure visions.

Just slightly beyond that cave on the same level lies the meditation cave of the great pandit Smriti Jnana. Located below is the cave of the demon tamer, Vajra Sagging Belly [Dorjé Drolö, one of the eight main forms of Guru Rinpoché], which contains an image of Vajra Sagging Belly holding his hand implements—a vajra and a dagger–and standing upon a tigress. Further in the same direction, there is a red syllable *Bom* above a fissure in the rock-face. In the crevice of a rainbow-colored syllable *Houng*, there is the impression of the footprint of the great master Humkara. This marks the location of his self-appearing throne, similar to the throne of the bodhisattva Chö-pak at Tsari.

On the far side of this throne lies a small cave with a form of White Kachari at its door. Again further in the same direction, there stands a rock in the shape of Vajra Sow. Vermilion flows like blood from her vagina. The vermilion stream that flows down the ridge on the far side of this rock resembles the Dark-Red Blood Lake [in Tsari]. Since this place is sacred to the red *dakini* of enlightened speech and to Ekajati, it is extremely wild: be careful there! All these locations are similar to Tsari: the water's essence, the earth's fertility, the medicinal nectar, and the substances of auspicious connection are all endowed with full potency. The songs, sounds, and music of gatherings of *dakinis* can sometimes be heard here.

Above this place is located the meditation cave of Ga the Translator, who visited here; his footprint in stone is visible. Above and to the left there is a self-formed mark of stability swirling to the right on the outer left face of a cave. Many meditation caves are located throughout this area.

This side of this sacred place is ideal for the meditation focused mainly on the stage of completion: the yoga practices of inner channels, circulatory energy, and vital essence.

Features of the Union Middle Hill

At the heart of the center of this hill stands the structure of the temple of Great Glorious *Héruka*. Above the temple a *bhatra* tree grows. If one looks south from the sheltering cliff close to the tree, one can see many self-arisen *Houng* syllables. These mark the place where the two masters [Vimalamitra and Humkara] compiled the teachings for three days. Below this, in a cave, there are two footprints in stone of the two masters and a white syllable *Houng*. In a seemingly concealed shelter in the cliff to the left of this lies the supreme place of Vimalamitra, his separate hidden residence. Within the cave one can find the syllables *Tam* and *Ha*, and a self-arisen sun and moon above the door. On auspicious occasions, this place is blessed by the visit of the vajra-bodied Vimalamitra, who appears in a display of timeless wisdom. Close to the edge of the cave one can see two footprints in stone, one large, one small: these were made by Vimalamitra and the *dakini* Déchen Gyalmo.[19]

Below this, on the face of the heart-shaped cliff, stands a self-formed likeness of the great master Humkara, one story in height. The cave to the left of this was the place where Jangchub Lingpa accomplished longevity [through meditation].

A pair of high rocks, one large and one small, below the heart of this place, and the tree which grows from them are the residence, outwardly, of the male and female Lion-Faced Demon Protectors; inwardly, of the realm protector, Great Terrifier; and secretly, of the spiritual warrior Vajra Light and the female spiritual warrior Powerful Woman of Lanka. On the face of this rock is a large image of the master from Oddiyana, in a form called Zahor-ma, beneath which are the twelve syllables of the *Vajra Guru* mantra. In front of the rock there appears a vajra and the three syllables and, below it on a flat rock, two or three clockwise swastikas and the syllables *Ha-Ri-Ni-Sa* are distinctly visible. The auspicious connection of these features ensures that if one meditates single-mindedly in this retreat center, one will be able to remain in retreat and reach the full limits of one's potential life span.

The stream on the right side of this hill flows with blessed washing water: to wash with it or to drink it creates a positive connection that leads to the eventual pacification of illness, demons, negative acts, and obscurations. If water from this stream is mixed with vase water consecrated by meditation, it becomes very potent. The left face of this hill, just over the outer circumambulation path, features cliffs that look like the *tormas* offered during a vajra feast, with trees that resemble parasols planted in the ground. One hundred and eight footprints of the *dakinis* in stone mark the side of these hills. In front of them stands the changeless spike [a tree], the residence of the realm protectress Co-Emergent Woman. Moreover, other palaces of Co-Emergent Woman are located elsewhere [on the land].

This central hill is said to be ideal for meditative absorptions that combine creation and completion phase meditations, such as Great Seal or Great Completion.

Features of the Pure Celestial Hill

This hill is identified in the source texts as the castle of Great Compassion. However since this cliff itself belongs to the local god, the great *genyen* Dorjé Palbar, the many self-formed features of this place are located in a very wild area. Because the time was not propitious for [Chokling] to introduce them to me, I have nothing to report concerning this hill.

Behind this hill is a white rock that resembles a horse's set of teeth. This is a place sacred to the guides of the three kinds of beings. Self-formed images of the three guides appear on the rock face: Chok-gyur Déchen Lingpa says that he saw them from the valley below. In the past, when Jangchub Lingpa lived here, it seems that a number of powerful practitioners who could fly through space came to this hill.

Features in the Surrounding Area

The Treasure-Text Guide to Tsadra states:

> Humkara and Vimalamitra
> And all accomplished masters
> Blessed this place with their form of pure timeless wisdom.

In this delightful land of caves and sheltering cliffs,
The three awareness-holders [Humkara, Vimalamitra, and Guru
   Rinpoché] made their meditation sites.

Amazing qualities abound,
Such as consecrated washing water, water of longevity,
   vermilion, and medicinal water.
This supreme place for attainment is indeed delightful!

This praise pertains to three hills—of skillful means, of wisdom, and of the union of the two. The medicinal water referred to in this passage is the water of [the stream] near Rimo-da, known to cure digestive ailments.

The ten wrathful ones who guard against obstacles reside in the many cliffs below the main center here. If you follow the lower stream uphill in a clockwise direction around the Plain of the Throne for Spiritual Teachings, a grassy plain which looks like the syllables É and *Vam* together lies on the left side of the Ra-chen Stream. To the right is a form of Buddha Eternal Life; to the left, Red Tara; and many other self-arisen images in the general vicinity of the Ra-chen Stream. In particular, the pillar-like cliff-face, known as Orub Flat Place, features a red Buddha Boundless Light and a very large image of eleven-faced Great Compassion. At Dong-po Gang, also called Dil, stands a palace that is the occasional residence of glorious Powerful Realm Protector. If you look up at the rock from below, you will see a self-formed image of Vajra Sow.

As you walk up along the Léringma Stream, you arrive first at the end of the path known as Tser. This marks the enclosure where *dakinis* play: it is forbidden to make fires here or to bring horses or donkeys through this area. Behind this, the landscape of the place called Né-dil is shaped in the self-arisen design of glorious Charitra. On its front side stands a very clear image of Padmasambhava; White Tara, Wish-Fulfilling Wheel; Nub-chen Sangyé Yeshé's handprint in stone; Nyak-chen Jnana's footprint; the impression of Sokpo [Dorjé] Lhapal's head; a white syllable *Ah*; a vajra; an elephant; a pair of golden fish; a white conch shell; the divine yak of Tsari; and, after it, the syllables *Ha-Ri-Ni-Sa*. On the face above are such features as Yeshé Tsogyal's footprint, called Rainbow; a syllable *Houng*; and the hoof prints of the Oath-Bound One's goat.

If you continue following the course of the stream uphill, you will reach a one-story tall stupa of great awakening. To the right of this is the footprint of Guru Rinpoché, a syllable *Houng*, a container for the vajra feasts of the *dakinis*, and three large rocks in the shape of skulls on either side of the stream. Above these is a self-formed conch shell. The water flowing from this "shell" is consecrated: drinking it or washing your head or body with it pacifies illness, demons, negative acts, and obscurations. Continuing your ascent from here, you will arrive at the residence of either Victorious Woman or of the white-bodied *dakinis*.

To the right of Conch-Shell Conduit [Kala Doung] Lake is the footprint of the precious master from Oddiyana; to the left is the footprint of the *dakini* Drowa Zangmo. By the lake on that side, you will find in ascending order an image of [the bodhisattva] Great Compassion, Emptier of Cyclic Existence; the footprint of a *dakini*; and a white image of Vajrasattva protruding from the rock. These cliffs, called the Black Rocks, are said to hold one hundred and eight amazing marks—images of the three sources, enlightened form; mantras, enlightened speech; and hand implements and stupas, enlightened mind. The area of these rocks is sacred to the noble woman Tara; thus, the place is called Tara Rock. Here there is the empowerment cave of Guru Rinpoché, where he performed the great practice of the Eight Great Configurations. Above and below this cave, there are self-formed images of the nine deities of Yangdak Héruka. The cave concealed by a cluster of juniper trees is the meditation cave of Noob-chen Sang-gyé Yeshé. The cave located at the junction of three rocks was the residence of Lha-cham Mandarava when she visited this place through her miraculous power. The cave situated below the rocks, which has rainbow-colored designs of various silk brocades, is the place where the glorious [First Karmapa] Dusum Kyenpa [1110-1193] stayed for three days on his journey from Kampo Gang-ra to central Tibet. [He later] blessed it mentally: the rocks show self-formed images of Marpa, Milarepa, Dawkpo [Gampopa], and Karmapa himself. The cave in the red cliff facing east was the residence of Jangchub Lingpa: his miraculous footprint can be found there. In the cliff shaped like a vase of longevity is the meditation cave of Tang-Tong Gyalpo. Other features of this area include many hand and footprints in stone.

If you ascend from the valley below Léringma, you will see along the path a self-formed image of Red Tara on the face of a rock. In the direction of Dorjé Tserchen [Mountain], there is a cave where accomplished masters of the mind section of Great Completion sometimes come to meditate. On the mountain of the Red Earth Pass there is a semi-circular castle of power, the color of power [i.e., red]. On its face, you can see distinct, self-arisen shapes of the vase of longevity and a hook. On the face of the rock to the right of the great enclosure's gate are three forms of the Buddha Eternal Life: one white, one red, and one who embraces his consort in sexual union. The plain that forms the top of the descending valley has the form of a syllable *Houng*. Following the path across the pass, Big-Head Hill on your left is marked in the right corner by an imprint of a *dakini*'s footprint in stone. In general it has been said that this area of sacred ground contains one hundred and eight such footprints of the *dakinis*. For example, on the upper part of the line of hills of Tsadra Rinchen Drak, the Glorious *Héruka's* head, there is a stone which has two very clear footprints, one large and one small, and the hoof-print of the magic mule on which the Glorious Goddess [Mahakali] rides. There are many such rocks in this area.

Over the pass, in Mar-yu, you can see to the north a white cliff, the residence of the harm-bringing spirit [*yaksha*], Muk-dzin Wongpo. The face of this cliff shows the self-arisen shape of a stupa. In front, there lies a flat rock that points east: on the rock face you can view the arrangement of the central mountain of this world-system and its surrounding continents. The rock below the cliff is shaped like a blazing, eight-sided jewel, marked by a symbolic syllable *Hri* and the Tibetan syllable *Trom*. On a rock above to the right, the sign of hidden treasure, a coil of joy, and a blazing vajra have been etched in the stone below a footprint of Guru Rinpoché in stone. In the rocks between this place and the Dzu-ru Valley, there are many syllables, such as a blue *Houng* in the rock face of Til-kar Chung.

All of the above features have been referred to in *The Treasure-Text Guide to Tsadra* in these words:

> This place has one hundred and eight representations of the
>   Buddha's body, speech, and mind;
> Four rivers resound naturally with the sounds of mantras;

Conch-Shell Conduit Lake holds consecrated washing water;
The skulls of the three forms of enlightenment serve as
    containers for vajra feasts;
Clouds of offerings that please the five senses emerge,
Great blissful Vajrasattva.
This is the immortal place of the Buddha Eternal Life.

"Four rivers resound naturally with the sounds of mantras": Pa-ok River, which makes the sound of Vajrasattva's mantra; the river by the hermitage, which makes the sound of the *Rulu* mantra; the Many-Headed Source and Ra-chen River, which make the sound of the six-syllable mantra; and Tser-mingma River, which makes the sounds of the mantras of the three deities of longevity [Boundless Life, White Tara, and Victorious Female Buddha].

Features of the Area in Front of the Héruka

To begin from the left, the cliffs connected with the meditation cave of Translator Ga are the palace of Four-Armed Mahakala and his eight attendants. This area, called Gorge of the Protector, includes the protector's spirit-tree, named Terrifying, and the cliffs' dense forests, where one hundred thousand black persons, black dogs, and black birds dwell.

Further, in stages, there are Ngonmo Ja-dré Chi Dré, and the self-arisen Raven-Head Cliff. Beyond La-gu Lung-gu, there is a self-formed image of Six-Armed Protector. On the far side of the Ridge Which Eradicates Confusion, there are self-appearing letters in stone, such as the six-syllable mantra. The cave at Bear's Home Gorge is the residence of the secret protector: meditation on this protector here brings rapid results. Here and at Tiger's Lair Gorge, there are meditation caves where the master from Oddiyana stayed. On the far side of the Passage to Decide Between Good and Evil, there is a self-formed image of the *dakini* Master of Bliss. In general in this front area, there are eight gorges formed by four ridges: these eight are palaces where reside the eight *mamos*, such as Gauri; the eight *tramen* spirits of the region, such as Singha-ma; and the four horse-headed gate-guardians [of each]. On the face of the stone hills, it is said that there exist forms, handprints, footprints, meditation caves, and water of accomplishment of each of the eight awareness-holders of the exalted land [India] and the nine Tibetan recipients of their instructions. Self-formed images of each of the *mamos,* their implements, and syllables (such as *Gom*), which represent their names, appear in stone there and a tree grows where each resides.

At the outer extremity of this area, charnel grounds appear spontaneously in a form identical to the charnel grounds that surround great configurations of deities. Within these, the little stream's path to the right of the Many-Headed Source clearly flows in the shape of a tantric staff and the face of the flat rock which points west shows the distinct image of the wisdom *dakini* Auspicious Master of Longevity, riding a lion. This rock is her residence.

All the features of this area described above have been recorded, without omissions or additions, directly from the speech of the emanated great treasure revealer [Chokling]. He either overtly visited these places himself or privately saw them with his vision of wisdom. In general, the features of this sublime sacred area and the pure vision of ordinary beings are inconceivable. [Sentient beings' recognition of the sacred features here through their development of pure vision] will make this area's features increasingly apparent and numerous.

Furthermore, *The Treasure-Text Guide to Tsadra* states:

> This sacred ground,
> Praised by all the joyful ones of the three times,
> Is the sacred ground of the radiant heart of enlightenment.
> Therefore, its earth, stones, rocks, and cliffs
> All resemble rainbow light and circles.

Although the earth, stones, rocks, and cliffs of this sacred ground have indefinite shapes and colors, they appear together like rainbow light or spheres, as stated here.

> Spiritual heroes and *dakinis* gather here;
> Guardians of the doctrine and their messengers perform activity
>   quickly.
> This sacred place separates good from evil.

The meaning of these words is borne out by the features of this place. Furthermore, *The Treasure-Text Guide to Tsadra* states:

> In the center stands the *bhatra* tree;
> In the east is the Jonpa tree; in the south, the Sal;
> In the west, the Hook; in the north, the Fruit-Bearing.
> These changeless trees are planted like spikes.

In the sublime sacred place of Dévikotri, there are said to be five changeless trees, the Five Spikes. The central *bhatra* tree grows at the heart of the Union Middle Hill. Its leaves are like silk thread; it is the support for the residence of Mantra Protectress. The Excellent Jonpa to the east is situated between Protector Gorge and Field Protector Gorge. It has a dark-red hue unlike any other tree in the area: it is the spirit-support of the protectors. To the south, a *sal* tree is located below [Palpung] Monastery. It has nine points at its top; it is the support for Lord of Death. To the west, the tree which resembles the hook of an *utpala* flower is located in the enclosure of Tara Rock; the tree was consecrated by Tara. These three trees all belong to the *sal* species. To the north, a fruit-bearing tree is located in the direction of Dzu-ru Valley. It is a juniper tree unlike any other in the area; it is the spirit-support of the *yaksha*.

Furthermore, along the outer circular route, the Ocean of *Dakinis* [described in the next section], all cliffs have the distinct shapes of enclosures of weapons, such as vajras, daggers, swords, and wheels. There are four gorges:

Protector Gorge
Raven or Field Protector Gorge
Tiger's Lair Gorge
Bear's Home Gorge.

There are four difficult passages:

Difficult Passage to Distinguish Between Virtue and Non-Virtue
Difficult Passage to Eradicate Confusion
Difficult Passage to Decide Between Good and Evil
Difficult Passage on the High Pass Between Cyclic Existence and Transcendence.

There are four plains:

Well-Arranged Mandala Plain
Dancing *Dakini* Plain
Fullest Happiness Plain
Expansive Wisdom Plain.

There are four passes:

Tara Pass

Field Protector Pass
Purification Pass
Spread of Spiritual Teachings Pass.

There are four ridges:

Freedom's Path Ridge
Prostration Ridge
Meeting the Deities Ridge
Reaching the Limit Ridge.

There are four hills of isolation:

Hill of Isolation from the Demons' Obstacles
Hill of Isolation from the Distractions of Desire and Anger
Hill of Isolation from Emotions of the Eight Worldly Concerns
Secret Hill of Isolation from Suffering and the Increase of Happiness.

There are five glens:

Glen of Clear Wisdom
Glen of Self-Arisen Nature of Reality
Glen of the Wide Expanse
Glen of the Single Vital Essence
Glen of the Changeless Mark of Stability.

Of these, the four passes are located to the right, the four gorges and the four passages to the left [as one walks in a clockwise direction]. All the other features [of Tsari] are present in the surrounding area: apart from the difference in size between the two places, all the features and the forms of this place are identical to those of glorious Charitra. Therefore, be confident in and feel inspired by this sacred ground and visit it with a respectful attitude.

The Temple, Kunzang Déchen Ösel Ling

The above has provided a detailed description of the features of the hills of this sacred place, the environment that supports the monastery and retreat center. The main monastic center has been foretold:

In the future in these sublime sacred places,
Many accomplished persons will gather;
A temple and a stupa will be constructed there.

This foretells the founding of the structure and contents of Palpung Toubten Chökor Ling and the congregation of persons who maintain them. In addition,

> When this guide appears on the earth,
> The body, speech, and mind of the *Héruka*
> Will arrive here from Highest Pure Land.

This foretells the construction of the structure and contents of the retreat center, Kunzang Déchen Ösel Ling [Place of the Ever-Excellent Luminosity of Great Bliss]. Both prophecies were clearly made in the adamantine speech [of Guru Rinpoché]: with an attitude of lucid and confident faith you should energetically increase your cultivation of merit and wisdom [at these sites].

That the self-formed images and other extraordinary features of this place are genuine is stated in *The Sealed Prophecy of the Spiritual Master's Quintessential Vision*:

> Sometimes emanations of all enlightened ones
> Will appear on the earth, stones, rocks, cliffs, paths, and passages
> In self-arisen manifestations of their body, speech, and mind.
> Whatever connection one makes with them—through sight,
>   sound, etc.—prevents rebirth in miserable existences.
> Where will these appear? Anywhere: in the cardinal directions,
>   in between, in the center, etc.
> Such concepts as near or far are irrelevant: they will appear
>   everywhere.
> Similarly, the time of their appearance is unfixed: they can
>   appear at any time.
> They aren't limited to any period: they will appear until the
>   wheel of life ends.

Further,

> Self-appearing forms, such as the six syllables, are inconceivable.
> These and other forms manifest in various ways
> To help the world and to spread the Buddha's teaching.

Therefore, as has been said, such self-arisen features appear not only in this sublime sacred place, but in every direction, high and low. Every self-formed image that exists has been created by the enlightened victors' and their spiritual heirs' inherently radiant wisdom. There is no difference between viewing these self-arisen forms and images with single-minded faith, devotion, and pure vision, and actually meeting these buddhas and bodhisattvas.

PART SEVEN: HOW TO PERFORM PILGRIMAGE AT THIS PLACE

This section has three parts:

1. The paths of circumambulation
2. The time for pilgrimage
3. How to perform pilgrimage

1. The Paths of Circumambulation

There are five[20] paths of circumambulation:

a. Outer
b. Inner
c. Secret
d. Summit
e. Upper

a. The Outer Path of Circumambulation, The Ocean of *Dakinis*

Outwardly, this sublime sacred place is arranged like the Ocean of *Dakinis*, the sacred configuration of deities that surround the central deity, Supreme Bliss. This path of circumambulation follows the inside of that configuration's vajra enclosure.

To begin, develop the mind of awakening and descend from Doung-kar Chudang to the Well-Arranged Mandala Plain. There recite the hundred-syllable mantra of Vajrasattva while washing with water from the Pa-ok Stream; then make outer, inner, and secret mandala offerings. At the Plain of the Throne of Spiritual Teachings, make burnt offerings and *serkyem* offerings to the guardian of the southern gate. While reciting the six-syllable mantra, wash with water from the stream that flows from Ra-chen, then follow the course of the stream uphill. On the Dancing *Dakini* Plain, sing and dance during the course of a vajra feast. Since the way is cut above Amna Ghost Cave, follow the stream uphill behind the self-arisen [replica of] Tsari.

On Tara Pass, you come to the vajra feast container of the *dakinis*: ordinary persons here offer whatever food or drink they can;

practitioners of tantra do the meditation of offering their own bodies as a symbolic form of outer, inner, and secret vajra feasts. Recite
the recollection formulae [Sanskrit, *dharanis*] of the three deities of
longevity while washing and drinking the self-arisen consecrated
water that flows here. However, because it is unfitting that impurities should be mixed with the stream's water, draw the water and
wash to the side. At Conch-Shell Conduit Lake, offer whatever pure
lake-offerings you have. At the top of Tara Pass, create an auspicious connection to the increase of your merit and longevity by
making a mandala offering and reciting prayers.

On Fullest Happiness Plain, create an auspicious connection to
future happiness by eating pure, delicious food and singing and
dancing to joyful songs. Make prayers for the happiness of the
whole country. On Freedom's Path Ridge, make prayers that all
beings enter the incontrovertible path to freedom. At the top of
Purification Pass, offer burnt offerings and *serkyem* to the guardian
of the western gate. This will create an auspicious connection for
your control of your mind and circulatory energy.

On Prostration Ridge, offer as many prostrations as you can while
bringing clearly to mind the sacred configuration of this supreme
place's environment, temple, and the temple's sacred contents. At
the top of Spread of Spiritual Teachings Pass, make prayers that all
beings' minds accept spiritual teachings. Offer burnt offerings and
serkyem here to the main guardian of the area, Dorjé Palbar. Shout,
"May the gods be victorious!" In front of the residence of Muk-
dzin Wongpo or close to the Fruit-Bearing Tree, honor the guardian of the northern gate by burnt offerings and *serkyem*; request the
power to attract good fortune and prosperity. As you pass by rocks
that resemble swords, make an auspicious connection to eradicate
the enemies and impediments in your spiritual life.

Continue in a clockwise direction, going from the Spontaneously-
Appearing Red Cliff on the left side of the self-formed Great Glorious *Héruka* until you are able to see the summit of the snow mountain. Once you reach Meeting the Deities Ridge, you can see the
configuration of the self-formed Great Glorious *Héruka*: offer a
mandala, a vajra feast, torma, and the recitation of the eight-part,
common prayer to acknowledge faults, etc. Make special prayers.
From this point until you arrive at Reaching the Limit Ridge, do

not make loud noises, such as cries or whistles, and do not urinate, defecate, spit, etc. You should walk with full awareness in a single-minded attitude of devotion.

As you pass through Ngonmo Ja-dré Chi-dré, you can sometimes hear the calls of vultures and ravens. Cross the Realm-Protector Pass; then, in front of the self-formed Raven's Head, offer torma and a vajra feast and request [the protectors'] enlightened activity. In front of the Feast Torma of the *Dakinis*, recite the eight-part service; offer outer, inner, and secret mandalas; and offer torma and a vajra feast. Make prayers for the attainment of supreme accomplishment. At the eastern Jonpa tree, honor the guardian of the gate by burnt offerings and *serkyem*.

Cross Lagu Lung-gu and make offerings at the self-formed image of Six-Armed Protector and request the protector's blessing. Descend to what is known as either Raven Gorge or Realm-Protector Gorge. Wash in the nectar water of the stream while reciting the *Rulu* mantra. Walk along the Passage to Distinguish Virtue and Non-Virtue until Tiger's Lair Gorge. It is here that a *dakini* manifests in the form of a tigress or leopard and devours evil persons. To other pilgrims, she growls or shows frightening forms: your fear will purify the obscuring effects of past negative acts.

On the right side of this area, there is a cave where you toss stones to make divinations foretelling good or bad fortune. At the end of the Passage to Eradicate Confusion, you can see the self-formed six-syllable mantra: think that in seeing it you are actually meeting in person the Bodhisattva All-Seeing Eyes. You then reach Bear's Home Gorge. Here lies the cave of the secret protector: ordinary persons are not permitted to enter it; persons who do the practice of Six-Armed Awakened Protector may enter carefully and make offerings and praises. Their wishes will be accomplished.

These gorges are actually branches of the sacred ground of Tsari. After crossing the Passage to Decide Between Good and Evil, you can see the form of the *dakini* Master of Bliss: make prayers of aspiration to achieve the celestial states. Once you have crossed over the Passage to Distinguish Between Cyclic Existence and Transcendence, you can take a short rest on the even ground of the Certainty of Cyclic Existence and Transcendence, the Plain of Expansive Wisdom. Practitioners of tantra should maintain their meditative experience and sing vajra songs of realization, offer a vajra feast, and make extensive offerings of mandalas. Ordinary men and women should sing the seven-syllable mantra of Wheel of Supreme Bliss and the *Vajra Guru* mantra [of Guru Rinpoché]. Once you arrive at Reaching the Limit Ridge, you should complete your circumambulation with auspicious wishes and seal it with prayers to dedicate the merit of your activity.

b. The Inner Path of Circumambulation of the *Héruka*

Start from Palpung Monastery and cross Tara Pass. Across the valley below Dorjé Tser Chenma, descend from Ra-chen Ka directly to Mar-yu and onto Meeting the Deities Ridge. From there, continue along the secret path of the plain, below the retreat center and the Field Protector Cliff, to the White Conch Ridge. This completes the knot [i.e., one tight circle] of this route.

c. The Secret Path of Circumambulation, Blazing Wisdom

This path can be traveled only by accomplished masters, vajra holders who possess the vows of the three levels of commitment, fully-ordained persons who have kept their vows purely, mantric practitioners who have kept their commitments, and women who have the signs of being *dakinis* of an excellent family of enlightenment. This path cannot be walked by ordinary persons.

d. The Summit Path of the Awareness-Holding Spiritual Master

From the Many-Headed Source, walk to the summit, the head of the *Héruka*, then descend from the flat ground there. From Field Protector Cliff, walk down to the White Conch Ridge.

e. The Upper Path of the Buddha Ever-Excellent

This path, walked above the configuration of deities, is accessible to those who maintain their meditation experience, but is beyond the range of experience of ordinary persons.

[Other Paths]

The path of circumambulation that follows an easy lower course along the foot-hills starts at the Plain of the Throne of Spiritual Teachings. Walk along Red Earth Pass and, from Dzina, descend to

Ngo Chen. Then follow the Pa-ok Stream upstream until the Throne Cliff at Well-Arranged Mandala Plain.

It is said that the following route must be walked to finish a circumambulation of the complete configuration of the three *hérukas*: Once you cross Sha-zhé Pass, go from Tsa to Tsézul Do. Then cross the Alo-ka Teng Pass. From Karong-ka, follow Jongé Pass of Lhamdo and enter Powerful Hero Cliff. Follow the secret path below Yudruk Pass and then descend to Dopu. Walk along the river, upstream, then cross Sidu Pass. From Rongmé, follow the main road until you reach this place.

2. The Time for Pilgrimage

This section has two parts:

> a. Ordinary time for pilgrimage
> b. The special time for pilgrimage

a. The Ordinary Time for Pilgrimage

This sublime sacred place has been consecrated as a site that will help others through any connection to it until the end of cyclic existence. Therefore, prostrations, circumambulations, offerings, etc. done here at any time, according to one's ability, will result in the corresponding benefits. Thus, pilgrimage can be done here at any time.

b. The Special Time for Pilgrimage

The Treasure-Text Guide to Tsadra states:

> Especially, in the Sheep Year, during the Monkey Month,
> The assembly of awareness-holders, meditation deities, and
> *dakinis*
> Gather from the ten directions and appear in this place.

As stated here, Sheep Years mark the special time when configurations of deities of the Three Sources assemble from the ten directions and gather in this sublime sacred place. Most particularly, the definite, special occasion during the year is the Monkey Month. The Monkey Month of a Sheep Year and the Monkey Month in any year are times when the blessing of this place is most intense. The Monkey Month has been interpreted [by different schools of Tibetan astrology] in three ways: as the fifth, sixth, or seventh lunar month. Since all three interpretations have been made by those who possess insight into spiritual teachings, none can be said to be mistaken. The compassion of the buddhas can enter the lives of their disciples: we receive their blessing to the extent that we live our faith. Therefore, these three months should be considered of equal importance.

3. How to Perform Pilgrimage

The information given above has provided complete details of pilgrimage in the specific context of this place. The following section describes general advice for pilgrimage according to the works of such authors as the second buddha, Rangjung Dorjé [the Third Karmapa]; and the realized master, Kachö Wongpo [the Second Zhamarpa, (1350-1405)].

You should accompany pilgrimage with three qualities of your bearing: physical, verbal, and mental restraint, as instructed in the Buddha's teachings on discipline; the development of the mind of awakening, as instructed in the teachings on the transcendent perfections; and the pure tantric commitments, as instructed in the teachings of Secret Mantra. Purify the obscuring effects of past negative physical acts by giving up such things as riding horses or wearing hats. Purify the obscuring effects of negative verbal acts by reciting prayers and singing praises. Purify the obscuring effects of negative mental acts by maintaining devotion, respect, and pure vision. In summation, while on pilgrimage give up all activity detrimental to spiritual life and be consistently attentive, mindful, and faithful.

On pilgrimage, renounce playful jokes and jests, raucous laughter, and idle conversation. Leave far behind any worldly concern, such as for food, drink, and fashion. In particular, scrupulously avoid such acts as intoxication, arguments, and loud shouting.

There is a strict year-round ban on killing deer or other animals, large or small, in this area: immediate punishment will be meted out if this ban is violated. Since rituals invoking the deities will even be performed in this case, offenders will certainly be punished. Therefore, in consideration of your own life and wealth, respect this ban conscientiously.

If you become tired climbing along passes, slopes, ridges, and gorges [of circumambulation routes], be glad of it since this exertion is unlike the difficulties you encounter in worldly work: effort during pilgrimage purifies your negative acts.

Don't place imaginary limits on the miraculous manifestations of spiritual heroes and *dakinis* in this place: regard everything you see, good or bad—human beings, animals, birds, mice, deer, or carnivorous animals—with faith and pure vision.

Don't be intimidated by fearful things, such as narrow passes, rain, wind, thickly forested gorges, carnivorous animals, lightning, or hail: pray to the Three Sources [master, meditation deity, and *dakinis*] and offer *torma* and *serkyem* to the area's guardians and command their protection. Regard your fear as like the alarm and anguish that accompany the period between death and rebirth: pray to be liberated from the passage between death and rebirth.

The representations of the deities and the self-formed images must never be struck, broken, or moved to another place: to do so causes obstacles, such as untimely death. Never be careless: develop the perception that these features really embody the Three Sources. Persons who behave improperly in the meditation caves will be punished. Visits to these caves should be used for offering vajra feasts or for meditation, acts that create positive connection to the site.

The Treasure-Text Guide to Tsadra states:

> This sacred site is not a place
> For those without commitments who behave badly.
> Fortunate persons who keep their tantric commitments,
> Practitioners who conduct themselves appropriately,
> Will attain accomplishment according to their connection:
> Have no doubt about this!

In conclusion, the awareness-holding spiritual master will bless those who accompany pilgrimage with devotion, respect, and prayer. The meditation deities will bestow accomplishment upon those who accompany pilgrimage with meditation and the recitation of mantras. The mother and sister *dakinis* will befriend those who accompany pilgrimage with joyous celebrations and vajra feasts. The protectors and guardians of the Buddha's teaching will perform the enlightened activity for those who accompany pilgrimage with offerings of consecrated substances and tormas. The owner-spirits and local gods will assist those who accompany pilgrimage with burnt offerings and *serkyem*.

Pilgrimage undertaken with difficulties and dedicated exertion purifies negative acts, unwholesome acts, and obscurations. Pilgrimage accompanied by offerings of mandalas and the recitation of prayers of aspiration leads to the fulfillment of any wish. Pilgrimage accompanied by very secret tantric discipline brings the attainment of stable great bliss. Pilgrimage accompanied by meditation without discursive thought fosters the attainment of supreme accomplishment. Therefore, even after one hundred circumambulations of this unsurpassable, indestructible configuration of deities, you still want to do more. Even if you were to live here for one hundred years, you will never feel regret or grow tired of it. Always cultivate trust and certainty toward this place; always stay here in a fully joyful state of mind: this will make your life meaningful.

PART EIGHT: THE BENEFITS OF PILGRIMAGE AT THIS PLACE

The description of the benefits of cultivating merit at a place that has such amazing qualities has three parts:

1. The general benefits of pilgrimage to sacred places
2. The specific benefits of cultivating merit in this great sacred place
3. The benefits of circumambulation along the various routes

1. The General Benefits of Pilgrimage

In general, indestructible great sacred places contain sublime, self-arisen representations of the deities that are not the product of human endeavor. They appear to those of pure vision as palaces of great liberation, and to those of impure minds as inert forms of earth, stones, rocks, and cliffs. It is stated in discourses and tantras that infinite merit is accrued by making prostrations and offerings to, and circumambulations of, representations of the Buddha's body, speech, and mind made from clay or other materials by a skilled artisan. Compared to that merit, millions of times more benefits result from prostrations, offerings, and circumambulations at these sublime sacred places. This can be proved by both logic and textual sources. Practitioners can create here various auspicious connections that lead to the tantric discipline of the Vajra Way. *The Sealed Prophecy* states:

> Similarly, the qualities that arise from meditation
> In the major sacred places and subsidiary places,
> The sacred regions, regions similar to them, and hidden regions
>   are unimaginable:
> One day of meditation in these places
> Brings one closer to attainment than a year of meditation in an
>   ordinary place.

This and other statements, similar in both style and content, can be found in the treasure texts in praise of the unlimited qualities of the great sites of sacred ground. On the subject of the great regions of sacred ground in Amdo and Kham, Guru Rinpoché writes of the benefits of pilgrimage to them in *The Location List of the Twenty-Five Major Sacred Sites of Amdo and Kham*:

> Prostrations and circumambulations done in these places close
>   the door to rebirth in the miserable existences.
> Service rendered here leads to rebirth in the higher realms.
> The offering of one vajra feast completes a great cultivation of
>   merit.
> A second offering of a vajra feast purifies all the ripened effects
>   of past acts.
> A third offering of a vajra feast ensures that you will meet me,
>   Lotus-Born Master from Oddiyana,
> In a symbolic form in real life, in meditation, or in a dream.
> One hundred vajra feast offerings lead to rebirth in the pure
>   celestial realms.
> If you wish to attain supreme accomplishment, practice single-
>   mindedly: you will attain it!
> How marvelous are these sublime sacred places that help others
>   through any connection to them!

2. The Specific Benefits of Cultivating Merit in This Great Sacred Place

The Treasure-Text Guide to Tsadra states:

> At all times, ordinary or special,
> One is protected from the *dukka* [suffering] of miserable
>   existences

By just reaching this sacred place
With stable faith and devotion.

By making offerings of outer, inner, and secret vajra feasts,
One completes a great cultivation of merit and wisdom.
Whoever makes prostrations and circumambulations here
Purifies all negative acts and obscurations.

One session of meditation here is more profound
Than a year of meditation done elsewhere.
Whoever meditates single-mindedly
Will attain ordinary and supreme accomplishment by the
    blessing of this place.

Whoever makes offerings at this sacred place
Will experience the full increase of longevity and merit.

As stated in this true, concise, unambiguous declaration, apart from the effect of prostrations, circumambulations, offerings, praises, mandala offerings, vajra feast offerings, and simple or complex meditations, just to reach this sacred place with faith and devotion is sufficient to ensure that one will avoid rebirth in the miserable existences!

Since this place is similar to the sacred ground of Charitra, pilgrimage to this place accrues all the special benefits of pilgrimage to Charitra. On that subject, the powerful victor, Rangjung Dorjé, states:

Charitra, principal among the twenty-four sacred places,
Is the palace of the Honored One, Wheel of Supreme Bliss.
Those who perform pilgrimage there with faith and devotion
Will later be reborn in the presence of the Buddha Boundless
    Light
In the pure land Great Bliss.

Further, the Seventh Karmapa, Chödrak Gyatso, states:

Fortunate persons will see directly
This great configuration of deities.
Those of middle or lesser fortune
Will see vividly or dimly
The deities, their implements, syllables of mantras,
Stupas, and charnel grounds, etc.

If one takes but a single step toward this sacred place
With the thought of making pilgrimage to it,
One's obscurations will be purified and obstacles cleared away,
And one will surely attain accomplishment.

Therefore, for a person endowed with faith and the tantric
    commitments,
Who has renounced wrong views and has conscientiously
Made pilgrimage to the entire area,
All disharmonious influences,
Such as sickness, demons, negative acts, and obscurations, will
    be pacified;
Wishes will be fulfilled; longevity and wealth,
Merit, happiness, and well-being will increase;
Control over the environment and beings will be gained;
Enemies and obstructions will be eradicated;
Most ordinary accomplishments will be attained;
And supreme accomplishments will gradually be realized.

These adamantine words are a sworn attestation of the benefits
of this pilgrimage. You will attain these benefits according to the
strength of your faith and devotion, and the extent of your spiritual connection.

Specifically, cultivation of merit and wisdom on the four plains
of this sublime sacred place purifies the four modes of being. Crossing the four passages purifies the four obscurations. Traveling
through the four gorges clears away the habitual clinging of the
four circumstances. Washing with, and drinking the water of,
the four streams infuses one with the power of the energy of the
four empowerments. Making the difficult climb to the four
passes makes one cross the four paths. Walking on the four ridges
causes the four meditation experiences to arise. Maintaining
meditative experience on the four isolated hills causes the attainment of the four realizations. To see the five glens causes the
dawn of the five wisdoms and the attainment of the five ultimate
bodies of enlightenment.[21]

Through pilgrimage, you create these auspicious connections that
infuse your mind with positive influences. It is also necessary for
each person to develop confidence in each sacred feature of the
land [for this to be effective]. In this way, the effect of one great

circumambulation done in the full, appropriate manner spontaneously creates the auspicious connection for a person with an ordinary body of the six elements[22] to complete the stages of maturation and liberation on the spiritual path and to achieve enlightenment in this very body and lifetime.

3. The Benefits of Circumambulation Along the Various Routes

Those persons of highest, middle, or ordinary capabilities who have entered the Buddha's Way [i.e., are ordained] or those men and women who are householders should do the circumambulations with whatever motivation and conduct are appropriate to their respective traditions. The completion of one round of the outer path of circumambulation, The Ocean of *Dakinis*, as described above, equals the effect of one hundred million recitations of whatever prayers or mantras one recites. For a person of the highest capability, the effect is immeasurable. Similarly, seven rounds of the inner path of circumambulation of the *Héruka*, one hundred rounds of the summit path of the awareness-holding spiritual master, or twenty-one rounds of the easy, foot-hill course all equal the benefits of one hundred million recitations.

Further, the benefit of one hundred offerings of mandalas, lamps, or vajra feasts in this sacred place equal three hundred such offerings elsewhere. The immeasurable difference in the effects of meditation and other forms of practice here as compared with elsewhere has been clearly described in the texts cited above. Therefore, wise persons who wish to make their human life fully meaningful should not delay increasing their cultivation of merit and wisdom at this sublime sacred place. Don the armor of a firm resolve to practice assiduously!

Dedication and Colophon

> The domain of the Buddha's wisdom is inconceivable;
> The bounds of the enlightened constituent [i.e., buddha-nature]
>   and interests of beings are equally immeasurable.
> The dancers who are intoxicated with the alcohol of great bliss
> Sing songs of the infinite vajra design.

> For those who are not exalted individuals, the eyes to see what is
>   hidden are veiled;

They can neither see such mysteries themselves, nor reveal them
  to others. Thus I just see a foggy blur.
Such difficult work should not concern me,
But due to the kindness of the accomplished one, I have written
  this for others' benefit.

Those who have eyes free from obscurations
Find right beside themselves the array of the buddhas' pure
  lands.
Those of such great minds perform oceans of bodhisattva deeds
And quickly reach the stage of omniscience.

Those endowed with vajra eyes to see hidden things
Have wisdom that comprehends subtle domains.
Whatever words they speak reflect the truth:
My writing mixes their fine silk brocade with my ordinary cloth.

May the many beings who have connection to this work follow
  the vajra path
And, once their impure obscurations are purified in the essence
  of buddha-nature,
In magnificent ways to help themselves and others,
May they impartially bestow the gift of perfect peace.

*In the Water Tiger Year [of the fourteenth sixty-year cycle, called]
Splendid Mind [1842], the master Vajra Bearer incarnate, the powerful
lotus, [Tai Situpa] gave me an auspicious silk scarf along with a gift to
accompany his repeated requests to write an extensive guide to this area
of sacred ground; however, this never came into my hand [i.e., from the
treasures].*

*Subsequently, in the Earth Sheep Year, called Accomplishment of Goals
[1859], the face of that same guide of the three worlds, the spiritual heir to
Karmapa, again blossomed [i.e., the new Tai Situpa returned to Palpung].
During that time, the great treasure revealer, king of spiritual teachings,
Chok-gyur Déchen Lingpa, kindly provided a definitive and clear description of the inner features of this place and gave me permission to write
this text.*

*Signed: the one who lives on this mountain slope, stable in the practice
of the meditation deities, Péma Gar-gyi Wong-chuk Lodrö Tayé [Jamgon
Kongtrul].*

May virtue and well-being increase!

NOTES

[1] This reference to Karmapa as Karma*ka* is not a typing error. The *ka* perhaps indicates "the first, the original".

[2] The word "liberated" here is a tantric code word for forceful separation of consciousness from the body and its transference to a pure realm, thus liberation.

[3] For mention of dismemberment and scattering of body parts to earth as a recurring theme in Indic religions, see Janet Gyatso, "Down with the Demoness" in J. Willis (ed.), *Feminine Ground.*

[4] Authority, enjoyment, and dissolution (in Tibetan, *bdag po; longs spyod; thim*) in this sentence refer to three movements of circulatory energy within the body that correspond to past, present, and future. This is discussed in context in the second section of Part Two of the *Pilgrimage Guide*, "Correspondence Between Outer and Inner Sacred Places," and in "The Inner Journey," above in the Introduction.

[5] The meaning of the term *drink-severer* is given below, in the second section of Part Four, entitled "The Literal Meaning of Its Names."

[6] Perhaps the original list counted the two Tibetan sites as two, rather than 1 and 1/2, to give the total of one hundred thirteen.

[7] These first thirty are listed in the Appendix.

[8] These two symbolize, respectively, male and female sexual fluids.

[9] The four kinds of magnificence (*phun tshogs sde bzhi*) refers to material and worldly splendor in four domains—spiritual teaching, wealth, pleasure, and freedom.

[10] In the original Tibetan wood-block, a circle has been drawn under the words glorious (*pal*) and mound (*pung*), to indicate that Kongtrul here is referring to Palpung Monastery (literally, Mound of Glory). What is not marked but is an equally obvious play on words is the mention of the four kinds of magnificence followed by the ten virtues of a region. Although Kongtrul is describing the Palpung area, by mentioning these two qualities he suggests the entire region of Dergé, the name of which is formed from a combination of the first and third syllables of those two qualities, *dé-zhi gé-chu* (*bde bzhi dge bcu*).

[11] Once again, the words "resembling Charitra" contain the name Tsadra.

[12] Kongtrul never explicitly reveals the identity of these seven. In the Guide below, he names these disciples of Guru Rinpoché as related to the features of the land: Mandarava, Bérotsana, Yeshé Tsogyal, Namké Nyingpo, Noob-chen Sangyé Yeshé, Nyak-chen Jnana Kumara, and Sokpo Dorjé Lhapal.

[13] A talismanic turquoise (la-yu; *bla gyu*) would represent the life-force of the spirit; offering it to the lama represented total submission to the lama's command.

[14] Kongtrul is too well-mannered to mention what many of his Tibetan readers understood. Jangchub Lingpa had founded at Palpung, probably in the twelfth century, a monastery of the Drigung Kagyu, a system that did not fare well under the Sakya administration of Tibet (1235-1349). The Drigung sponsor, Kublai Khan's brother, attacked Sakya in 1285, for which Drigung was razed in 1290.

[15] Kongtrul was recognized as a reincarnation of this lama soon after his arrival at Palpung.

[16] See Huber, pp. 66-68 for this story, and p.241, n. 33 for their identity.

[17] The four modes of liberation are taught at the first level of Great Completion practice: primordial liberation, natural liberation, direct liberation, and liberation from extremes.

[18] Among bodhisattvas, Manjushri guides the gods; Avalokiteshvara, the nagas; and Vajrapani, humans.

[19] The text names the *dakini* as Déchen Gyatso. This is likely an error, as Gyatso is exclusively a man's name. I believe Kongtrul refers here to Déchen Gyalmo, a common name of Yeshé Tsogyal, who lived at Tsadra at the same time as Vimalamitra, Guru Rinpoché's teacher.

[20] Although four is written in the text, five are clearly listed here and below.

[21] Of the many numbers mentioned here, the ones I have been able to identify are the following: the *four obscurations* are of karma, negative emotions, habitual patterns, and ignorance; the *four circumstances* are those of the waking state, sleep, dream, and sexual intercourse; the *four empowerments* are vase, secret, wisdom through transcendent knowledge, and precious word; the *four paths* are cultivation, application, seeing, and meditation; the *four realizations* are of the single basis, seed syllables, blessing, and direct perception; the *five wisdoms of enlightenment* are of the absolute expanse, mirror-like, equality, discernment, and accomplishing.

[22] The six elements are the basic five—earth, air, fire, water, and space—plus that of consciousness.

Appendix

This appendix has four parts:

1. A list of the twenty-five regions of sacred ground in Kham and Amdo
2. Translations of the passage from Chokling's first treasure text that mentioned Tsadra as sacred ground and of *The Treasure-Text Guide to Tsadra*
3. Two invitations to Tsadra addressed to pilgrims by Kongtrul and Kyentsé Wongpo
4. Kongtrul's concise genealogy of the Dergé royal family

EASTERN TIBET'S TWENTY-FIVE REGIONS OF SACRED GROUND...
OR WAS THAT FORTY-TWO... OR EIGHTY-FIVE?

The Location List of the Twenty-Five Major Sacred Sites of Amdo and Kham, a treasure text revealed by Chok-gyur Déchen Lingpa in 1857, marked the first mention of eastern Tibet's regions of sacred ground. Although these sites are often referred to as "the twenty-five," closer inspection reveals thirty important places. To these, the text adds twelve others: four special places and eight sites whose enlightened activity manifests to tame beings, thus forty-two in all.

In 1867, Kongtrul wrote "a short clarification" of Chokling's original proclamation of the "twenty-five" places. Kongtrul goes through the list, identifies each place, and relates any significant spiritual history at each location. He remains uncertain of some locations, including one near his hometown. He states that in addition to the forty-two places mentioned in the original text, forty-three others were included in the network as auxiliaries to those first named. He reports that Chokling had visited and opened fourteen among the forty-two. He further claims that, apart from a formal visit by the treasure revealer, they had all been ultimately opened, presumably by virtue of their inclusion on the original treasure text's list.

Gyurmé Dorjé's *Tibet Handbook* includes a list of the basic thirty sites. (For a more detailed map of the location of each, please refer to that book, a very wise investment for anyone interested in any location in all regions of Tibet, as well as Bhutan and Nepal.) The thirty locations are each related to the body, speech, mind, attributes, or activity of enlightenment, in a fashion reminiscent of a configuration of buddhas or deities. Thus, Tsadra is related to the mind of the attributes (or qualities) of enlightenment. Gyurmé Dorjé writes,

> Pilgrimage is as important here [in Kham] as in Central Tibet. When Buddhism was established in the eighth century, Padmasambhava roamed throughout East Tibet in the company of his students, and he is reputed to have concealed his teachings as *terma* in many parts of the country. Twenty five such ancient pilgrimage sites are esteemed above all others in East and Northeast Tibet. They are considered to have special affinity with either buddha-body, speech, mind, attributes or activities.

> Buddha-body

> **Kyadrak Senge Dzong** in the Upper Yalong valley is the main site. It has five aspects, viz.

>> 1. **Chijam Nyinda Puk** in the Yalong valley (body)

>> 2. **Lotu Karma** (speech)

>> 3. **Nyen** in the Yangtze valley (mind)

>> 4. **Khala Rongo** in Nangchen (attributes)

>> 5. **Hekar Drak** (activities).

> Buddha-speech

> **Powo Gawalung** is the main site. It also have five aspects, viz.

>> 1. **Mt. Kawa Karpo** in Tsawarong (body)

2. **Pema Shelri** (speech)
3. **Nabun Dzong** in Nangchen (mind)
4. **Yegyel Namka Dzong** near Riwoche (attributes)
5. **Hor Tresho** or **Chakdu Khawa Lungring** near Kanze (activities).

Buddha-mind

Dentik Shelgi Drak in Ma-khok, Amdo, near the Huangho River is the main site. Its five aspects are:

1. **Zhara Lhatse** in Minyak (body)
2. **Warti Trak** (speech)
3. **Dorje Drak** in lower Machu (mind)
4. **Khandro Bumdzong** in lower Nangchen (attributes)
5. **Po-ne Drakar** near Riwoche (attributes).

Buddha-attributes

Rudam Gangi Rawa is the main site, ie the mountain Trori Dorje Ziltrom above Dzogchen. Its five aspects are:

1. **Ngulda Podrang** in front of Derge Lhundrupteng (body)
2. **Pema Shelphuk** in lower Mesho Dzomnang (speech)
3. **Tsandra Rinchen Drak** at Pelpung (mind)
4. **Dzongsho Deshek Dupa** in Dzing (attributes)
5. **Dzomtok Puseng Namdrak** by the Yangtze (activities). All these sites are in Derge district.

Buddha-activity

Katok Dorjeden is the main site. Its five aspects are:

1. **Ngu** (body)
2. **Tsangshi Dorje Trolo** (speech)
3. **Tashi** or **Kampo Kangra** (mind)
4. **Hyelgi Trak** (attributes)
5. **Drakri Dorje Pungpa** (activities). These sites are in and around Katok in southern Derge. (*Tibet Handbook*, pp. 377-378)

THE TREASURE TEXTS RELATING TO TSADRA

As mentioned often in the Introduction and in the *Pilgrimage Guide*, Chokgyur Déchen Lingpa revealed two treasures that identified

Tsadra as an area of sacred ground. These gave Tsadra a vital source of recognition and authenticity. Kongtrul carefully wove passages from the two treasure texts into his pilgrimage guide, but the constraints of his work forced him to quote them out of order. In this section, I have re-arranged the passages as they appear in the original texts. The first is an excerpt from *The Location List of the Twenty-Five Major Sacred Sites of Amdo and Kham*, where each site is described briefly. The second text is *The Treasure-Text Guide to Tsadra* in its entirety.

The Passage that Mentions Tsadra Within *The Location List of the Twenty-Five Major Sacred Sites of Amdo and Kham*

> To present the supreme sacred place of the heart of enlightened
>   qualities,
> It is situated at Dri, within the Amdo and Kham regions of Tibet.
> Its glorious mountain is shaped like the crest of an elephant's
>   head
> And it reflects the nature of the nine *hérukas*.
> Lotus-Born's meditation cave, which resembles a blossoming
>   lotus, is located there.
> On the side of the cliff are self-arisen forms of the peaceful and
>   wrathful deities.
> There is also the half-moon shaped supreme meditation place
> Of the heart awareness-holder, Namké Nyingpo:
> Those who wish for supreme attainment should meditate single-
>   mindedly there.
>
> In particular, the supreme sacred place
> Blessed by my crown [i.e., spiritual master], Vimalamitra, is
>   hidden to one side.
>
> A cave close to the *bhatra* tree, the place sacred to Mantra
>   Protectress,
> Is the site of the residence of myself, the master from Oddiyana.
> While I was staying there, the heart awareness-holder, Humkara,
>   arrived
> And spent three days compiling the teachings.
>
> The two masters [Vimalamitra and Humkara] left clear self-
>   arisen forms of themselves
> And impressions of their wisdom-bodies feet [in stone].
> Such marvellous special features can be found in this place!

(*The Collected Works of Chokgyur Déchen Lingpa*, vol. 60, pp. 28.5-29.6)

The Treasure-Text Guide to Tsadra

I bow to the *Héruka*.

In the sphere of enlightenment, the completely pure land,
Appears a spontaneous array
Of the great exaltation and wisdom of perfect rapture
That equals the limits of space.

Among its many miraculous appearances,
Both pure and impure emanations are possible,
However the entire infinite expanse of the cosmos
Constitutes a spontaneous pure land of the manifest body of
    enlightenment.

In this pure land, our world-system [known as] Endurance,
Many emanated buddhas have appeared.
In particular, in our realm, the region of the Land of Jambu,
The perfect Buddha, Shakyamuni,
Demonstrated twelve deeds.

The spiritual influence of his body, speech, and mind
Consecrated all the illusory features of inanimate nature —
Mountains, cliffs, and lakes—in both central lands and outlying
    areas
As enlightened body, speech, and mind.

I, Lotus-Born [Padmasambhava],
His manifestation, who took miraculous birth,
Have complete control of all appearing phenomena
And thus have lit the lamp of the spiritual instructions of Secret
    Mantra.

Moreover, I have sealed inanimate earth and rocks
With the marks of the body, speech, and mind of enlightenment
To aid all beings with the four means of liberation.

I have meditated and given my blessing
At the twenty-four sacred places, the eight cemeteries,
The sacred places of all lands, central or outlying;
And in particular here in Tibet —
At the one hundred and eight meditation sites of Ü and Tsang
    [central and western Tibet],
And the twenty-five great sacred places of Kham [eastern Tibet],

So that any connection to them will be meaningful to one's
    spiritual life.

The sublime place of enlightened mind, where signs of
    accomplishment arise quickly,
This place [called] Tsadra Rinchen Drak,
Is shaped like the channel-spokes of the wheel of great bliss.
It is called Vajra Chitta Kotri.

Its central cliff is the *Héruka*,
Surrounded by the eight Gauri goddesses.

In the center stands the *bhatra* tree;
In the east is the Jonpa tree; in the south, the Sal;
In the west, the Hook; in the north, the Fruit-Bearing.
These changeless trees are planted like spikes.

This place has one hundred and eight representations of the
    Buddha's body, speech, and mind;
Four rivers resound naturally with the sounds of mantras;
Conch-Shell Circuit [Kala Doung] Lake holds consecrated
    washing water;
The skulls of the three forms of enlightenment serve as
    containers for vajra feasts;
Clouds of offerings that please the five senses emerge,
Great blissful Vajrasattva.
This is the immortal place of the Buddha Eternal Life.

Humkara and Vimalamitra
And all accomplished masters
Blessed this place with their form of pure timeless wisdom.

In this delightful land of caves and sheltering cliffs,
The three awareness-holders made their meditation sites.

Amazing qualities abound,
Such as consecrated washing water, water of longevity,
    vermilion, and medicinal water.
This supreme place for attainment is indeed delightful!

In the future in these sublime sacred places,
Many accomplished persons will gather;
A temple and a stupa will be constructed there.

When this guide appears on the earth,
The body, speech, and mind of the *Héruka*
Will arrive here from Highest Pure Land.

Especially, in the Sheep Year, during the Monkey Month,
The assembly of awareness-holders, meditation deities, and
     dakinis
Gathers from the ten directions and appears in this place.

At all times, ordinary or special,
One is protected from the *dukka* [suffering] of miserable
     existences
By just reaching this sacred place
With stable faith and devotion.

By making offerings of outer, inner, and secret vajra feasts,
One completes a great cultivation of merit and wisdom.
Whoever makes prostrations and circumambulations here
Purifies all negative acts and obscurations.

One session of meditation here is more profound
Than a year of meditation done elsewhere.
Whoever meditates single-mindedly
Will attain ordinary and supreme accomplishment by the
     blessing of this place.

Whoever makes offerings at this sacred place
Will experience the full increase of longevity and merit.

This sacred ground,
Praised by all the joyful ones of the three times,
Is the sacred ground of the radiant heart of enlightenment.
Therefore, its earth, stones, rocks, and cliffs
All resemble rainbow light and circles.

Spiritual heroes and *dakinis* gather here;
Guardians of the doctrine and their messengers perform activity
     quickly.
This sacred place separates good from evil.

This sacred site is not a place
For those without commitments, who behave badly.
Fortunate persons who keep their tantric commitments,

Practitioners who conduct themselves appropriately,
Will attain accomplishment according to their connection:
Have no doubt about this!

This precious catalogue was concealed as a treasure
With profound instructions
And supreme relics of all transcendent ones,
Means to aid the world —
The excellent physical remains [of the buddhas],
Concentrated as sacred substances in precious pills.
May these [treasures] reach someone who has a connection to
    them!

Samaya gya gya! [Commitment seal, seal]

*On the tenth day of the Monkey Month of the Sheep Year, the emanation
of enlightenment, the great treasure revealer, Orgyen Chok-gyur Déchen
Lingpa retrieved consecrated precious pills, together with this yellow
parchment, from the heart of the secret cave of Guru [Rinpoché], on the
right side of the central cliff, a self-arisen image of the Glorious One, the
sublime sacred place, Tsadra Rinchen Drak. In the hermitage of Kunzang
Déchen Ösel Ling, I, Péma Garwong Lodrö Tayé, transcribed the definitive version of this text from the miraculous letters that were written on
the parchment one half hand-span long and four finger-widths wide.*

May virtue and well-being increase!

TWO INVITATIONS TO TSADRA ADDRESSED TO PILGRIMS

In the section above entitled "An Invitation and a Supplication," I
mentioned that Kongtrul wrote or co-authored three letters of invitation to pilgrims to visit Tsadra on the years commemorating
the sacred ground's inauguration. Tsadra's "birthday" celebration
took place every twelve years; thus, the three letters were written
in Sheep Years 1871, 1883, and 1895. The above-referenced section
contained the text of the second invitation; the first and third appear here. Kyentsé and Kongtrul co-authored the first two invitations (Chokling died in 1870), and Kongtrul wrote the last alone
since his master and friend, Kyentsé, had passed away in 1892.

Each of these three documents presents Tsadra slightly differently, yet we see in all of them the basic concepts of pilgrimage and
sacred ground that these masters wished to present to pilgrims.

Sheep Years continue to be important to Tsadra: my first visit to Tsadra in 1991 was in a Sheep Year. The two most important spiritual leaders of Palpung Monastery and Tsadra Retreat Center, Tai Situpa and Jamgon Kongtrul (the Third), visited that year and attracted large crowds of the faithful.

The First Notice of Gathering at the Sacred Place [1871]

With complete respect in thought, word, and deed, I take refuge in and bow at the pure lotus feet of the illustrious knowers of the three times, the king of spiritual instructions from Oddiyana and his consort [Guru Rinpoché and Yeshé Tsogyal]!

The second buddha, Padmakara's [Lotus-Born Master's] three mysteries of enlightenment [i.e., his body, speech, and mind], his qualities, and his enlightened activity consecrated an inconceivable number of adamantine sacred places. Those that are well-known include the especially holy twenty-one meditation places of Ü and Tsang and the twenty-five sacred areas of Kham, all primordially renowned locations. Among the twenty-five sacred areas of Kham, this supreme sacred place represents the heart of enlightened qualities.

[Concerning its history,] to begin with, in the Fire Dragon Year of the fourteenth cycle [1856], the full ritual of the practice and empowerment of *The Spiritual Master's Quintessential Vision* was performed in Palpung Monastery's Hall of Pure Fragrance, which contains the shrine of new statues, Gloriously Flaming Blessing. On that occasion, I heard in a vision the *dakinis'* secret instruction, "This sacred place is a third Dévikotri!" Later that same year, as the beginning of the new Fire Snake Year [1857] approached, Terchen Chok-gyur Déchen Lingpa retrieved before a crowd of people the treasure text *The Location List of the Twenty-Five Major Sacred Sites of Amdo and Kham* from Powerful Hero Cliff. On the thirteenth day of the waxing moon of the first lunar month, he introduced us to the features of the essence of the great sacred area along the paths of circumambulation around Tsadra Rinchen Drak.

On the tenth day of the fifth lunar month of the Sheep Year [1859], at the time the victorious one and his spiritual heir [Karmapa and Tai Situpa] of the Kagyu Lineage appeared, Terchen Rinpoché retrieved profound treasures of outstanding spiritual instructions and consecrated objects from Tsadra Rinchen Drak. On the same occasion, he unveiled this sacred area and gave a detailed and definitive description of its features. This proclamation of its magnificent qualities marked the beginning of this area's enlightened activity. Therefore, the effects of virtuous acts performed here—meditation practice, vajra feast or other offerings, prostrations, circumambulations—whenever they are done—are multiplied one hundred thousand times. This is stated firmly in texts of the adamantine speech [of Guru Rinpoché].

Now especially, from the first day of the sixth month of the Iron Sheep Year [1871] until the new moon, the palace and the deities of the circle of wisdom from the supreme sacred place of Charitra will actually come here. During this period the effect of one circumambulation around the outer extremity of this area will certainly equal that of seven hundred million recitations of the six-syllable mantra or the *Vajra Guru* mantra; similarly, three such circumambulations equal that of a circumambulation of the whole area of Charitra; one circumambulation of the intermediate path of the *Héruka* equals the merit of three hundred million recitations of [the *Héruka's*] heart mantra; and seven circumambulations on the summit path equal the benefits of three hundred million recitations of mantras.

Your physical, verbal, and mental behavior along these routes should not be mixed with non-virtuous acts: be whole-hearted in your faith, respect, and devotion and make offerings of incense, vajra feasts, *torma*, and other offerings as you walk. If you exert yourself in creating as positive a connection as possible through prostrations, circumambulation, etc., your life as a human being will become meaningful. The effect of each vajra feast offering you make will definitely be multiplied one hundred thousand times.

In particular, in the retreat center, Kunzang Déchen Ösel Ling, resides a statue of the noble lady, holy Tara. This statue, called The Speaking Image of Tara, is indivisible from Tara's wisdom form. If you regard Tara with great faith and respect and recite *The Twenty-One Praises of Tara* and her heart mantra while doing prostrations and circumambulation [of the retreat center], all your immediate troubles and difficulties will be pacified and your longevity, merit, and wisdom will increase. Further, her influence will pacify the threat of terrible border conflicts. Ultimately, your prayers create an auspicious connection for holy Tara's continual nurturing of your spiritual life.

At the summit of the sacred ground there dwells a profound concealed treasure of an image of the holy Lord of the World, Great Compassion [i.e., the bodhisattva commonly known as Avalokiteshvara in Sanskrit, Chenrézi in Tibetan].[1] This image was originally used by the *dakini* Lékyi Wongmo and Master Nagarjuna as their meditation support and then given to Guru Rinpoché. It is like a wisdom form and a sacred support of the Buddha's doctrine. Therefore, if you recite the heart mantra of this bodhisattva, the six-syllable mantra, while exerting yourself at prostrations, making offerings, and circumambulations, the negative effects of the five acts of immediate fruition will be purified and the connection made through your practice will lead you to rebirth in the pure land, Blissful. Further, your longevity, merit, social standing, wealth, and wisdom will all increase. Since this is clearly stated in the texts of Guru Rinpoché's adamantine words, be single-minded in your faith and devotion. If you apply yourself diligently in thought, word, and deed to such acts as prostrations, circumambulation, offerings, and recitation of *The Prayer of Excellent Conduct*,[2] all circumstances will be virtuous during this and later lives and you will be certain to accomplish every goal. We ask that everyone keep these things in mind.

This letter to encourage virtuous practice has been written in the small meditation room in Dzongsar Tashi Lhatsé on the thirteenth day of the waxing moon of the fourth month of the Iron Sheep Year of the fifteenth cycle [1871] by both Jamyang Kyentsé Wongpo, Péma Ösel Do-ngak Lingpa; and [Jamgon Kongtrul] Chimé Ten-nyi Yung-drung Lingpa. May the radiance of virtue and well-being always pervade every time and direction!

Sarva Daka Laya Nam Mangalam Bhavantu

The Third Notice of Gathering at the Sacred Place [1895]

> To the sole refuge of all in the Himalayan region,
> The second buddha, Lotus-Born Master,
> And to his consort of the absolute expanse, Queen of Great Bliss,
> I bow and pray, and ask for your blessing.

This world, the Land of Jambu, where the primordial twenty-four major sacred places and thirty-two supreme regions were consecrated by the glorious *Héruka*, includes the land of Tibet, which has only one sacred place where the configuration of the deities of the honored one, Wheel of Supreme Bliss, actually reside: glorious Charitra. That site is replicated in Dévikotri, Tsadra Rinchen Drak, as foretold by Lord Marpa the Translator [to Milarepa]:

> To the east, lies a great sacred place related to both Dévikotri and
> Tsari [but the time to open it has not come]. In the future someone
> who preserves your children's spiritual lineage will appear there.

Accordingly, Palden Jangchub Lingpa, heart-son of Kyob-pa Jikten Soumgon, founded a temple here that flourished. Later, the omniscient Situ Chökyi Jungné made this his principal residence and founded what is now well-known as Palpung Monastery.

Among the twenty-five great sacred places of Amdo and Kham, this place definitely represents the sacred ground of the heart of enlightened qualities. In the past, this has been concealed; now its time to aid the world has arrived. First, the all-knowing spiritual master Péma Ösel Do-ngak Lingpa received a prediction of this from the wisdom *dakinis*. Then, in response to my earlier and later requests, the manifestation of enlightenment, the great treasure revealer, Chok-gyur Déchen Lingpa, retrieved from their concealment places the treasure text of *The Location List of the Twenty-Five Major Sacred Sites of Amdo and Kham* and *The Treasure-Text Guide to Tsadra*. Further, the noble precious master Jamyang Kyentsé Wongpo retrieved the treasure text of *The Additional Proclamation*. Following the instructions of these texts, this sacred place was inaugurated.

Now at any time, the effect of any virtuous practice done here, such as prostrations or circumambulations, is multiplied one hundred thousand times, since the configuration of the wisdom deities dwells in this place. Moreover, the special time [for pilgrimage] is specifically mentioned in *The Treasure-Text Guide to Tsadra*:

> Especially in the Year of the Sheep, during the Monkey Month,
> The assembly of awareness-holders, meditation deities, and
> *dakinis*
> Gathers from the ten directions and appears in this place.

As stated, during the fifth, sixth, and seventh lunar months (based on the three methods to calculate the Monkey Month) of this Wood Sheep Year, the infinite gathering of the Three Sources from all great sacred places in general and from the configuration of glorious Charitra in particular will actually appear here and the spiritual heroes and heroines of these configurations will participate in tantric gatherings. Therefore at this time, one circumambulation of the extremity will multiply any positive act, such as recitation of the six-syllable or the *Vajra Guru* mantras, seven hundred million times. One intermediate circumambulation multiplies the effects of good acts three hundred million times, as does seven circumambulations of the summit. Three circumambulations of the extremity definitely equal the effect of one circumambulation of the great region of Charitra.

Further, the treasure text states:

> In the future in these supreme sacred places,
> Many accomplished persons will gather;
> A temple and a stupa will be constructed there.

This foretells the founding of the structure and contents of Palpung Toub-ten Chökor Ling, which contains many unique sacred supports of the Buddha's body, speech, and mind. In addition, *The Treasure-Text Guide to Tsadra* states:

> When this guide appears on the earth,
> The body, speech, and mind of the *Héruka*
> Will arrive here from Highest Pure Land.

This foretells the retreat center, Kunzang Déchen Ösel Ling, which contains outstanding sacred supports, unmatched anywhere, of the body, speech, and mind of the *Héruka*. The retreat center also houses such images as The Speaking Image of Tara, inseparable from Tara herself. On the right of the area, there is an auspicious knot of eternity, and on the left, the imprint of Guru Rinpoché's body in stone. These are the principal ones among an infinite number of self-arisen marks of enlightened influence and Buddhist signs that aid one through any connection to them. The benefits of making a positive connection to them are described in the treasure text:

> At all times, ordinary or special,
> One is protected from the *dukka* [suffering] of miserable
>   existences
> By just reaching this sacred place
> With stable faith and devotion.

> By making offerings of outer, inner, and secret vajra feasts,
> One completes the great cultivation of merit and wisdom.
> Whoever makes prostrations and circumambulations here
> Purifies all his negative acts and obscurations.
> One period of meditation here is more profound
> Than a year of meditation done elsewhere.
> Whoever meditates single-mindedly
> Will attain ordinary and supreme accomplishment by the
>   blessing of this place.
> Whoever makes offerings at this sacred place
> Will experience the full increase of longevity and merit.

The knot of eternity is specifically mentioned in *The Additional Declaration*:

> The obscurations of acts of immediate result are purified by
>   seeing it:
> Imagine the benefits of making a positive connection to it!
> Just one offering of a vajra feast and torma
> Pacifies one's obscurations and impediments, and increases one's
>   merit.
> If one offers outer, inner, and secret gifts
> To please all *dakinis*
> On the meadow of the *dakinis* at the base of this sacred place,
> One will become free from movement of the body's inner
>   channels, circulatory energy, and vital essence.

The imprint of Guru Rinpoché's body is also mentioned:

> By seeing, touching, or recalling this
> With faith and supreme commitment,
> One will attain in seven lifetimes
> Irreversible vajra wisdom.
> Just imagine the benefits of honoring it with faith!

As explained in detail in *The Location List of the Twenty-Five Major Sacred Sites of Amdo and Kham*, considerable benefits are accrued by prostrations, circumambulation, offerings, mandala offerings, vajra feasts, prayer flags, etc. at this place and time. Similarly, this text warns against unvirtuous acts, such as cutting the grass or trees, displacing the rocks, killing animals on this mountain, swearing or shouting loudly. To have done these things will break your connection with the Buddha's doctrine during this life. Further, the effects of negative acts done here are multiplied, just as are the effects of positive acts. The enhanced force of such negative acts will cause rebirth in the hell realms. Of this, you should have no doubt! Therefore, wise persons should believe and attentively follow the sound advice given in the adamantine speech of the second buddha, the master from Oddiyana. You should strive intently, without indifference, to create a positive connection with the special features of this sacred place. In this and future lives, this will cause the glorious qualities of virtue and well-being to swell like the rising moon.

This letter to encourage virtuous practice has been written by Chimé Ten-nyi Yung-drung Lingpa [Jamgon Kongtrul], motivated by the noble intention to help others. May it prove meaningful! May virtue and well-being increase!

KONGTRUL'S CONCISE GENEALOGY OF THE DERGÉ ROYAL FAMILY

Kongtrul included the following concise genealogy of Dergé's ruling family in a catalogue he wrote for a temple built under the patronage of the Dergé queen mother. Dergé and its royal family's history have interest for us in that it stood at the heart of Kham and acted as a magnet for the spiritually high and the politically mighty of eastern Tibet. Kongtrul, Kyentsé, and Chokling were all regular visitors to Dergé and all were welcomed and sponsored by the ruling family.

The memory of Dergé's royal family continues to have importance for the natives of Kham: two modern Tibetan editions of *A Genealogy of the Kings of Dergé* have been printed in China in recent years (1985 and 1989). Tséwong Dorjé Rikzin, one of the kings of the line, wrote the book in 1828. (The queen for whom Kongtrul wrote the temple catalogue was Tséwong Dorjé Rikzin's daughter-in-law.)

In his introduction to a Western edition (in 1968) of the same Tibetan work, Josef Kolmas gives the most detailed view of Dergé to appear in English. He counts the rulers starting from the family member who had been a disciple of Guru Rinpoché and had immigrated from central to eastern Tibet. From that ancestor, Kolmas counts forty-four generations until the author of the genealogy.[3] In the case of the following concise story, after Kongtrul identifies the

family's origins, he begins his account with the twenty-third generation (according to Kolmas's schema), and he seems to consider
the true line of Dergé kings as having begun with the king of the
thirty-first generation, who invited Tang-Tong Gyalpo to Dergé to
found its main monastery, Lhundrup Teng. By all accounts, Dergé's
religious, cultural, and political powers reached their zenith during the reign of Tenpa Tsering, (the fortieth of the line according to
Kolmas, 1678-1738). This was an improbable time for the kingdom
to flourish: the Fifth Dalai Lama (1617-1682) had recently united
Tibet under his power and many parts of Tibet hosted scenes of
unseemly settling of scores and brutal battles for power into the
early eighteenth century. It was not an auspicious time to be a semi-
independent king of non-Gelug persuasion (the kings of Dergé were
Sakya). Kolmas explains the Dergé kings' survival:

> The lamas of Amdo and Kham chose Kalzang Gyatso (1708-1757),
> a native of Li-thang in Eastern Tibet, as the Seventh Dalai Lama.
> Kalzang Gyatso had to be hidden for some time lest Lha-zang
> Khan's [Mongol ruler of central Tibet, who had installed a differ-
> ent child, Yeshé Gyatso, as the Seventh Dalai Lama] emissaries,
> searching everywhere for the child, should find him out; during
> this time, the young Dalai Lama who, with his family had to leave
> Li-thang and move to Amdo, was granted a temporary asylum in
> Derge by Sonam Puntsok [Tenpa Tsering's father]. When, after the
> fall of Lhazang Khan and his puppet Dalai Lama in 1717, the le-
> gitimate Dalai Lama again took office in Lhasa, he repayed Derge
> monastery generously for the help it had given him. (p. 36)

This relative peace allowed Tenpa Tsering to pursue other projects
besides war, defense, and politics: he sponsored the construction
of the Dergé Printing Press in 1729, the publishing of the Buddhist
Canon (Tib.: *Kangyur*) in 1733, and the Collection of Indian Buddhist Treatises (Tib.: *Tengyur*), completed in 1743, after his death.
The editor-in-chief of the Dergé edition of the Canon was the Eighth
Tai Situpa, Chökyi Jungné, who had recently founded a monastery
at Palpung, in 1727. It is this same edition of the collections of the
Canon and Treatises that was reprinted in New Delhi in the 1980s
through the wishes of the Sixteenth Karmapa. Those books have
now traveled throughout the world and are venerated wherever
they dwell, King Tenpa Tsering's enduring gift to us all.

A mere hundred years and five generations of Dergé monarchs separated that great king from Kongtrul's time. The reader will note that Kongtrul assiduously avoids any mention of politics when writing of that period, although he would have known of the events in detail from both written and oral accounts.

The line of kings ended soon after Kongtrul's time. He mentions in glowing terms the young princes he knew and admired. It seems that the next generation, the forty-sixth, was the last. Kolmas relates:

> [Dergé's] ruling family exercised both temporal and religious control over about 78,000 square kilometers on both sides of the Chin-sha River, constituting a "kingdom," the largest and most influential of its kind in Kham. In 1909 the so-called kingdom of Derge came to came to an end when the Chinese intervened to terminate a fratricidal war which had been raging in Derge for some fifteen years: they deposed the "King" Dorjé Sengé (1877-1926) and exiled him to Chengdu, while the other claimant, Jampa Rinchen, fled to Lhasa. The area was then divided into five administrative units under Chinese magistrates. (*Ibid.*, p. 22)

Two notes on this passage: First, to get an idea of the extent of Dergé's approximately 78,000 square kilometers, we can compare them to the 77,166 square kms. of Scotland or the 79,940 square kms. of the American state of Maine. Second, I question the pretext for the Chinese intervention. Not only would Dorjé Sengé have been but seventeen years old at the outset of what Kolmas refers to as the "raging fratricidal war," the Chinese warlord responsible for the Chinese intervention was none other than the notorious Zhao Erfeng. It was he, future Imperial Commissioner in Tibet (this was still the Manchurian Ching Dynasty), and his brother, future Viceroy in Sichuan, who were charged by the Empress to assimilate Tibet back into China following the English invasion and occupation of Lhasa in 1904. They decided to begin with the eastern Tibetan regions, Amdo and Kham, which were named as the Chinese provinces Chinghai and Xikang. In 1905, Zhao Erfeng invaded Kham. Heather Stoddard, in her wonderful biography of Gendun Chöpel, *Le Mendiant de l'Amdo*, writes of Zhao's ends and means:

For the Dalai Lama and the Tibetans, what distinguished Zhao
Erfeng was his declared intention to destroy Tibetan Buddhism.
An old-school Chinese mandarin, who had received a modern
military training, he was resolutely anti-religious. His troops razed
monasteries, massacred monks, and beheaded Tibetan officials in
their path to replace them with Chinese. His plan aimed first to
colonize Kham with the impoverished peasants of Sichuan. This
represented a radical transformation in Manchu policies, which
had exercised authority over Tibet and Mongolia essentially
through the Lamaist Church. (p. 51, translated from the French)

It is clear that the Chinese intervened in Dergé, but their mo-
tives probably had little to do with settling a feud in the ruling
family. Zhao met his own end two years after he ended the rule of
the Dergé kings. He was executed in Chengdu by anti-dynasty,
pro-Republic troops in 1911, the year the Manchu Dynasty ended.
Unfortunately, Zhao's radical new policy toward Kham, Amdo, and
Tibet outlived him.

The Translation

The following account describes the family lineage of the worldly
victors, leaders of mankind, the great religious kings of Dergé. In
this province called Do-Kham or greater Tibet, there are four great
clans—Ga, Dru, Dra, and Dong—and a fifth, called Go-lha-dé
Karpo. This family belongs to this last one, the Go-lha-dé Karpo
clan. Of the eighteen groups of Ngu-chen Gyalmo, they are de-
scendents of the Gar family.

Among this family's members, the great Gar Yeshé Zangpo was
given dominion over the lower six Do [corners]. His younger brother,
Damchö Dingpa, a disciple of Drigung Jikten Soumgon, attained
great accomplishment [in meditation]. Yeshé Zangpo's son, Sonam
Rinchen, served as private secretary to the guide of beings, Chögyal Pakpa [1235-1280], and was given an edict by the Mongolian
king [Hopula Khan/Hubi Li 1215-1294]. The high lama's secretary gave [Sonam Rinchen's] nephew Nguguru's son, Dawa
Zangpo, the position of lord over one thousand men at Samar.
His son was Ngu Gyalwa Zangpo; his son, Péma Ten-soung; and
his son, Kar-chen Jangchub Boum. His son, Ngu Chökyi Dorjé,

held the long tradition of Katok and became a highly accomplished meditator.

His brother, Déchen Sonam Zangpo, on the prophetic advice of [the Seventh] Karmapa Chödrak Gyatso [1454-1506] and Ngu Chökyi Dorjé, followed the Dri River upstream and arrived before the chief of Ling. He received the name of Dergé.[4] Of his four sons, Bo-tar (also known as Tashi Sengé) invited Tang-Tong Gyalpo to the area. This marked the inauguration of the family's royal power and the founding of Lhundrup Teng Monastery.

Tashi Sengé had two sons, Lama Palden Sengé and Gyaltsen Boum. The latter's son, A-nga, had seven sons, of whom Namka Dorjé assumed the throne. His son, Lhundrup, had six sons: The eldest, the accomplished master Kunga Gyatso, was foretold in religious texts as the holder of the great treasure revealer Jatson Nyingpo's instructions. The second was Ön Lupel. The third, Lama Jampa Puntsok, was a lord of great merit and power. The fifth, Lama Lha-soong, and the sixth, Lama Karma Samdrup, exerted themselves in meditation and religious affairs. Karma Samdrup upheld the Karma Kamtsang lineage of philosophy.

Many treasure texts foretold that Ön Lupel's grandson, Trichen Sangyé Tenpa (Önchen Kunga Puntsok's son), would be a reincarnation of Chokro Lu'i Gyaltsen [a disciple of Guru Rinpoché]. After Ön Lupel's reign, his nephew, Lama Sonam Puntsok (son of Ön Lupel's older brother, Orgyen Tashi), assumed the throne. His brother, Wong-chen Gonpo, had a son, the religious king Tenpa Tsering [1678-1738], whose life's work has left an incomparable impression on this kingdom. Even today it is nectar for the eyes and ears. Wise masters of all traditions scattered praises on him like flowers:

> The kings of the past who are famous
> Attained mirror-like speech.
> Even though they have not remained close-by,
> Look: they remain unchanged!

For example, this [ancient praise by an Indian poet] describes him as he is.

Tenpa Tsering had three sons, of whom Sonam Gonpo stayed in the family home and Lama Puntsok Tenpa assumed the throne. He followed the advice of the testament of his father, the religious king, and had a great influence on Buddhism, including sponsorship of the printing of *The Collection of the Precious Indian Buddhist Commentaries*. He was followed by Sa-kyong Lodru Gyaltsen; he by his son Sa-kyong Sawong Zangpo; and he by his son Tséwong Dorjé Rikzin. He increased the enlightened activity of Buddhism and the kingdom through such feats as employing the Buddhist protectors as his servants. His three sons—Sawong Damtsik Dorjé, a lama-son, and the youngest son—all displayed extraordinary lives like those of bodhisattvas who rule as Buddhist kings.

Damtsik Dorjé and the person who initiated this excellent work [the temple for which this catalogue was written], the queen Sa'i Wongmo, had two sons. The first, Palden Chimé Tak-pé Dorjé, has assumed the golden throne and now protects Buddhism and the kingdom. His life has been predicted in the adamantine words of the precious master from Oddiyana [Guru Rinpoché] in treasure texts retrieved by the undisputable and great treasure revealer of our time, Chokgyur Déchen Lingpa: he is said to be an emanation of Prince Mutik Tsépo, Séna Lek-jin-yon. He has become the chief holder of a number of treasure teachings, *The Heart Practice to Dispel All Obstacles* principal among them. Further, the spokesman for Lotus-Born Master, the fearless great master Péma Ösel Do-ngak Lingpa, otherwise known as Jamyang Kyentsé Wongpo, has praised him and empowered him to be the chief inheritor of his teachings, [a choice] in accord with written [predictions]. If we look back over his life, since his infancy he has shown respect toward those who are worthy of veneration, spiritual masters and the Three Jewels. He has never evinced pride in his family or position, but applied himself diligently to his education in general and specifically to Buddhist study, reflection, and meditation. He has given full protection to the weak out of his love and compassion. He has shown impartial veneration and has rendered great service to the precious doctrine of the Buddha, including his own tradition. His thought is very profound, so it is difficult to plumb the depths of his mind. He is consistently honest: he deals with everyone fairly, regardless of their proximity to his family. In brief, his holy qualities are not hidden, but are conspicuously apparent to all.

His younger brother, who is a lama, has an extensive knowledge of all aspects of study and has read, studied and reflected upon the second Buddha's historical tradition, that of Ngor Évam Chöden. He devotes his life to the cycle of meditation of a renunciant. His peaceful, restrained, compassionate, and loving nature make him worthy of praise as a holy person who upholds the Buddhist tradition.

In conclusion, each member of this line of sovereigns of enlightened activity and legacy has acted as patron to the entire doctrine of the Buddha through wide-ranging sponsorship of Buddhism and protection of the many persons in their domain according to royal laws in harmony with tradition. Among Dergé's rulers, those dating from the religious king Tenpa Tsering have been conferred sovereignty over the land by the god of heaven, the great emperor [of China]. The emperor further bestowed edicts granting them the rank "Tu-zhu Dergé Xuan-wei-shi,"[5] a title that has become manifestly renowned from the great ocean in the east [i.e., the Chinese Pacific Coast] to the fields where nutmeg grows in the west [i.e., India]. (*Dergé Temple Catalogue*, pp. 330-335)

Names Mentioned in Kongtrul's Account with Generation Numbers from J. Kolmas

23. Gar Yeshé Zangpo
    Damchö Dingpa
[24. Palgyi Gyaltsen]
25. Sonam Rinchen
    his nephew, Nguguru
26. Dawa Zangpo
27. Ngu Gyalwa Zangpo
28. Péma Ten-soung
29. Kar-chen Jangchub Boum
30. Ngu Chökyi Dorjé
    his brother, Déchen Sonam Zangpo
31. Bo-tar or Tashi Sengé
32. Gyaltsen Boum
    Lama Palden Sengé

33. A-nga (son of Gyaltsen Boum)

[34. Ya-gyal Pel]

35. Namka Dorjé

36. Lhundrup (six sons)

37. Kunga Gyatso
    Ön Lupel
    Lama Jampa Puntsok
    Lama Lha-soong
    Lama Karma Samdrup

38. Önchen Kunga Puntsok
    Trichen Sangyé Tenpa
    (Orgyen Tashi, older brother of Sangyé Tenpa, did not reign)

39. Lama Sonam Puntsok
    (Wong-chen Gonpo, brother of Sonam Puntsok, did not reign)

40. Tenpa Tsering (three sons)

41. Lama Puntsok Tenpa
    Sa-kyong Lodru Gyaltsen

42. Sa-kyong Sawong Zangpo

43. Tséwong Dorjé Rikzin

44. Sawong Damtsik Dorjé, married Sa'i Wongmo

45. Palden Chimé Tak-pé Dorjé

NOTES

[1] It is a mystery to me why the authors state that this statue dwells "at the summit," unless they use this as an unusual allusion to the retreat center, for it is there that both statues mentioned—Tara and Great Compassion—still reside. Their survival is thanks to Omdzé Zopa, who concealed them during the dark days of the Cultural Revolution.

[2] This prayer ends *The Flower Ornament Scripture* (translated by Thomas Cleary, pp. 1511-1518). Pilgrims would be hard-pressed to find a monastery or retreat center in the Himalayas where Tara's *Praises* or this prayer are not recited on a daily basis.

[3] Modern Tibetan scholars in China differ only slightly: according to *The Great Tibetan-Chinese Dictionary*, Tenpa Tsering was the forty-second generation of the Dergé royal line (p. 1472, entry for Dergé Printing Press); J. Kolmas, *A Genealogy of the Kings of Dergé, passim.* By such calculation, the author of the genealogy would be the forty-fifth in the line.

[4] The longer version has family members receiving this name from other dignitaries over the centuries, Chögyal Pakpa first among them.

[5] This was hardly the honor Kongtrul seems to suggest. Kolmas reports that the title, literally "Local Chief of Dergé; Commissioner for the Propagation of Pacification" (Kolmas has "Commissioner of Tranquillisation"), was one of five ranks, and not the highest, given by the Manchu court to local officials in the hinterlands. King Tenpa Tsering received it in 1733 and it remained in usage until 1909 (Kolmas, pp. 38-39 and p. 70, n. 51).

Persons Mentioned by Jamgon Kongtrul

Jamgon Kongtrul mentions many persons in his writing and it is difficult for even those of us who read Tibetan to keep track of them and to recall their historical period. The following list contains the persons Kongtrul refers to in this book, a transliteration of their name in Tibetan if their name is from that language, a translation of Buddhist names (not place or clan names), and an indication of their historical period, if I have been able to find that information.

Bengar Kunkyen (*ban gar kun mkhyan;* Omniscient One of Bengar) wrote a praise of the Seventh Karmapa, Chödrak Gyatso.

Bérotsana, (eighth century) one of the principal disciples of Guru Rinpoché, meditated at Tsadra. He is considered to be one of Kongtrul's previous incarnations.

Chimé Ten-nyi Yung-droung Lingpa (*'chi med bstan gnyis gyung drung gling pa;* Deathless Swastika of the Two Doctrines) was the name Jamgon Kongtrul received for his activity as a treasure revealer.

Chökyi Wongchuk (*chos kyi dbang phyug;* Master of Spiritual Instruction) (1212-1270), usually called Guru Chöwong, was one of the early great treasure revealers.

Chödrak Gyatso (*chos grag rgya mtsho;* Ocean of Renown in Spiritual Instruction) (1454-1506) was the Seventh Karmapa.

(Orgyen) Chok-gyur Déchen Lingpa (*o rgyan mchog gyur bde chen gling pa;* Oddiyana, Supreme Great Bliss Island) (1829-1870). This great treasure revealer master, Kongtrul's disciple and friend, unveiled Tsadra.

Chökyi Jungné (*chos kyi 'byung gnas;* Source of Spiritual Instruction) (1700-1774) was the Eighth, and by all accounts, greatest Tai Situpa. He founded the modern Palpung Monastery.

Dabzang Rinpoché (*lza bzang*; Excellent Moon) refers to a series of reincarnate masters, one of whom was Jamgon Kongtrul's spiritual master.

Da'o Zhonnu (*lza 'od gzhon nu*; Moonlight, Youth) is a common name of Gampopa.

Déchen Sonam Zangpo (*bde chen bsod nams bzang po*; Great Bliss, Excellent Merit) (fifteenth century) was the first king of Dergé.

Déchen Gyalmo (*bde chen rgyal mo*; Queen of Bliss) is a common name of Yeshé Tsogyal, who meditated at Tsadra.

Dharmakara is the Sanskrit translation of the name of the Eighth Tai Situpa, Chökyi Jungné.

Dorjé Zi-ji Tsal (*rdo rje gzi brjid rtsal*; Adept of Adamantine Brilliance) is a name of Jamyang Kyentsé Wongpo.

Drakpa Gyaltsen (of Nangchen) (*grags pa rgyal mtshan*; Victory Banner of Renown) (dates unavailable) is mentioned as one of Jamgon Kongtrul's illustrious ancestors.

Drigung Jikten Gonpo: see **Jikten Soumgon**

Drimé Özer (*dri med 'od zer*; Pure Light) was a name of Longchenpa.

Dudul Dorjé (*bdud 'dul rdo rje*; Demon-Conquering Vajra) (1733-1797) was the Thirteenth Karmapa. His divination led to the construction of a retreat center above Palpung Monastery

Durjaya-chandra, an Indian tantric adept, is mentioned for his style of presentation of the phases of creation and completion. Dates unavailable.

Dusum Kyenpa (*dus gsum khyen pa*; Knower of the Three Times), the First Karmapa (1110-1193), stayed in Tsadra for three days on his way to central Tibet.

Ga the Translator. Dates and information unavailable. A meditation cave at Tsadra is said to be his.

Gampopa (*sgam po pa*) (1079-1153) was the foremost disciple of Milarepa and the master of the First Karmapa.

Gar was the principal minister of Tibetan king Song-tsen Gampo (seventh century) and the distant ancestor of the Dergé royal family.

Gar Dampa (*gar dam pa*; Holy One of the Gar clan) (thirteenth century) was one of the three tantric adepts instrumental in inaugurating Tsari.

Guru Rinpoché (eighth century) is the Indian master responsible for the implantation of tantric Buddhism throughout the Himalayan region; his presence continues to permeate spiritual life there.

Gyalwa Lorépa (*rgyal ba lo ras pa*; Victor, Cotton-Clad Yogi) (1185-1250) was a great meditator of the Drukpa Kagyu tradition. His vision led to one inauguration of Tsari.

Humkara (eighth century), an Indian meditation master, was one of the main contributors to what became known in Tibet as the Ancient (Nyingma) Instruction Lineage. He visited Tsadra with Guru Rinpoché.

Jamyang Kyentsé Wongpo (*'jam dbyangs mkhyen brtse dbang po*; Gentle Melody, Power of Wisdom and Love) (1820-1892), like his disciple and friend, Jamgon Kongtrul, was one of the foremost meditation masters and writers of nineteenth-century Tibet.

Jangchub Lingpa (*byang chub gling pa*; Island of Awakening) (late twelfth-early thirteenth centuries), a Drigung Kagyu master, was the orginal founder of a monastery at the site of Palpung.

Jatson Nyingpo (*'ja' mtshon snying po*; Heart of the Rainbow)(1585-1656) was a great treasure revealer. Jamgon Kongtrul quotes from one of his treasures in his *Pilgrimage Guide to Tsadra*.

Jikten Soumgon (*'jig rten gsum mgon*; Protector of the Three Worlds) (1143-1217) founded the Drigung Kagyu monastic system. He sent Jangchub Lingpa to found a monastery at the site of present-day Palpung.

Kachö Wongpo (*mkha' spyod dbang po*; Powerful One of the Celestial Realms)(Second Zhamarpa, 1350-1405) wrote advice on pilgrimage that Jamgon Kongtrul uses as a basis for his counsel.

Kagyu Tenzin (*bka' brgyud bstan 'dzin*; Holder of the Kagyu Lineage) (also known as Satsa Lodrö) (eighteenth century?) meditated at Tsadra before Kongtrul's time and continued the Shangpa Kagyu lineage at his monastery at Satsa.

Karchen Polgyi Wong-chuk (*kar chen dpal gyi dbang phyug*; Illustrious Powerful One) (eighth century) was one of Guru Rinpoché's main disciples, whose meditation cave is situated at Tsadra.

Karma Drubgyu Tenzin Trinlé (*sgrub brgyud bstan 'dzin phrin las*; Enlightened Activity, Holder of the Doctrine of Meditation) (nineteenth century) was a reincarnate master at Palpung Monastery who participated in Tsadra's inaugural consecration.

Karma Dudul Gyalpo (*bdud 'dul rgyal po*; King who Tames Demons) (eighteenth century?) was a reincarnate master who identified a cliff in the vicinity of Palpung Monastery as sacred.

Karma Ngédon (*nges don*; Definitive Meaning) (nineteenth century) was the retreat master at Palpung Monastery's three-year retreat center at the time of Tsadra's consecration.

Karma Pakshi (1204-1283) was the Second Karmapa.

Karma Ratna (nineteenth century) was the vajra master of Palpung Monastery at the time of Tsadra's consecration.

Karma Sidral (*srid bral*; Free from Existence) seems to have been a master before Jamgon Kongtrul's time, an emanation of the Eighth Karmapa. His reincarnation in Kongtrul's time accompanied the Fourteenth Karmapa when he consecrated Tsadra.

Karma Tenpa Rab-gyé (*bstan pa rab rgyas*; Full Blossoming of the Doctrine) (eighteenth century?) was a reincarnation of Dabzang Rinpoché, resident of Palpung Monastery. He is mentioned as having buried treasure vases above Tsadra.

Kyégom (or **Kyébu**) **Yeshé Dorjé** (*ye shes rdo rje*; Adamantine Wisdom) (twelfth century) was an emanation of Guru Rinpoché's disciple, Namké Nyingpo, and a disciple of Gampopa. He was the first to open what is called Old Tsari.

Lama Ten-gyé (*bstan rgyas*; Spread of the Doctrine) (eighteenth century?) was the chief lama at Tsadra at a time when a retreat center existed there before the construction of a three-year retreat center at Palpung.

Langdro Translator, Konchok Jungné (*dkon mchog 'byung gnas*; Source of the Rare and Sublime) (eighth century) was one of the twenty-five main disciples of Guru Rinpoché. He is mentioned as the source of the reincarnate masters called Öntrul Rinpoché.

Lha-cham Mandarava (eighth century) was one of the principal Indian disciples of Guru Rinpoché, said to have visited Tsadra through her miraculous powers.

Lochen Dharmashri (1654-1718), the younger brother of Ter-dak Lingpa, the founder of Min-ling Monastery, was a great master and writer, here mentioned for his version of the Tibetan calendar.

Lodrö Tayé (*blo gros mtha' yas*; Boundless Intellect) is Jamgon Kongtrul's bodhisattva name.

Longchenpa or **Longchen Rabjam Zangpo** (*klong chen rab 'byams bzang po*, Infinite Vast Expanse of Excellence) (1308-1363) was an outstanding scholar and meditation master of the Nyingma Lineage. Kongtrul often quoted him in his work.

Longsal Nyingpo (*klong gsal snying po*; Essence of the Clear Expanse) (1685-1752) was a great treasure revealer, here mentioned as the source of one series of reincarnations.

Lotus Skull-Garlanded Adept (*pad ma thod phreng rtsal*) is one of Guru Rinpoché's many names.

Luhipa was an Indian adept whose meditation of Wheel of Supreme Bliss was preserved in Tibet and was used to consecrate Tsadra.

Manjushri-mitra was a great Indian master of Great Completion, reincarnated as Jamyang Kyentsé Wongpo.

Marpa the Translator (1012-1097) was the father of the Kagyu Lineage in Tibet.

Milarepa (*mi la ras pa*) (1040-1123) was Tibet's great yogi-poet, disciple of Marpa and master to Gampopa.

Nagarjuna was the greatest Indian Buddhist philosopher.

Namké Nyingpo (*nam mkha'i snying po*, Heart of the Sky) (eighth century), one of the principal disciples of Guru Rinpoché, meditated at Tsadra.

Ngari Penchen (also known as **Péma Wong-gyal**—*pad ma dbang rgyal*; Lotus King of Power) (1487-1543) was an important writer of the Nyingma tradition, here mentioned for his calendar.

Ngok-pa (also known as **Chö-ku Dorjé**—*chos sku rdo rje;* Vajra of the Body of Ultimate Enlighenment) (1036-1102) was one of Marpa's main disciples.

Nub-chen Sangyé Yeshé (*sangs rgyas ye she;* Wisdom of Enlightenment) (eighth century) was one of Guru Rinpoché's main disciples who meditated at Tsadra.

Nyak-chen Yeshé Zhonnu (*ye shes zhon nu;* Youthful Wisdom) (eighth century) was one of Guru Rinpoché's main disciples who meditated at Tsadra.

Nyak Jnana Kumara is the Sanskrit translation of the above name.

Nyö Chenpo Gyalwa Lhagangpa (thirteenth century) was one of the three tantric adepts instrumental in inaugurating Tsari.

Ön Sampel Chok-trul (*dbon bsam phel mchog sprul;* nephew, Supreme Reincarnation of Sampel, Wish-Fulfilling Gem) seems to have been an honorific reference to Karma Drubgyu Tenzin Trinlé, one of the reincarnate masters of Palpung.

Ön Samten (*dbon bsam gtan;* nephew, Meditation) (nineteenth century) seems to refer to another reincarnate master of Palpung Monastery who participated in Tsadra's inaugural consecration.

Öntrul Rinpoché, Wong-gyal Dorjé (*dbang rgyal rdo rje;* Adamantine King of Power) (eighteenth century) was a reincarnate master who administrated Palpung Monastery and directed the construction of its three-year retreat center.

Orgyenpa (true name is **Rinchenpal**—*rin chen dpal;* Jewel Glory) (1230-1309) was a disciple of the Second Karmapa. In 1288, he was responsible for the recognition of the first "tulku" in Tibet, the Third Karmapa, Rangjung Dorjé. He is mentioned as the founder of the Tibetan transmission of a lineage called the Intensive Practice of the Three Vajras.

Padmakara is one of Guru Rinpoché's many names.

Palchen Chöyé (*dpal chen chos yas;* Illustrious Boundless Qualities) (thirteenth century) was one of the three tantric adepts instrumental in inaugurating Tsari.

Palden Lhundrup (*dpal ldan lhun grub;* Illustrious Spontaneous Presence) (dates unavailable) is mentioned by Kongtrul as being the last of the Sakya lamas to head Palpung Monastery, after which the institutions there were abandoned until Chökyi Jungné's re-founding of the monastery in 1727.

Pamo Drupa (full name is **Pamo Drupa Dorjé Gyalpo**—*rdo rje rgyal po;* Vajra King) (1110-1170) was the disciple of Gampopa and the teacher of Jikten Soumgon. He founded a monastery called Pamo Dru.

Pandit Rong-zom Chökyi Zangpo (*chos kyi bzang po;* Excellent One of Spiritual Life) (1012-1088) is one of the most outstanding writers of the Nyingma tradition, cited in this book by Kongtrul on the subject of consecration.

Péma Garwong (*pad ma gar dbang;* Lotus Master of the Dance) was Jamgon Kongtrul's tantric name.

Péma Kunzang Chökyi Gyalpo (*padma kun bzang chos kyi rgyal po*; Lotus, Ever-Excellent, King of Spiritual Life) (1854-1885) was the Tenth Tai Situpa, an infant at the time Tsadra was consecrated.

Péma Nyinjé Wongpo (*pad ma nyin byed dbang po*; Lotus, Powerful Sun) (1774-1853), the Ninth Tai Situpa, was the principal spiritual master of Jamgon Kongtrul.

Péma Ösel Do-ngak Lingpa (*pad ma 'od gsal mdo snags gling pa*; Lotus Clear Light Island of Discourses and Tantras) was Jamyang Kyentsé Wongpo's name as a treasure revealer.

Péma Sang-ngak Tenzin (*padma gsang sngags bstan 'dzin*; Lotus, Holder of the Doctrine of Secret Mantra) (nineteenth century) was a master who assisted with the consecration of Tsadra.

Pol (*dpal*: Illustrious) **Jangchub Lingpa**: see **Jangchub Lingpa**.

Rangjung Dorjé (*rang byung rdo rje*; Self-Arisen Vajra) (1284-1339) was the Third Karmapa and the first reincarnate master recognized in Tibet. Kongtrul cites him as an authority throughout his writings.

Ratna Lingpa (Jewel Island) (1403-1479) was a great treasure revealer.

Rikzin Dorjé Drakpo (*rig 'dzin rdo rje drag po*; Awareness-Holder Wrathful Vajra) (eighteenth century), emanation of King Tri-song Dé'u-tsen, was a master who consecrated the ground for the construction of the main three-year retreat center at Palpung Monastery.

Rikzin Rolpé Dorjé (*rig 'dzin rol pa'i rdo rje*; Awareness-Holder Playful Vajra) (seventeenth century) was a treasure revealer, here mentioned as the previous incarnation of Dudul Gyalpo, a master who lived at Palpung Monastery in the eighteenth century.

Ripa Chok-trul Darjé Gyatso (*ri pa mchog sprul dar rgyas rgya mtso*; Wide and Spreading Ocean) (nineteenth century) was a reincarnate master from Ripa Monastery who participated in the consecration of Tsadra.

Rolpé Dorjé (*rol pa'i rdo rje*; Playful Vajra) (1340-1383) was the Fourth Karmapa.

Saroruha-vajra was an Indian master here mentioned for his style of teaching the phases of creation and completion.

Shakya Lodrö (*blo gros*; Intellect) (1002-1062) is mentioned, in treasure texts revealed by Chokling, as a previous incarnation of Jamgon Kongtrul.

Sokpo Dorjé Lhapol (*sog po dro rje lha dpal*; Vajra Glorious God) was one of Guru Rinpoché's disciples who sojourned at Tsadra.

Tang-Tong Gyalpo (*thang stong rgyalpo*; King of the Plain of Emptiness) (1385-1509) was a great meditation master who figures in a number of Tibetan lineages of tantric meditation. He is mentioned in this text as having founded Lhundrup Teng Monastery at Dergé in 1448.

Tegchok Dorjé (*theg mchog rdo rje*; Vajra of the Supreme Way) (1798-1868), the Fourteenth Karmapa, was one of the main masters to consecrate Tsadra.

Ten-nyi Lingpa: see **Chimé Ten-nyi Yung-droung Lingpa**

Tenpa Nyinjé (*bstan pa nyin byed*; Sun of the Doctrine): see **Chökyi Jungné**

Tenpa Tsering (*bstan pa tshe ring*; Doctrine, Long-Life) (1678-1739) is remembered as one of the greatest kings of Dergé.

Terchen Rinpoché (*gter chen rin po che*, Precious Treasure-Revealer) is the title Kongtrul uses in referring to Chok-gyur Déchen Lingpa.

Tsangpa Gyaré Yeshé Dorjé (*ye shes rdo rje*; Vajra of Wisdom) (1161-1211) inaugurated Tsari. Considered to be an emanation of the Indian master Naropa, he continues to reincarnate as Druk-chen Rinpoché.

Tsangpa Lha'i Métok (*tsangs pa lha'i me tok*; Flower of the Pure Gods) was an initiation name of King Tri-song Dé'u-tsen, who invited Guru Rinpoché to Tibet in the eighth century.

Tsultrim Özer (*tshul khrims 'od zer*; Light of Ethical Conduct) (dates unavailable) was the first Sakya lama to lead Palpung Monastery after it passed from Drigung Kagyu control.

Vam-teng Tulku Tsok-nyi Lek-drup (*tshogs gnyis legs drub*; Perfect Accomplishment of the Two Cultivations) (eighteenth century) was a disciple of the Eighth Tai Situpa. He recalled his past life as a meditator in the Palpung area.

Vimalamitra (eighth century) was a teacher of Guru Rinpoché who visited Tsadra. Jamyang Kyentsé Wongpo was his reincarnation.

Virupa (eleventh century) was one of the great, accomplished masters of Indian tantric Buddhism, here mentioned as the source of the teaching Jamyang Kyentsé gave to consecrate Tsadra.

Wongchuk Dorjé (*dbang phyug rdo rje*; Powerful Vajra) (1555-1603) was the Ninth Karmapa.

Yeshé Tsogyal (*ye shes mtsho rgyal*; Queen of the Lake of Wisdom) (eighth century) was one of the principal disciples of Guru Rinpoché.

Yonten Gyatso (*yon tan rgya mtsho*; Ocean of Qualities) is Jamgon Kongtrul's monastic name.

Yoru Nyonpa (*yo ru snyon pa*; Crazy One of Yoru) was a master (eighteenth century?) who attained accomplishment in meditation while in retreat at Tsadra.

Yung-drung Tsultrim (*gyung drung tshul khrims*; Swatika, Ethical Conduct) (nineteenth century) was a relative of Jamgon Kongtrul who contributed to the construction of Tsadra.

Yu-tok-pa (known as **Yutok Yonten Gonpo**—*gyu thog yon tan mgon po*; Turquoise Roof, Protector of Qualities) (twelfth century) was a major source of the Tibetan medical tradition; he is mentioned as a past life of Palpung's Öntrul Rinpoché.

Bibliography

WESTERN LANGUAGE PUBLICATIONS

Aris, Michael. *Bhutan*. Warminster: Aris & Phillips Ltd., 1979.

Cleary, Thomas, translator. *The Flower Ornament Scripture*. Boston and London: Shambhala, 1993.

Dorje, Gyurme. *Tibet Handbook*. 2d ed. Bath, England: Footprint Handbooks, 1999.

Farrow, G. W., Menon, I., and Krsnavajrapada. *The Concealed Essence of the Hevajra Tantra with the Commentary Yogaratnamala*. Delhi: Motilal Banarsidass, 1992.

Ford, Robert. *Wind Between the Worlds*. Berkeley, CA: Snow Lion Graphics,1987.

Grey, Anthony. *Peking*. Boston, Toronto: Little, Brown & Company, 1988.

Gyatso, Janet. "Down With the Demoness: Reflections on a Feminine Ground in Tibet," in *Feminine Ground: Essays on Women and Tibet*, pp. 33-51, ed. Janice D. Willis. Ithaca, NY: Snow Lion Publications, 1995.

Hilton, James. *Lost Horizon*. New York: William Morrow, 1936.

Huber, Toni. *The Cult of Pure Crystal Mountain*. New York and Oxford: Oxford University Press, 1999.

Huber, Toni. "Where Exactly Are Caritra, Devikota, and Himavat? A Sacred Geography Controversy and the Development of Tantric Buddhist Pilgrimage Sites in Tibet." *Kailash, A Journal of Himalayan Studies*, vol. 16, nos. 3-4 (1990), pp. 121-165.

Kolmas, Josef, ed. and introd. *A Genealogy of the Kings of Derge*. Prague: Oriental Institute in Academia, 1968.

Kongtrul, Jamgon. *Buddhist Ethics*, translated by the Sonada Translation Committee. Ithaca, NY: Snow Lion Publications, 1998.

Kongtrul, Jamgon. *Creation and Completion*, translated by Sarah Harding. Boston: Wisdom Publications, 1996.

Kongtrul, Jamgon. *Enthronement*, translated by Ngawang Zangpo. Ithaca, NY: Snow Lion Publications, 1997.

Lessing, Doris. *The Sirian Experiments*, the third of her five-part series Canopus in Argos: Archives. London: Grafton Books, 1987.

Patrul Rinpoché. *Words of My Perfect Teacher*, translated by the Padmakara Translation Group. San Francisco, London: HarperCollins, 1994.

Ricard, Matthieu. *Journey to Enlightenment: The Life and World of Khyentse Rinpoche, Spiritual Teacher from Tibet*. New York: Aperture, 1996.

Sogyal Rinpoché; Gaffney, Patrick; and Harvey, Andrew. *The Tibetan Book of Living and Dying*. San Francisco: HarperCollins, 1993.

Spence, Jonathan D. *God's Chinese Son: The Taiping Heavenly Kingdom of Hong Xiuquan*. New York, London: W. W. Norton & Co., 1996.

Stearns, Cyrus. "The Life and Teaching of the Tibetan Saint Thang-stong rgyalpo, King of the Empty Plain." Master's thesis, University of Washington, 1980.

Stoddard, Heather. *Le Mendiant de l'Amdo*. Paris: Société d'Ethnographie, 1986.

Trungpa Rinpoché, Chögyam. *Born in Tibet*. New York: Harcourt, Brace and World, 1968.

Tsering, Tashi. "Nyag rong mGon Po rNam rGyal: A Nineteenth-Century Khamspa Warrior," in *Soundings in Tibetan Civilization*, pp. 196-214, ed. Barbara Nimri Aziz and Matthew Kapstein. New Delhi: Manohar, 1985.

Walshe, Maurice. *The Long Discourses of the Buddha: A Translation of the Digha Nikaya*. Boston: Wisdom Publications, 1995.

Vasubandhu. *Abhidharmakoshabhasyam*, 4 vols. Translated into French by Louis de la Vallée Poussin and from French into English by Leo M. Pruden. Berkeley, CA: Asian Humanities Press, 1988.

Zabs-dkar Tshogs-drug-ran-grol. *The Life of Shabkar: The Autobiography of a Tibetan Yogin*, translated by Matthieu Ricard. Albany, NY: State University of New York Press, 1994.

TIBETAN LANGUAGE PUBLICATIONS

Works by Jamgon Kontrul in Tibetan

The volume and page numbers from *Collected Works of Jamgon Kongtrul* and *Treasury of Rediscovered Teachings* refer to the editions published by His Holiness Dilgo Kyentsé Rinpoché.

The Autobiography of Jamgon Kongtrul (Phyogs med ris med kyi bstan pa la 'dun shing dge sbyong gi gzugs brnyan 'chang ba blo gros mtha' yas kyi sde'i byung ba brjod pa nor bu sna tshogs mdog can). Collected Works of Jamgon Kongtrul, Volume 16, pp. 59-478.

Dergé Temple Catalogue (Thub dbang rten gsum mthong grol lha khang dzam gling bkra shi 'od 'bar gyi dkar chag rdzogs ldan dpyid kyi dbyangs snyan). Collected Works of Jamgon Kongtrul, Volume 10, pp. 297-438.

Encyclopedia of Buddhism (Shes bya kun la khyab pa'i gzhung lugs nyung ngu'i tshig gis rnam par 'grel ba legs bshad yongs 'du shes bya mtha' yas pa'i rgya mtsho). Beijing: People's Press, 1985.

Lives of the Treasure Revealers (Zab mo'i gter dang gter ston grub thob ji ltar byon pa'i lo rgyus mdor bsdus bkod pa rin chen bedurya'i phreng ba). Treasury of Rediscovered Teachings, Volume 1, pp. 291-760.

My Past Lives ('Dus shes gsum ldan spong ba pa'i gzugs bsnyan padma gar gyi dbang phyug phrin las 'gro 'dul rtsal gyi rtogs pa brjod pa'i dum bu smig rgyu'i bdud rtsi). Collected Works of Jamgon Kongtrul, Volume 15, pp. 261-342.

Music of the Celestial Realms: A Long Prayer to Tsadra Rinchen Drak, the Sublime Sacred Place of the Heart of Enlightened Qualities (Yon tan thugs kyi gnas mchog tsa 'dra rin chen brak gi gsol 'debs rgyas pa mkha' spyod rol mo). Collected Works of Jamgon Kongtrul, Volume 1, pp. 206-210.

Pilgrimage Guide to Tsadra Rinchen Drak (Thugs kyi gnas mchog chen po de vi ko tri tsa 'dra rin chen brag gi rtogs pa brjod pa yid kyi rgya mtsho'i rol mo). Collected Works of Jamgon Kongtrul, Volume 11, pp. 477-546.

A Small, Short List to Clarify the Proclamation of the Do-Kham's Twenty-Five Major Sacred Places and Their Auxiliary Sites (mDo khams gnas chen nyer lnga yan lag dang bcas pa'i mdo byang gi gsal byed zin thung nyung ngu). Although written entirely by Jamgon Kongtrul, this text is included in *The Collected Rediscovered Teachings (gter ma) of Gterchen Mchog-gyur-glin-pa*, Volume 60, pp. 41-67. New Delhi: Patshang Lama Sonam Gyaltsen, 1975.

Song of the Messenger of Spring: A Short Poem in Praise of Glorious Charitra (dPal gyi tsa ri tra'i bsngags brjod mdor bsdus dpyid kyi pho nya'i mgrin dbyangs). Collected Works of Jamgon Kongtrul, Volume 11, pp. 461-476.

By Other Authors

Chok-gyur Déchen Lingpa. *Location List of the Twenty-Five Major Sacred Sites of Amdo and Kham (Bod kyi gnas chen rnams kyi mdo byang dkar chags o rgyan gyi mkhas pa padma 'byung gnas kyis bkos pa). The Collected Rediscovered Teachings (gter ma) of Gterchen Mchog-gyur-glin-pa,* Volume 60, pp. 1-40. New Delhi: Patshang Lama Sonam Gyaltsen, 1975.

Chok-gyur Déchen Lingpa. *Treasure-Text Guide to Tsadra (gSang thig snying po'i skor las thugs kyi gnas mchog tsa 'dra rin chen brag gi dkar chag). The Collected Rediscovered Teachings (gter ma) of Gterchen Mchog-gyur-glin-pa,* Volume 60, pp. 109-116. New Delhi: Patshang Lama Sonam Gyaltsen, 1975.

Longchenpa. *The Treasury of Philosophies (Grub mtha' mdzod).* The page numbers mentioned in this text are those from the edition published by Tarthang Tulku, Dharma Publishing.

Sakya Pandita. *A Thorough Delineation of the Three Vows (sDom pa gsum gyi rab tu dbye ba).* Delhi: Sherig Parkhang.

Sanskrit and Tibetan Bilingual Dictionary (Sam bod skad gnyis shan sbyar gser gyi phreng mdzes). Gansu, PRC: Gansu Nationalities Publishing House, 1989.

The Great Tibetan-Chinese Dictionary (Bod rgya tshig mdzod chen mo), 4th edition. Beijing: People's Press, 1998.

OTHER BOOKS TRANSLATED BY NGAWANG ZANGPO

Jamgon Kongtrul's Retreat Manual

Enthronement

AS A MEMBER OF THE SONADA TRANSLATION COMMITTEE:

Myriad Worlds

Buddhist Ethics